ABANDONED VEHICLES OF NEW HAMPSHIRE

RUST IN PEACE

JERRY LOFARO

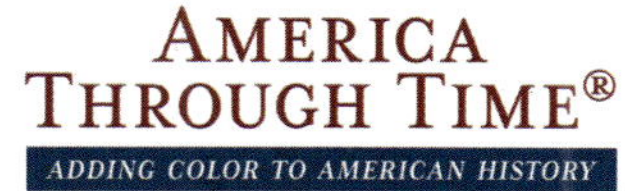

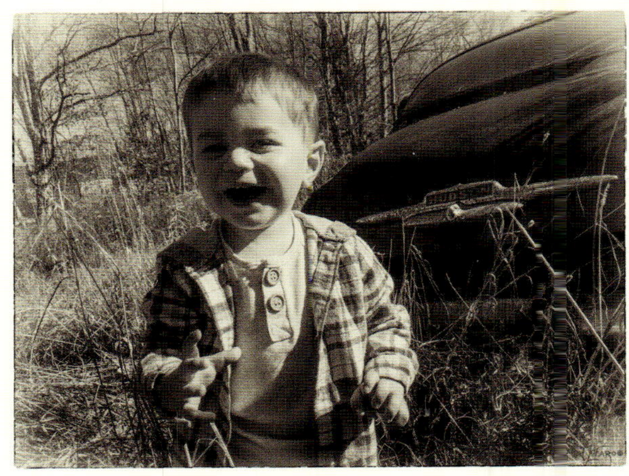

I believe this book's existence was preordained by my grandson Hudson, and it is with great love and joy that I dedicate it to him.

Select photos from this book will be available as limited edition premium archival prints from IntaglioEditions.com

A large selection of photos and art are available as high-quality prints at fineartamerica.com/profiles/jerry-lofaro/shop

For more info about Jerry and his photography, please visit: jerrylofarophotography.com

For more info about Jerry and his art, please visit: jerrylofarodesigns.com

America Through Time is an imprint of Fonthill Media LLC
www.through-time.com
office@through-time.com

Published by Arcadia Publishing by arrangement with Fonthill Media LLC
For all general information, please contact Arcadia Publishing:
Telephone: 843-853-2070
Fax: 843-853-0044
E-mail: sales@arcadiapublishing.com
For customer service and orders:
Toll-Free 1-888-313-2665

www.arcadiapublishing.com

First published 2021

ISBN 978-1-63499-296-1

Typeset in Trade Gothic 10pt on 15pt
Printed and bound in England

CONTENTS

About the Author **5**

Introduction **6**

Foreword **9**

1 In and Around the State **10**

2 Blanchard Auto Salvage **28**

3 Lane's Garage **44**

4 The Truck Stops Here **58**

5 Meet the Beetles **78**

6 School's Out … Forever **86**

7 Lincoln Slept Here **94**

8 Color, Detail and Texture **100**

9 The Hudson **114**

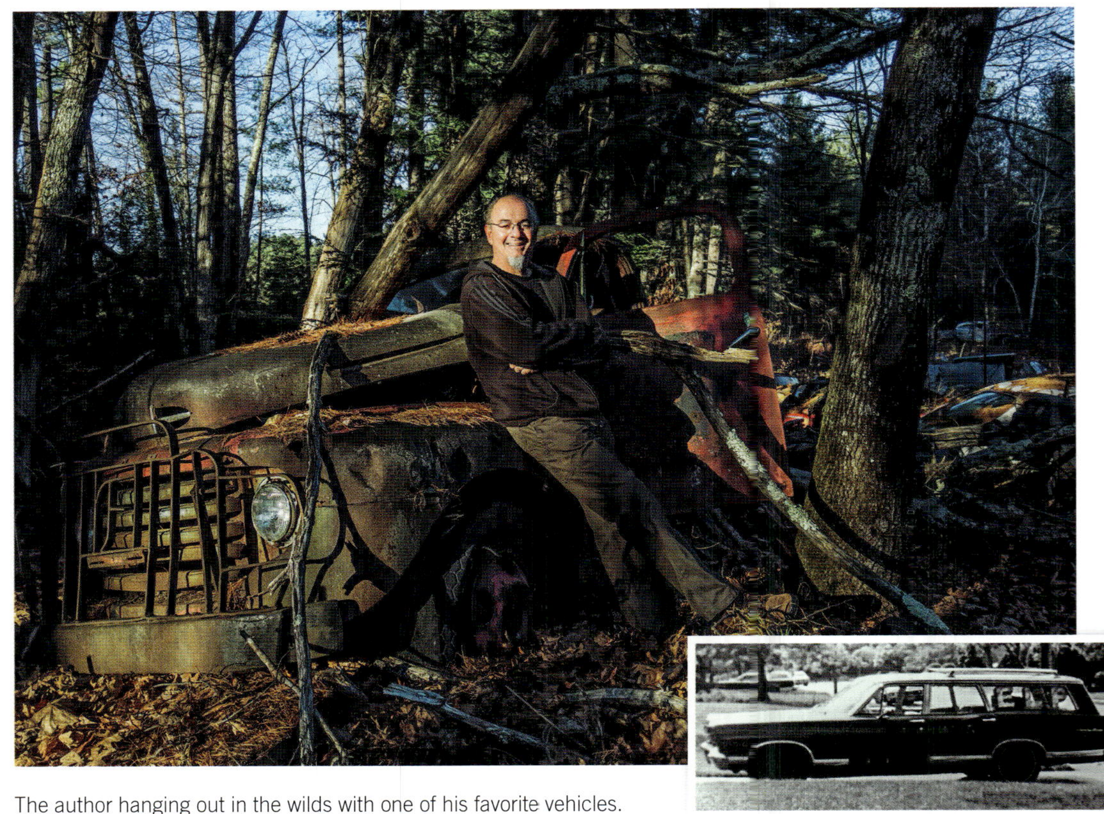

The author hanging out in the wilds with one of his favorite vehicles.

Inset: This 1967 Ford Country Sedan station wagon was my first car, given to me by my dad once he got another vehicle for his roofing and siding business. Years of carting too many bundles of shingles and ladders to job sites, as well as countless smears of tar and caulking, already made it ready for the junkyard. However I couldn't have been prouder cruising to Jones Beach in it with my friends! My favorite band, Emerson, Lake & Palmer, is represented in the back window with their famous initials cut out of an album sleeve. Given the state of this car, it was only natural that the musically un-indoctrinated always asked me where the "H" was.

ABOUT THE AUTHOR

JERRY LOFARO was born in 1959 in Farmingdale, New York, and has employed his lifetime interest in dinosaurs, animals, fantasy, art history and literature into a long career as an illustrator. The recipient of many awards, Jerry's art has adorned the covers of most major book publishers, along with countless advertising and promotional projects for Aflac, Claritin, Purina, Coca Cola, Dole Foods, Minolta, Disney, MGM Grand Hotel, and more. He is particularly renown for the scores of tea box illustrations he created for Celestial Seasonings over a twenty-year period. Jerry is also a popular instructor, having conducted airbrush workshops around the country, as well as teaching at the Fashion Institute of Technology in New York City and the New Hampshire Institute of Art in Manchester, New Hampshire. Finally, his growing passion and skills with a camera combined with his love of music and musicians has resulted in his current status as the official photographer at the Tupelo Music Hall in Derry, New Hampshire.

INTRODUCTION

Where did this fascination—okay, obsession—with photographing old vehicles begin? Though I started taking pictures with a Kodak Instamatic while in high school during the 1970s, I never regarded myself as a photographer. In fact, most of my shooting since 1986 was done as reference for creating illustrations, and rarely for its own sake. It was just a few years ago that I began to take photography seriously—first with an iPhone at concerts, and then with a Canon Rebel. In the last two years, I've hit my stride using the high-resolution Light 16 camera, which has been perfect for capturing the texture and detail in this book's subject matter.

So to speak, I've never actually been a "car" guy; but, in the course of my career as an illustrator, I developed many interests that were galvanized by assignment research. In one such case, I created book covers for the late author, Tom Powers, in which both novels revolved around growing up in the 1950s. Depicting cars from that time period helped capture the essence of the stories, and was the beginning of my appreciation for them. When I worked on the infamous Joe Camel campaign in the early 1990s, I fell in love with "fin" cars like the Newport and Chrysler 300, with the latter also inspiring my prehistoric fantasy piece, *Rapt Patrol.*

Every time I went out to photograph vehicles, it was with the feeling I was embarking on a great adventure. It is incredibly inspiring to wander in peaceful silence among the relics and discover dramatic abstract compositions along with unearthly combinations of color. Many are lying in various stages of decay that are both enhanced and softened by nature's blanket, and it's sometimes hard to discern where the mechanical ends and the organic begins. Contemplating a rusting hulk beneath layers of vines, branches, and moss brings out the child in me—it's tantamount to discovering the remains of an ancient beast, and I even dubbed one of my locations *Carassic Park.* However, even in my enthusiasm, I'm very aware that these cars and trucks have stories to share; and, with so many crushed and twisted remains, it appears that many did not end well. With deep hollow sockets staring blankly from missing headlights, and chrome grills with downward swooping mouths, some of the cars bear anguished, human-like expressions. While my photo expeditions can be breathtaking and exhilarating, at times they are also somber journeys into the past.

Automobiles have long been a major part of societal development in the world; and America, in particular, has a never-ending love affair with them. Everyone remembers the first time they learned how to drive, and many mark the plateaus in their lives with stories of the car they owned at the time. Vehicles from the 1950s and 1960s are lovingly ingrained in people's memories, and are even romanticized in movies such as *Rebel Without a Cause* starring James Dean; and, later, George Lucas's *American Graffiti*, starring Richard Dreyfuss and a pre-Han Solo Harrison Ford. With that in mind, I turned over most of the captioning in this book to my wide circle of notable art, music and photography friends. For each person, I selected a photo they responded to with a memory, a poem, lyrics, or purely a reaction to the mood or construct of the photo. I'm grateful that so many wanted to take part, and each person is credited with their discipline noted.

I reviewed thousands of photos in the process of creating this book, and discovered my increasing familiarity with the subjects allowed me to experience real "moments" with them. Sometimes it was a well-placed shaft of late afternoon light, or a glint off a chrome bumper in a sea of rust. Other times it was discovering a late-blooming flower, or quietly observing an insect moving about. I thought of the latter as life signs on a decaying hulk, very much like man-made reefs created to promote undersea ecosystems.

In closing, I can't help but pine for the ones that got away, as I was denied permission to shoot on a few properties that I can best describe as the "Elephant's Graveyard" for old car enthusiasts. It's a shame not to have those collections respectfully chronicled in this book, but I'll just to have to try again another day.

Jerry LoFaro

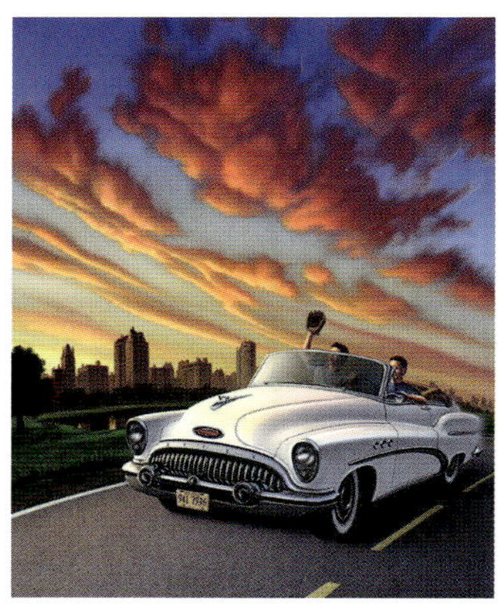

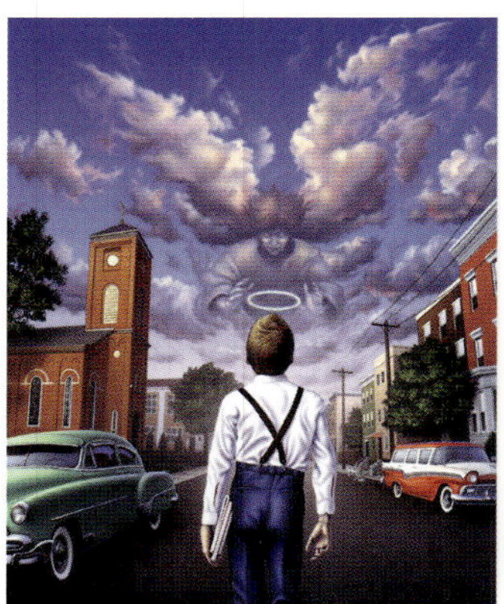

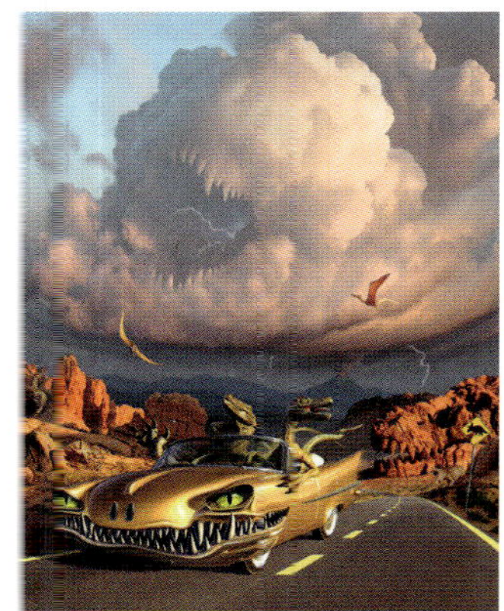

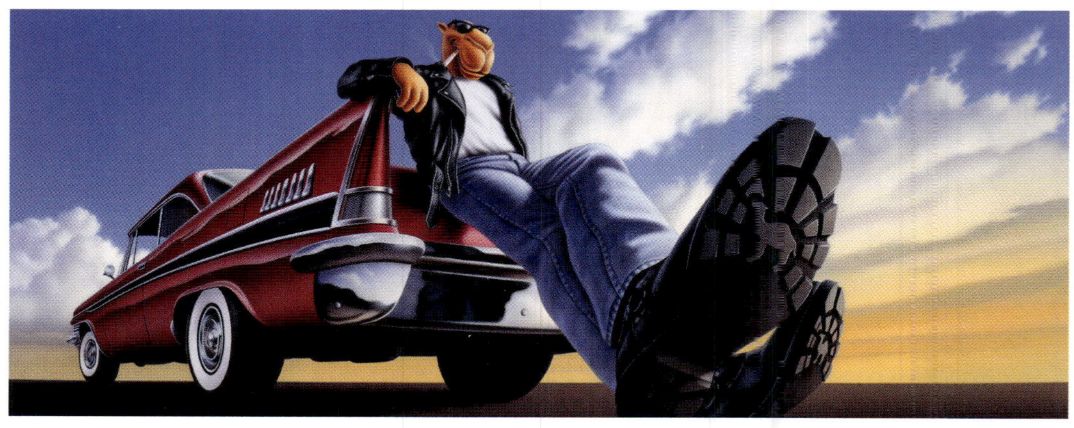

Top Left: *"The Junk Drawer, Corner Store, Front Porch Blues"* by John Powers; Top Middle: *"The Last Catholic in America"* by John Powers; Top Right: *"Rapt Patrol,"* inspired by the 1959 Chrysler 300E; Bottom: Camel campaign billboard illustration depicting a 1957 Chrysler New Yorker.

FOREWORD

THE AMERICAN DREAM

Consider this. Lurking in hidden, out-of-the-way places of America are the abandoned remains of a not-so-distant past. Look hard enough and you will find what is left of that essential possession of almost every American—the automobile. No matter what part of the country you come from, the car was your dream and your goal. It was rite of passage into adulthood, a path to a career, and a ticket to freedom. The open road and its possibilities have long been the desire of the American people, and books like *On the Road* and movies like *Easy Rider* celebrate that road, and its excitement of unknown adventure. Industry, progress, and the need for the new is our way, leaving a history of restless, constant movement. We use these cars to work, to play, to go on vacations, or in many cases to "just go."

The United States, a relatively young country with ruins dating back only a few centuries, has designated our past with iron and steel, not marble and stone. In junkyards, in fields and forests, and hidden in garages and barns, you will find the burial grounds of so many vehicles. Grand creatures of the recent past, they lie in repose, having succumbed to the passing of time, neglect and weather.

It is in this book that artist and photographer Jerry LoFaro pays homage to the golden age of automobiles. His attention is focused not on the pristine artifacts found in museums and collections, but to those found in a state of deterioration. These are the leviathans, half-buried and rusting, waiting to be discovered by history seekers before they become fully claimed by nature.

Take the journey as the past is uncovered and imagine what it was like to cruise on the open highway in ancient luxury transports of chrome, steel and eight cylinders. It is with his keen eye for detail and drama that LoFaro navigates these recesses as found in New Hampshire, and he invites you to come along for the ride.

Francis Klaess, Graphic Designer, Art Director and College Professor

1

IN AND AROUND THE STATE

So, where to start? I've never written a book before, and organizing chapters, thoughts, photos and captions into something interesting and coherent was quite challenging. This is especially so for the creative guy who didn't pay much attention in school, and barely squeaked by his senior year in order to graduate. My teachers would certainly be proud of me, but more likely shocked and amazed!

Of course, it all begins with the photos. I already had a couple of mainstay locations tucked in my belt, and they will actually have their own dedicated chapters, because I did so much shooting at both (in fact, I hope to do entire books about them). However, this is all about what lies around New Hampshire, and a more extensive effort was required to give a fuller picture. Once I started scouting additional places to shoot, I was thrilled to discover just how many relics are strewn around my beautiful adopted home state—the fifth smallest in the Union. In a modern-day version of a scavenger hunt, I would even routinely magnify areas on Google maps, searching promising tracts of land for signs of rusting hulks. I was also lucky enough to receive tips from people about places to shoot, and some of them resulted in most excellent adventures!

I want to point out that despite the title on the front cover, a sizable majority of the vehicles on these pages are actually "stored" rather than technically abandoned. However, with their rusted state of being, my criteria for shooting them is more than satisfied. Here they lie, basking in the elements season after season—just waiting to be rescued and lovingly returned to their former glory.

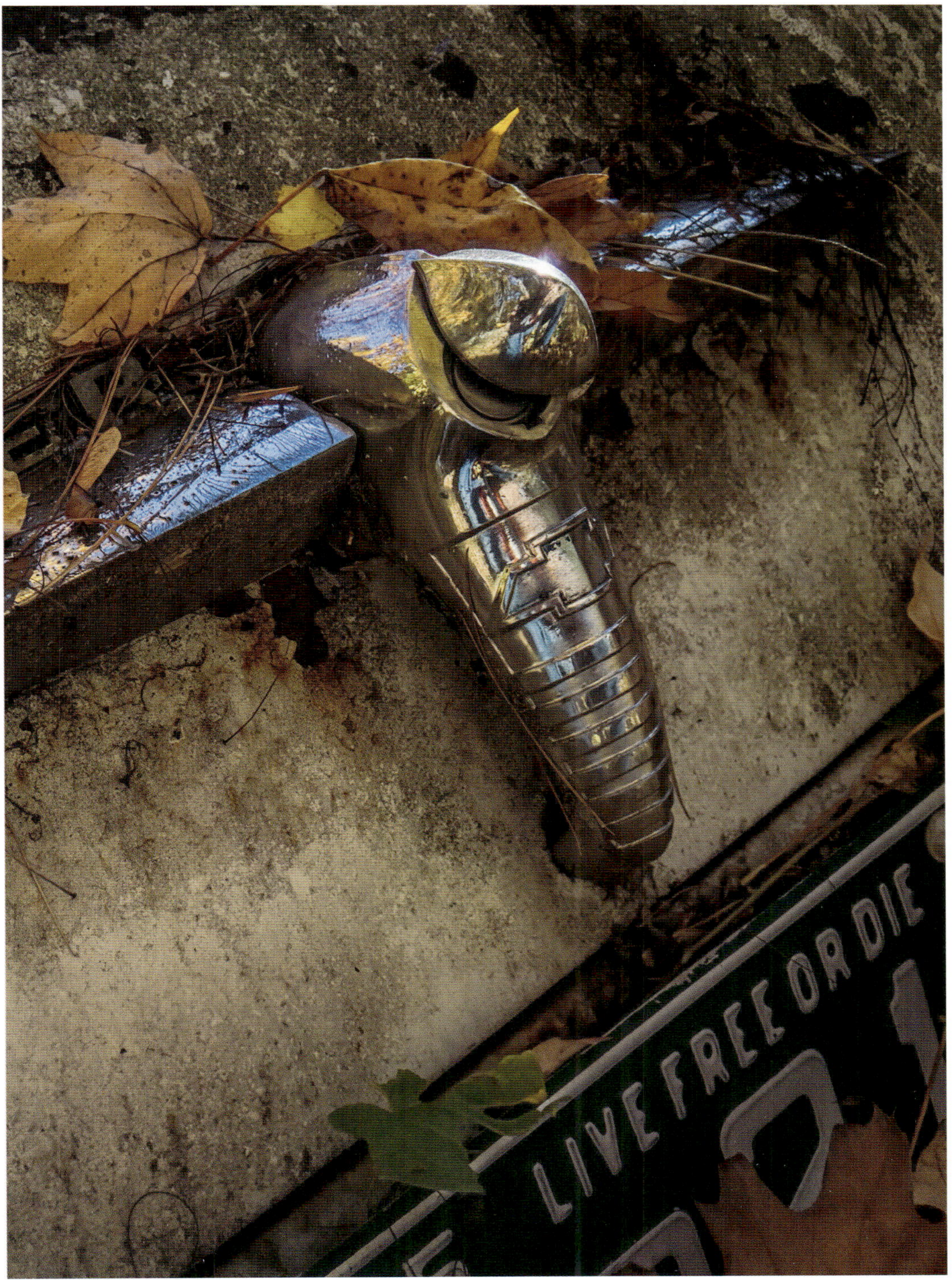

This 1950 Chevy Deluxe Powerglide's beautiful rear ornament, and hidden trunk keyhole, catches the sun, while the state's motto proudly exerts itself above the fallen leaves. I couldn't think of a better person to jumpstart this book with his following thought. "Someone's imagination, someone's treasure, someone's disappointment, someone's discovery." *Gary Sampson, Artist Laureate of New Hampshire, Photographer, Filmmaker, Retired NHIA Professor and Photography Department Chair*

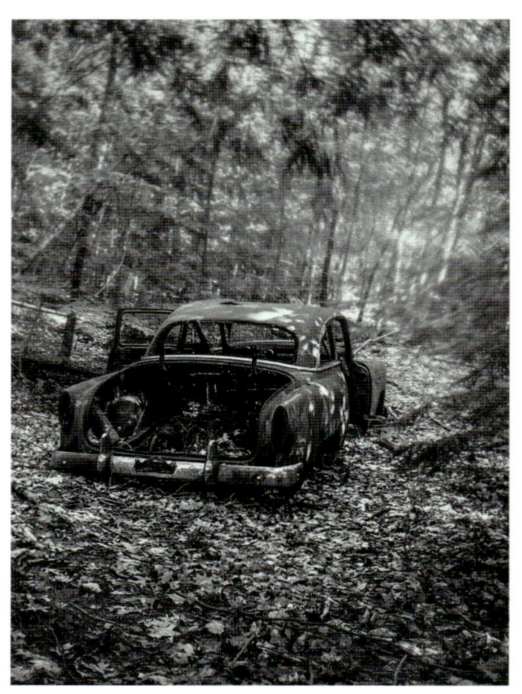

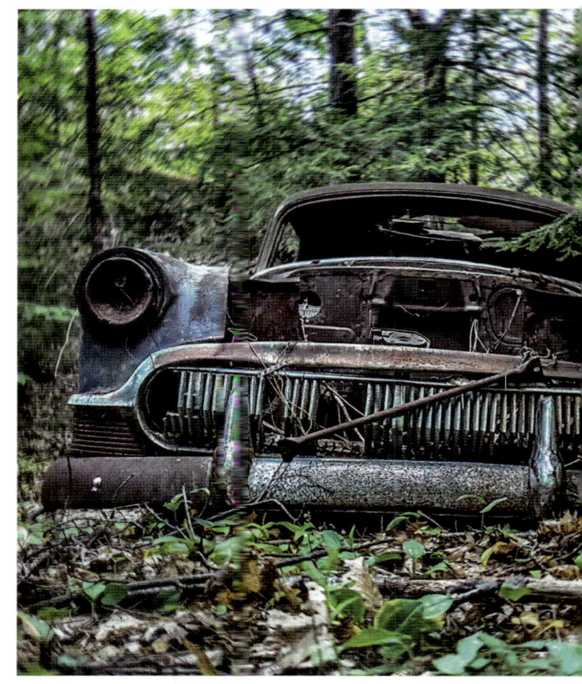

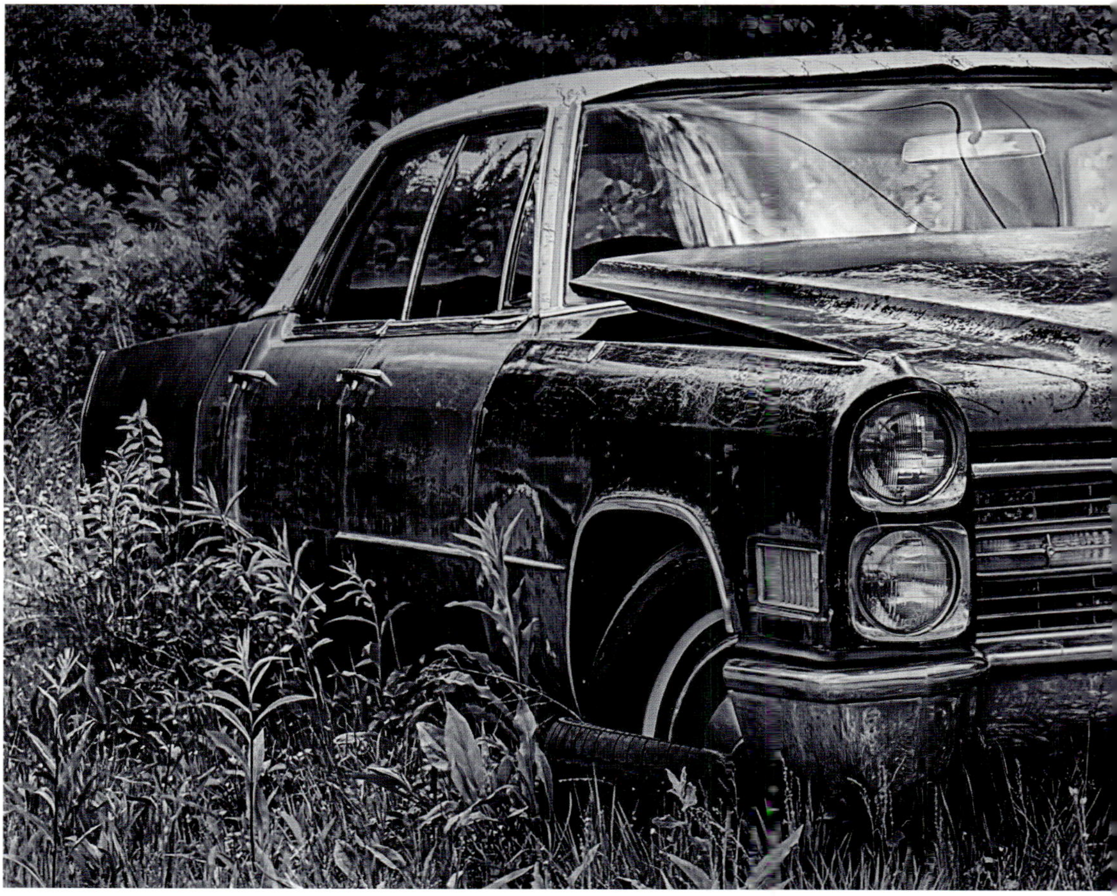

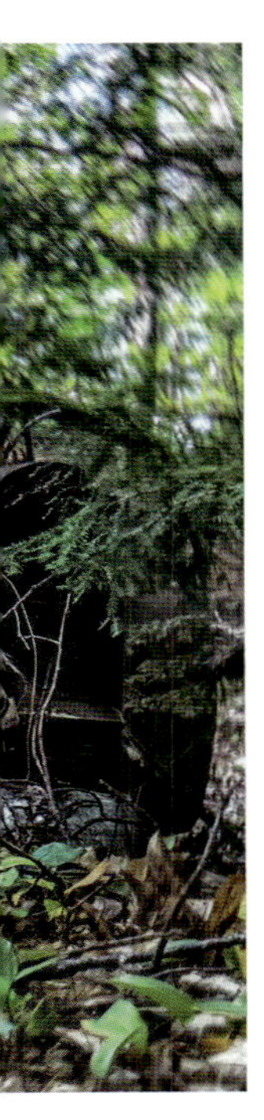

Left: *"Close To Home"* These are actually the last photos I took to include in this book, and I was thrilled to make an exciting discovery only two minutes away in my Henniker neighborhood. I was at the local lumberyard one day, and I happened to ask Dave (the fellow that works there) if there were any relics on the large property. He said no, but then told me of a nearby car that he remembered seeing forty years ago while out hunting. Immediately, I went to go find it, but despite his directions I realized I was way off the mark. While getting eaten alive by mosquitos far out in the woods in ninety-degree heat, I finally decided to call Dave for help. Once he redirected me, I backtracked quite a distance and, well—there she was! No known story, but it's definitely a curiosity how it ended up so far from the road. I went crazy trying to identify this car, and the grill totally threw me off. After some excellent sleuthing by J. D. Kelly (who shows up in the next chapter), we decided it to be a 1953 Chevy. But boy oh boy, that grill—it either belongs to a 1965 Dodge Coronet, a 1964 Mercury Monterey, OR … perhaps it's a dish drainer that was crudely modified to fit!

Bottom: *"Caddy Whacked"* This grand Cadillac sat stoically out in a field all by itself off Route 9/202 in nearby Stoddard for many years before it was finally removed. I believe it's either a 1966-7 Coupe, or Sedan de Ville.

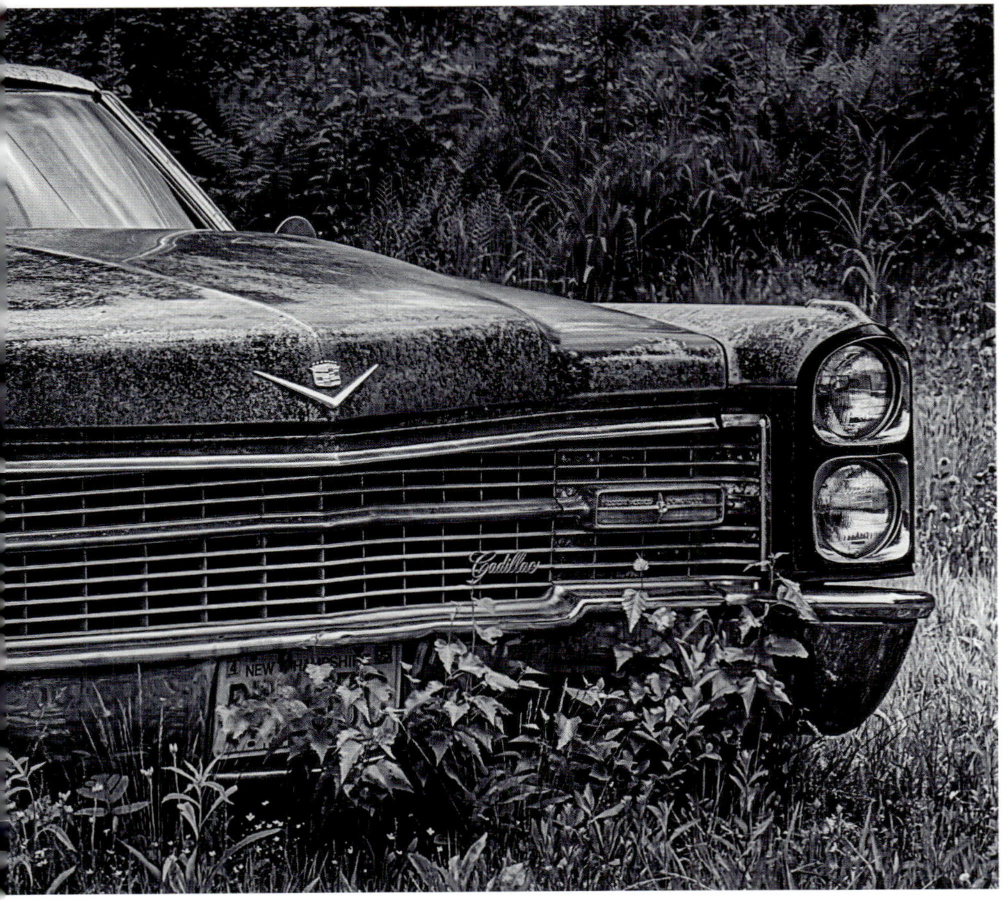

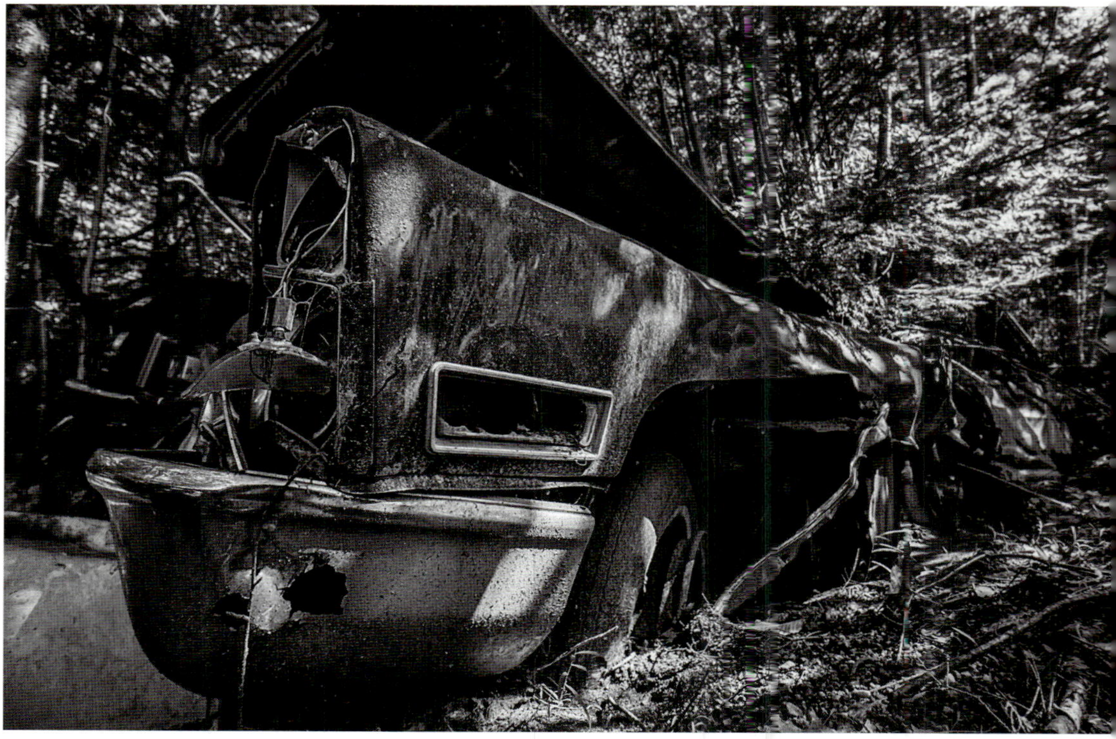

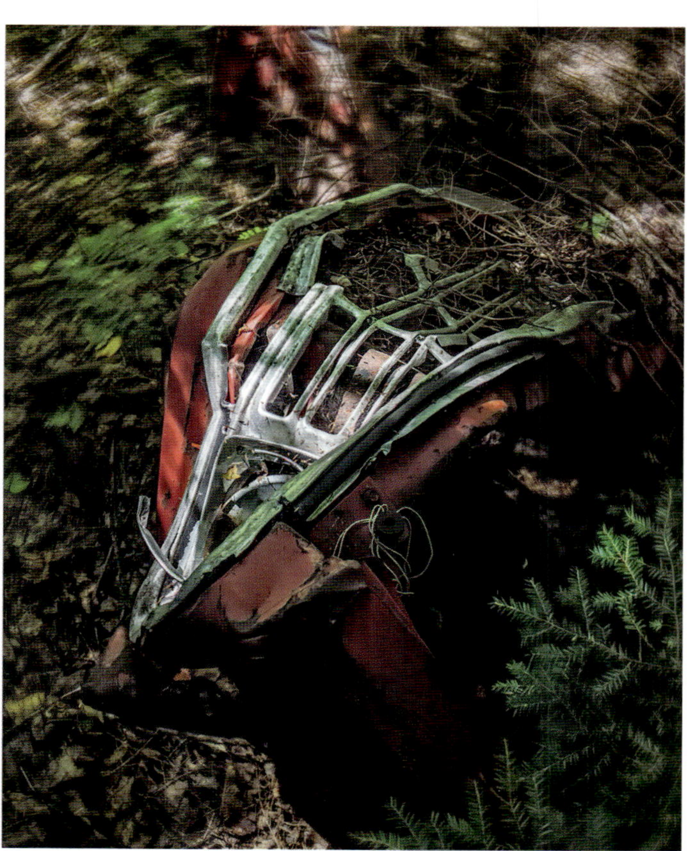

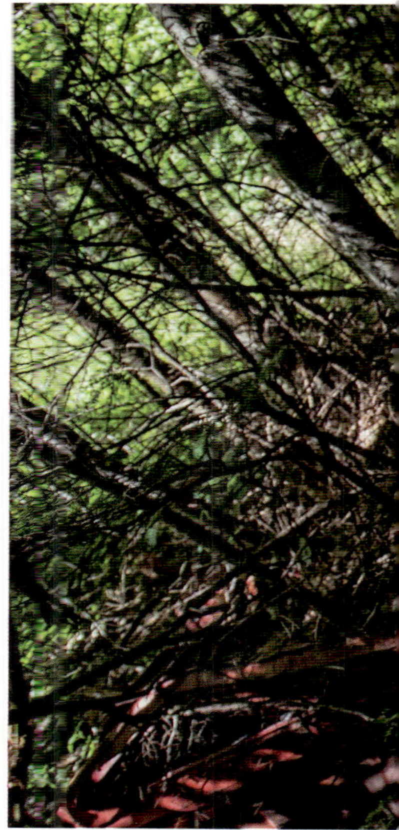

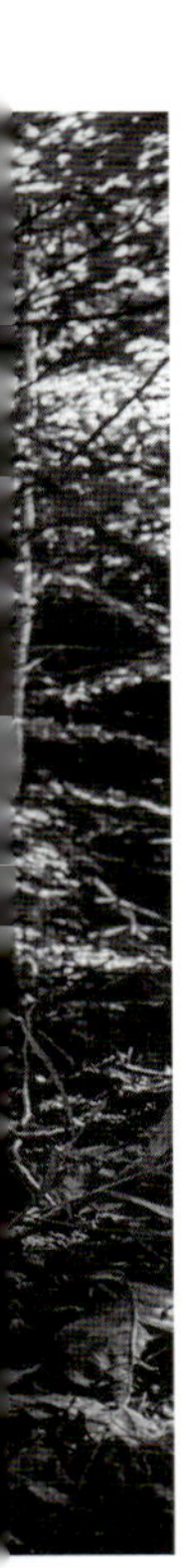

"The Swamp Caddies of Canterbury" One beautiful fall day, my friend José Cambrils took me out for an adventure on his remote property to get a load of these relics lying off to the side of a Class VI road. Interestingly, this was a Concord stagecoach road, and we passed by the foundations of centuries-old dwellings on our outing. The story that José learned from some "old timer" hunters was about a hermit that lived in a camp far into the woods. He regularly drove his two new Cadillacs up and down this difficult road (as well as the pickup truck below), and people thought he was crazy to do so. These days it's only passable with a four-wheel drive or ATV, and it's hard to imagine those vehicles were capable of driving this road. Apparently, his camp burned down sometime in the late 1970s, and he abandoned the area and left all three vehicles in a small swamp, though only one of the caddies is visible. They now serve as a landmark and target practice for local hunters, and a fascinating curiosity for anyone else that happens by.

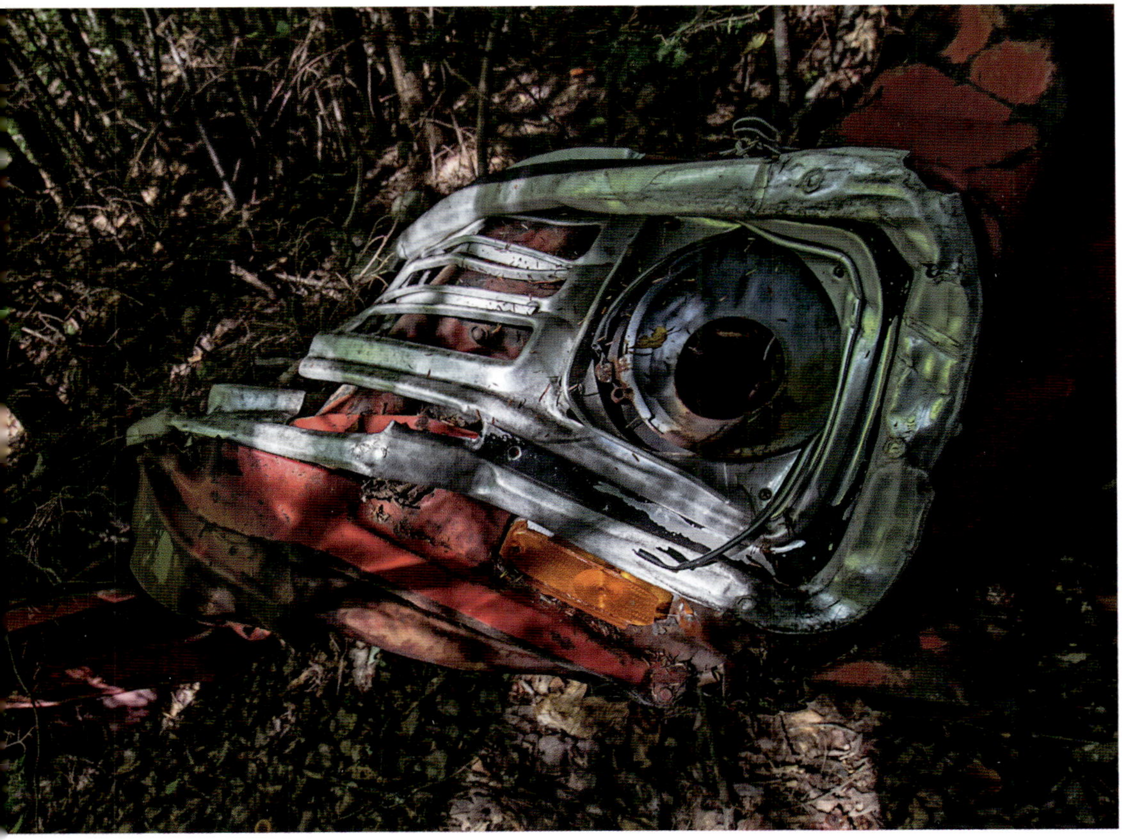

Bottom Left: On a tip from my former NH Institute of Art student, I hiked deep into the woods outside of Wolfeboro to shoot this mangled 1955 Chevrolet Bel Air. The details are hard to come by, but Emily was able to provide the following account. "According to local legend, this car was crashed by a pair of criminals who robbed a local bank. During a wild chase, they drove up Tumble Down Dick Mountain and were cornered by police from both Wolfeboro and Brookfield. In a desperate attempt to escape, they turned off the main road and began driving down a path through the woods, where they careened off a small cliff, rolled the car, and hit a large tree. The vehicle still rests there today, and no, there's no cash left over from their misadventure … I checked the trunk!"
Emily Marsh, Artist, Former NHIA Student

Right: Barely visible from the road, these assorted Chevys (1950 Styleline Deluxe, Customline) repose on a rural property in Loudon, oblivious to the maple sapping going on around them. The earthy palette made me think of my longtime friend, and greatly accomplished peer in illustration, to add a thought. "Such excitement arises from the purchase of a new car. One has planned and saved, and is envisioning a new version of themselves driving, waving, and being seen flying in this steel chariot by others. The interior is new, crackling when you sit on the seat, and it moves as smooth as silk on the road. Small dings and scratches happen and you fret over them, but one day there is a dent, then a broken window, a lost hubcap, some engine issues, then inevitably, thoughts move towards the next new car. The beloved car is parked, keys are taken, and it starts to become part of the earth again."
Tim O'Brien, Illustrator, Teacher, Past President of The Society of Illustrators of NY

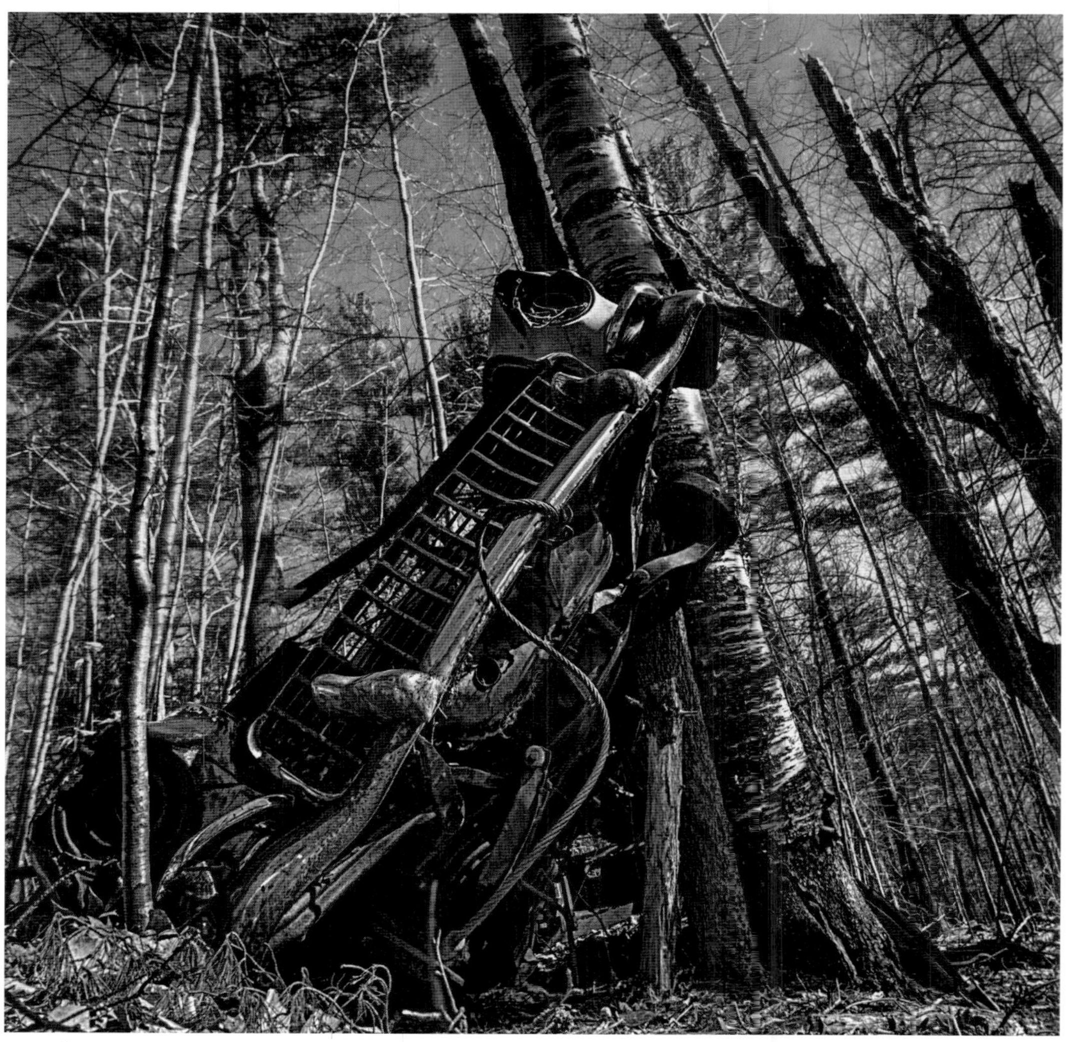

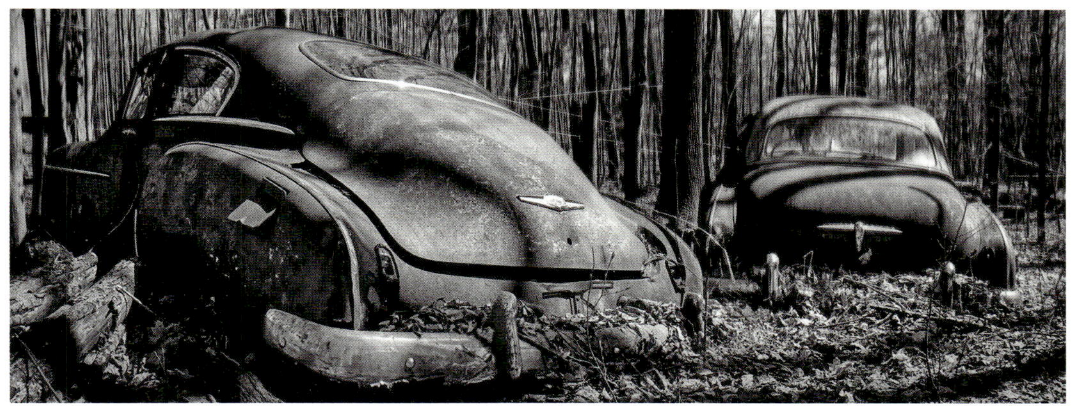

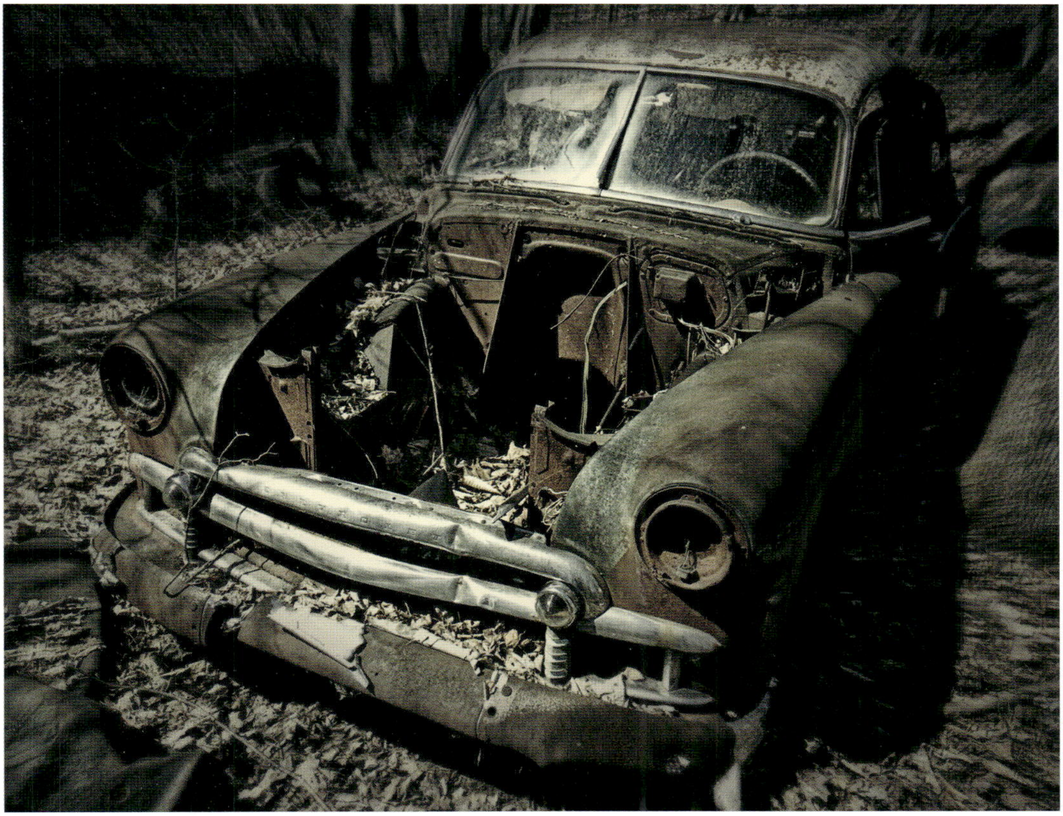

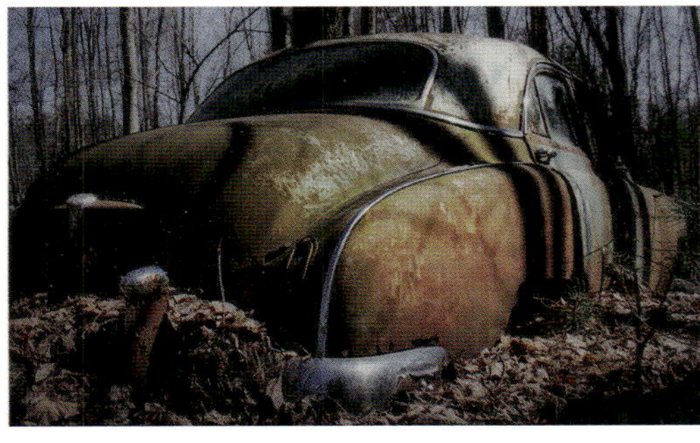

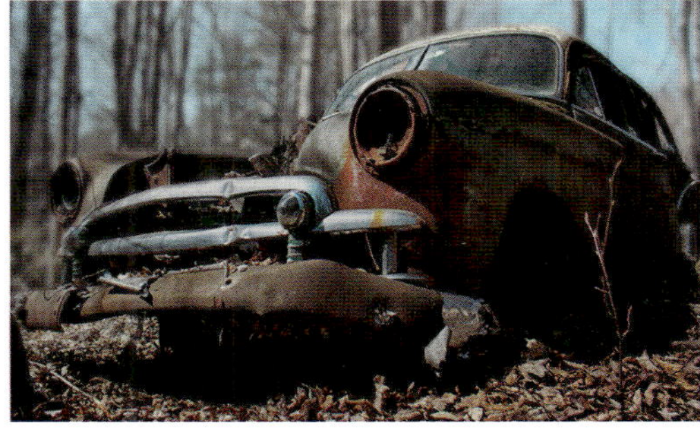

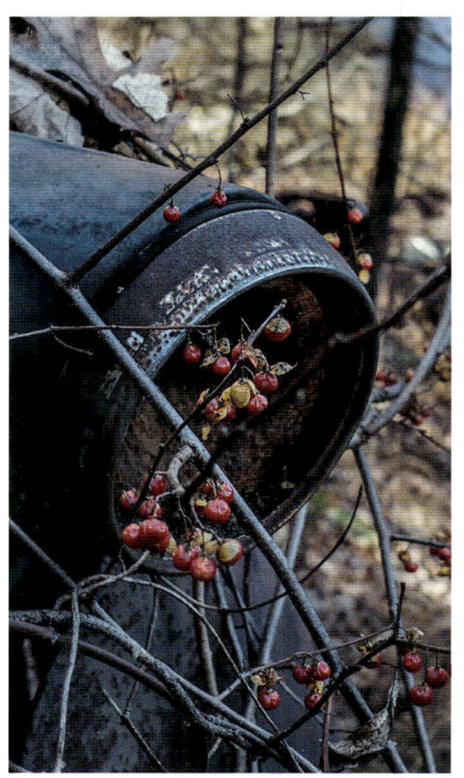

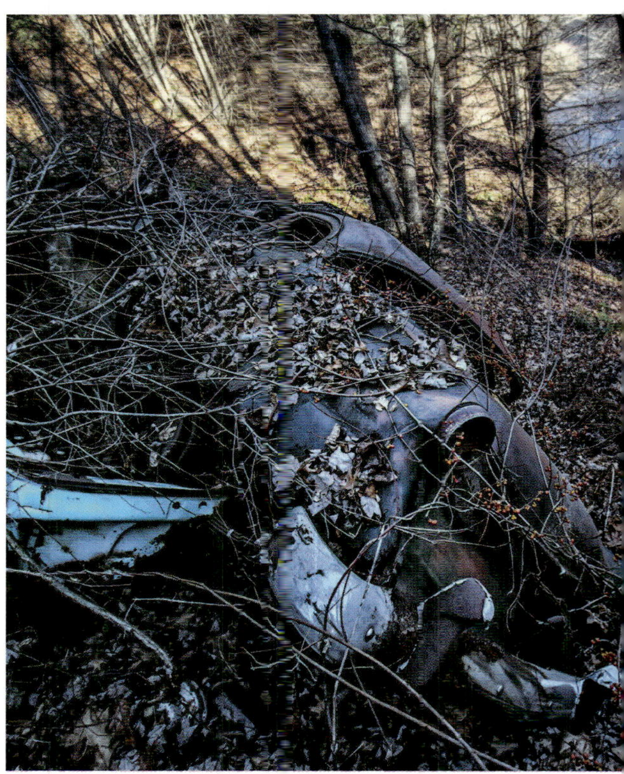

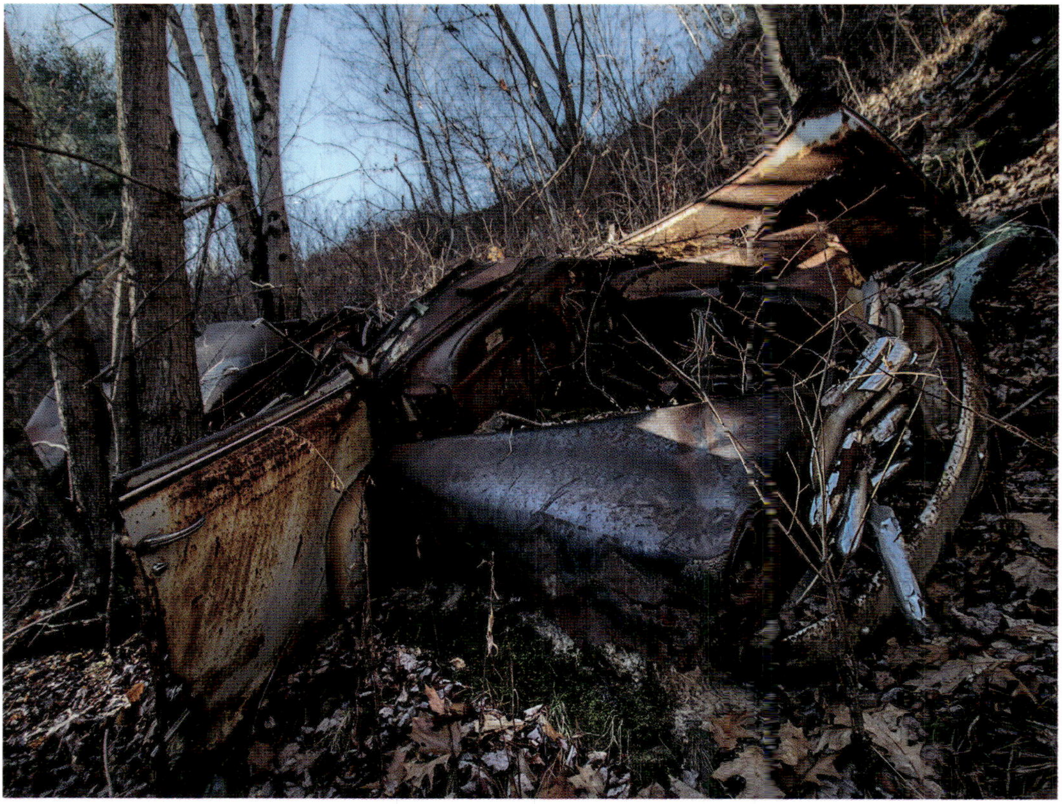

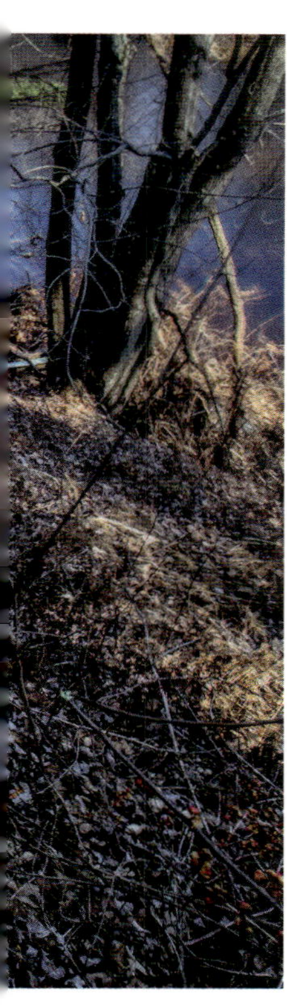

Someone told me about abandoned cars in Concord that were located behind a shuttered house on busy Route 106, right by the Steeplegate Mall. I went to find them on a crisp, but beautiful late November day, and was advised to go around and follow a trail along the river because "it's kind of steep back there." This turned out to be a HUGE understatement, as I soon found myself standing at the edge of what I can only describe as the Grand Canyon of Concord! Feeling adventurous, I decided to discard the warning and instead head straight down, which I could only do by holding onto trees and vines while often sliding on my butt. It was a long way down, but I was finally rewarded when I walked around a bend in the river and discovered my quarry illuminated by the late afternoon light. They were likely rolled over the cliff edge in the 1960s, and came to a rest about halfway down. While I was shooting the bottom right photo of a 1948 Chevy (Fleetline or Stylemaster), I was sitting on the ground braced by a tree so I wouldn't topple over. At that exact moment, my friend and youthful art mentor called to say hello, so it seemed perfect to have him remark. "Heartbreaking. The graceful patina of ashes to ashes." *Frank Foster Post, Artist*

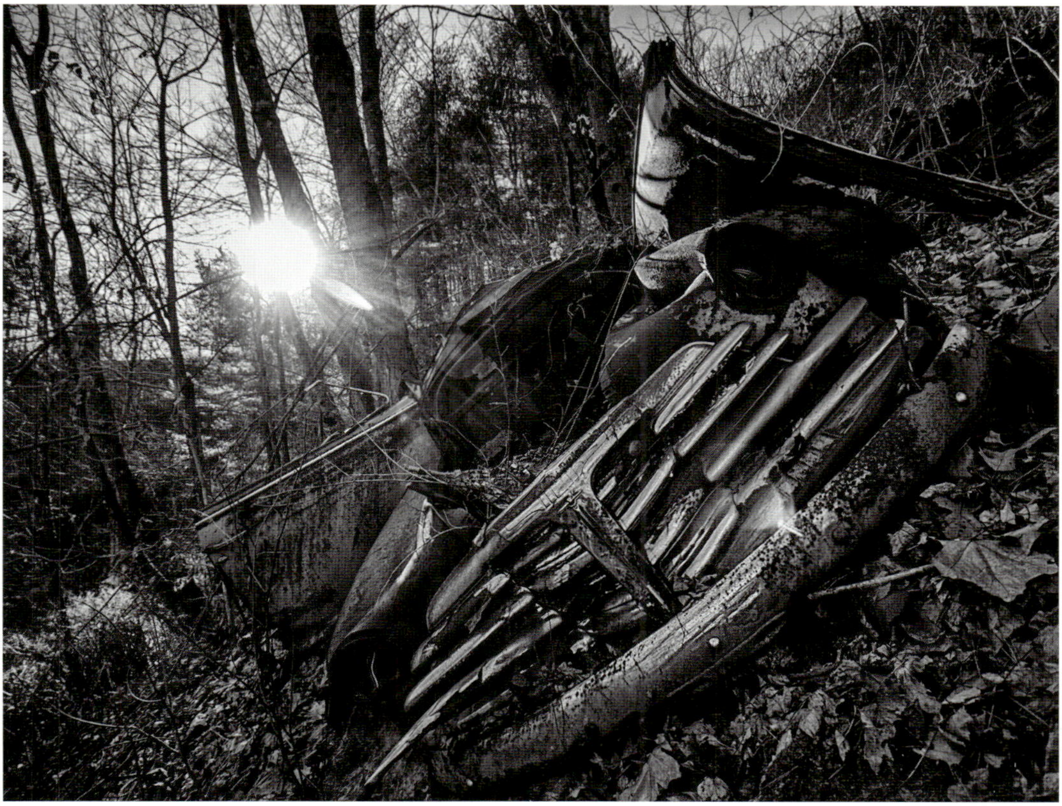

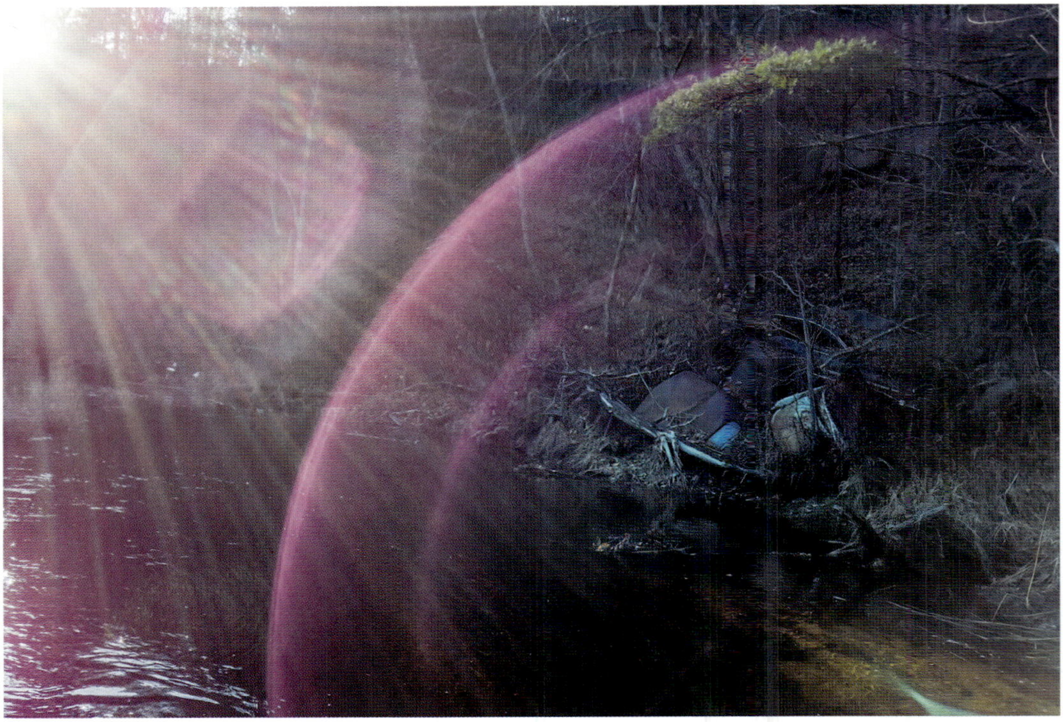

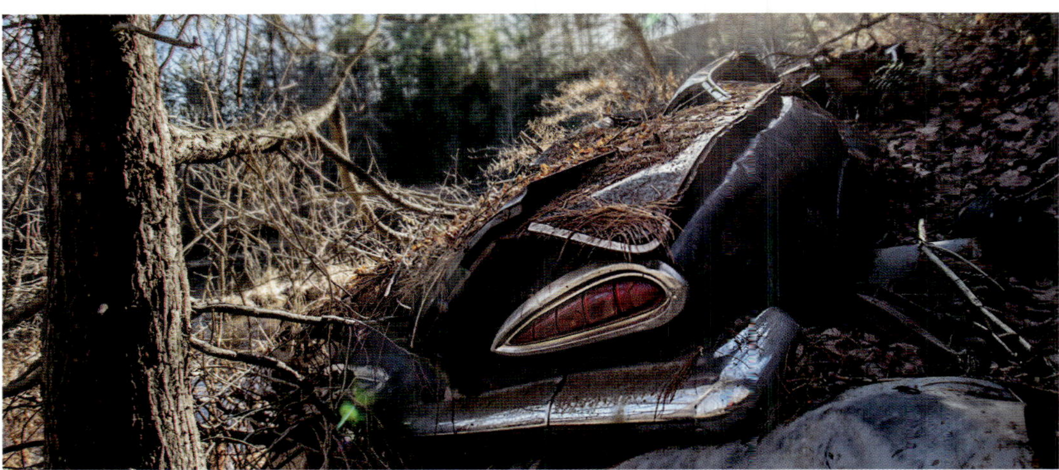

This pile-up rested far below the cars on the previous pages, and right at the edge of the Soucook River. The 1959 Chevrolet Impala was the most intact, and it's possible that the remains of three or more vehicles are tangled up in this cluster. To get the shots I wanted required me wading into the very cold water, but it was well worth it to be able to bask in the magic and serenity of this scene while capturing the incredible light peeking over the cliff top. Many years ago, I illustrated an album cover for Columbian/Latin music superstar Carlos Vives called *La Tierra Del Olvido* (The Land of Oblivion), and these photos reminded me of that concept. With that, I'm grateful that Carlos quoted some of the lyrics to the beautiful title song of that album for me after viewing this spread.

"*Como naufragan mis miedos si navego tu mirada,*
como alertas mis sentidos con tu voz enamorada"
(Like a shipwreck, my fears navigated into your eyes;
how you alert my senses with your loving voice.)
Carlos Vives, Singer, Songwriter, Actor

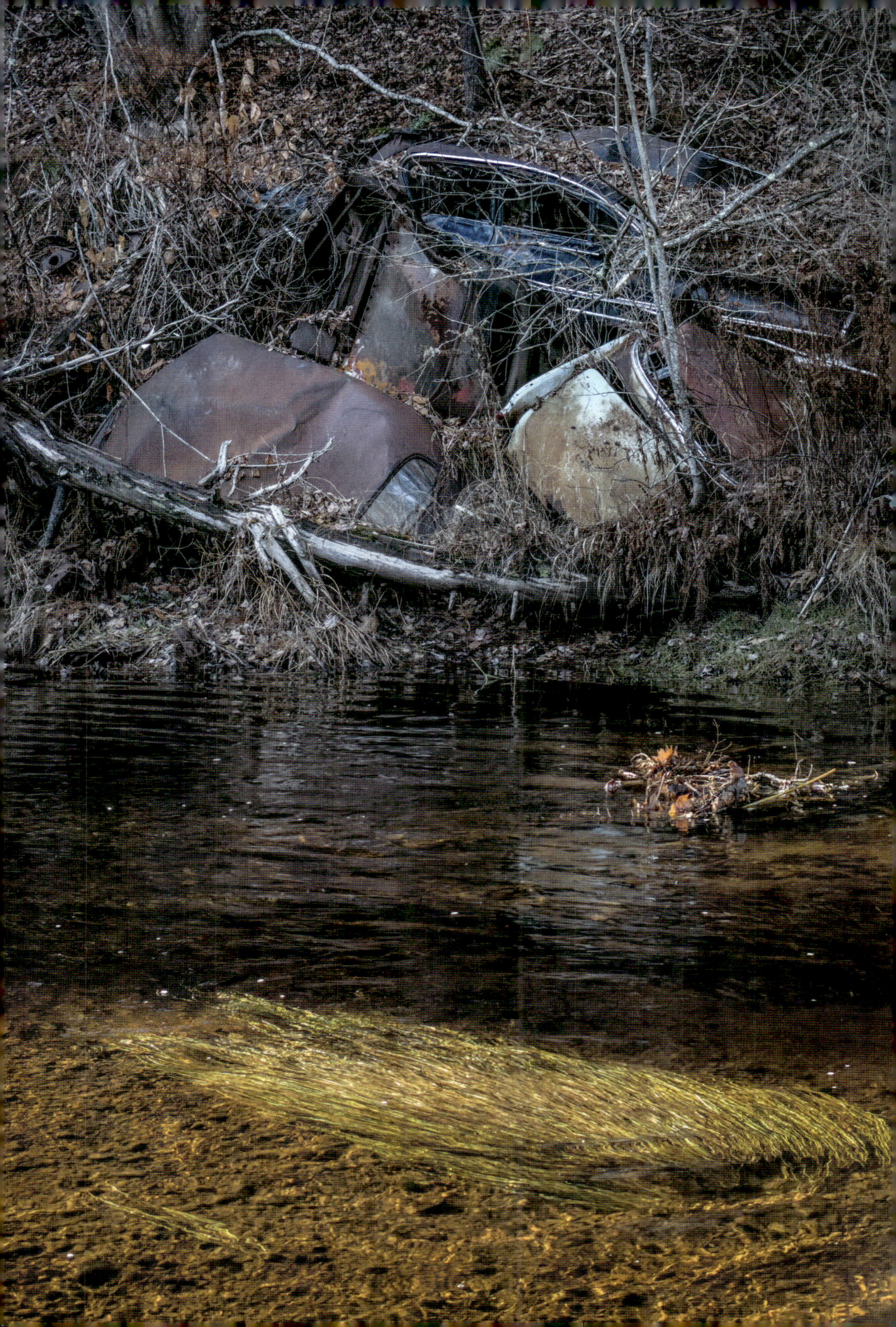

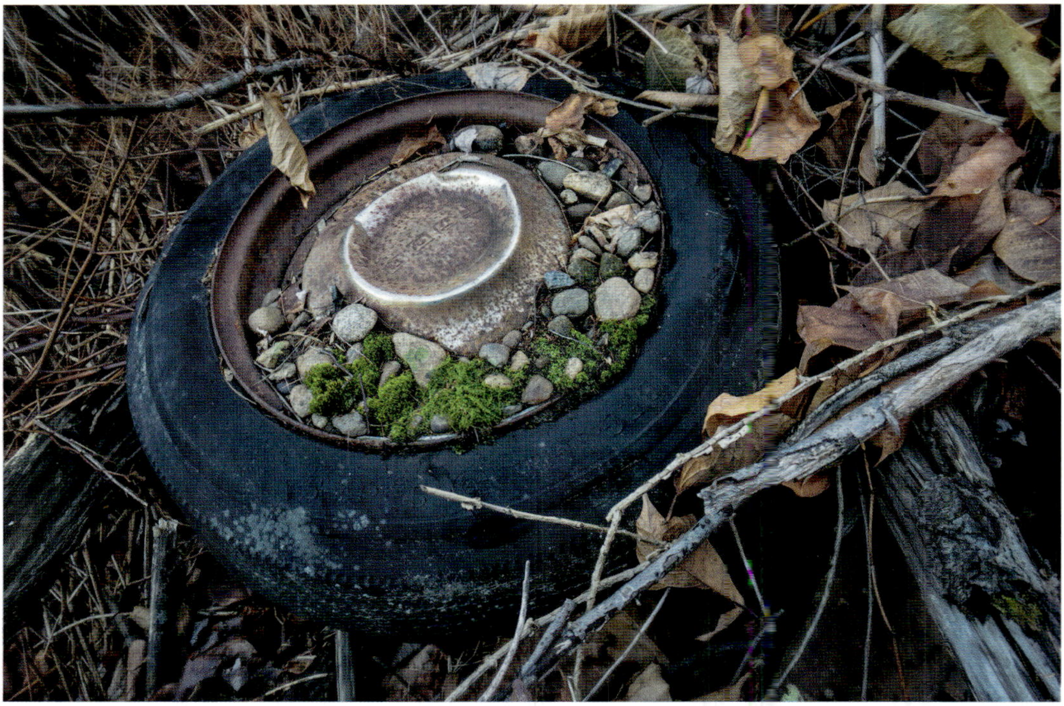

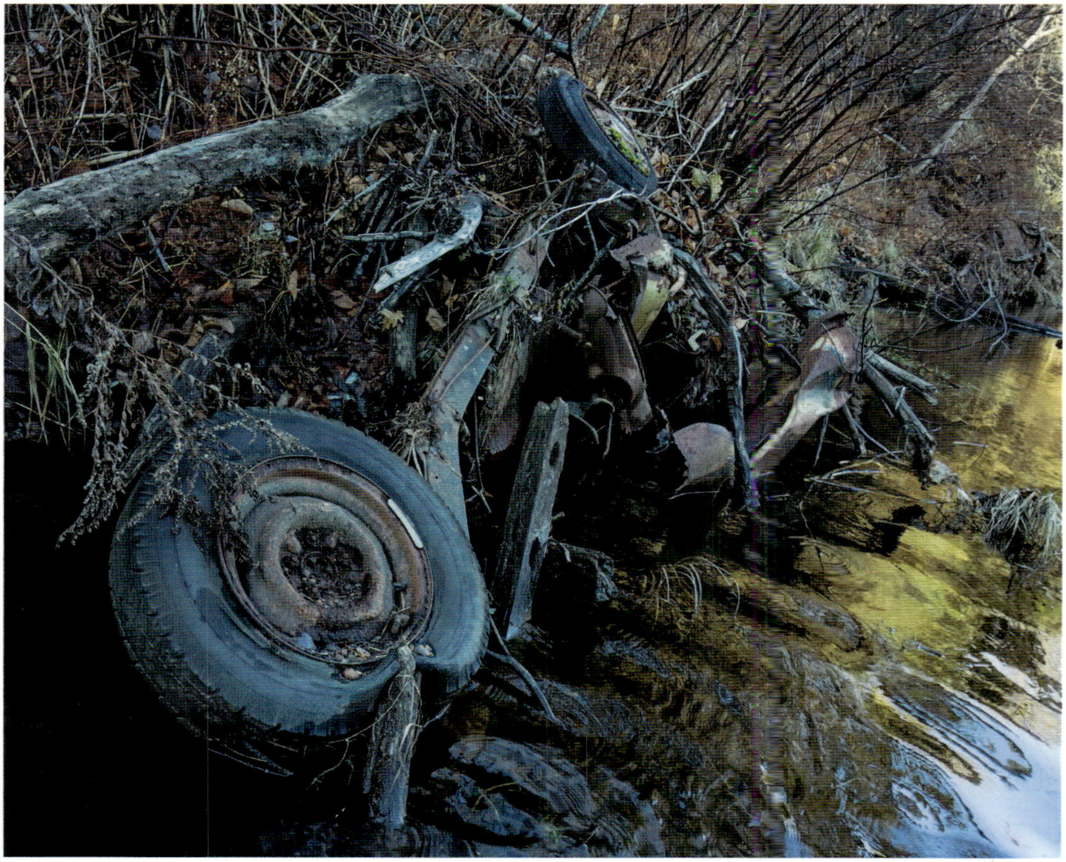

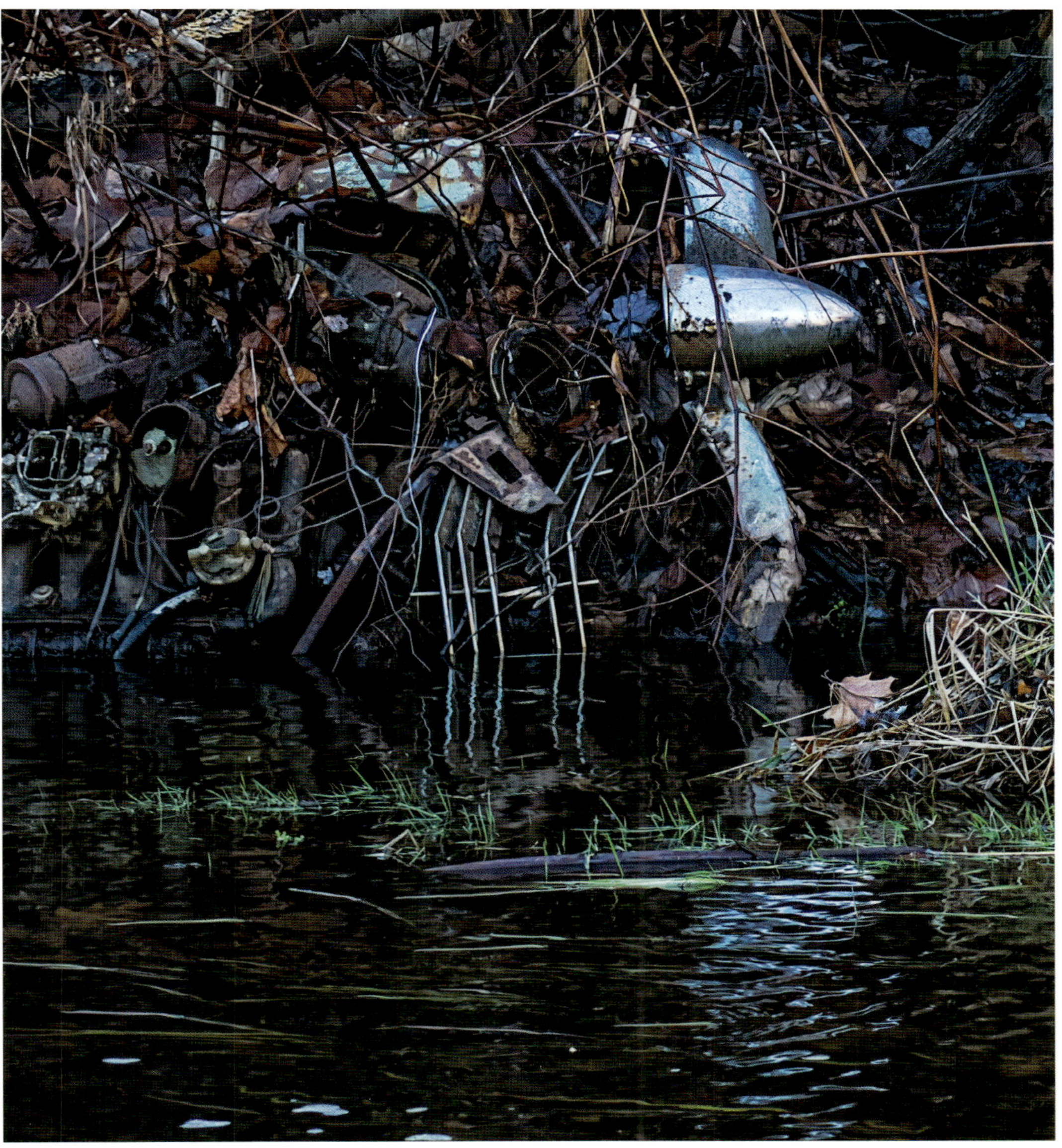

Even more automobile remains are strewn downstream along the river from those on the preceding pages. At this point, I was in the freezing water way too long, but I couldn't help but continue shooting. Wouldn't you know it—while I was up to my thighs in the river, I got a call from another friend wanting to confirm my studio shoot with his band. Therefore, it made sense to have him comment below, which he did so very colorfully. Anyway, by the time I waded out of the river, the sun had disappeared over the top and it had become very cold. My feet were now completely numb, and it felt like I was walking with blocks of concrete encasing them. This big oaf's crawl out of the canyon was longer, and much more challenging than I wanted, but I finally made it. I'm also going to pat myself on the back for good timing—the next day it snowed quite a bit! "These photos remind me of growing up in The Fens of East Anglia (England), and I was always fascinated by rusting metal machines left in the fields. When my son and daughter were children, I use to take them to a huge West London scrapyard. We'd watch those cranes equipped with massive grabbers like primeval behemoths holding cars down in the mud with their tracks, and ripping them in half with their grabbers; the innards dangling, and liquid pouring out as they flung them onto a humongous pile of car bodies. Then another crane would throw them on to a conveyer belt, and into a hopper where they would be pulverized. Hours of fun!" *Rupert Greenall, Musician, Keyboard Player (The Fixx)*

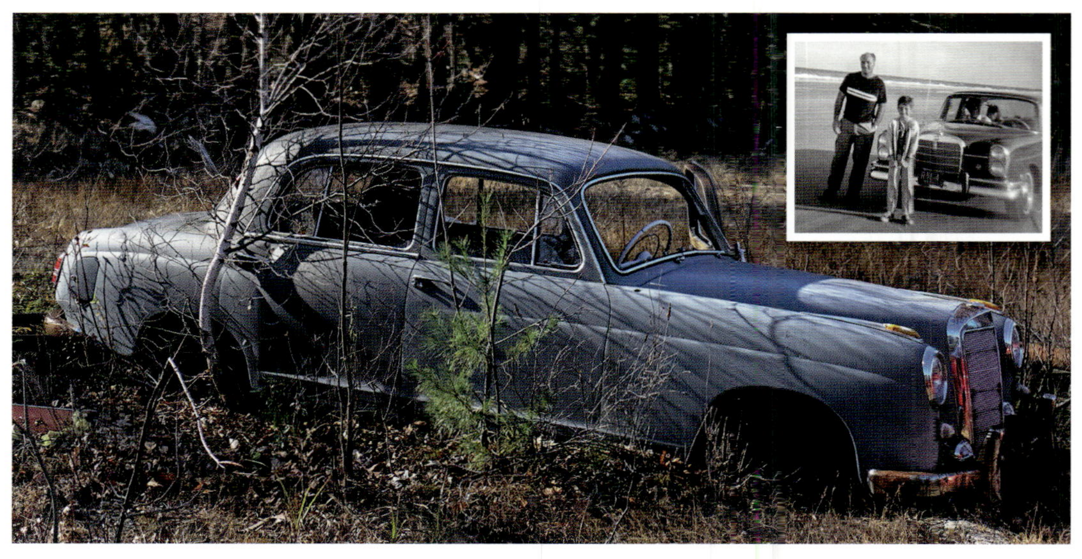

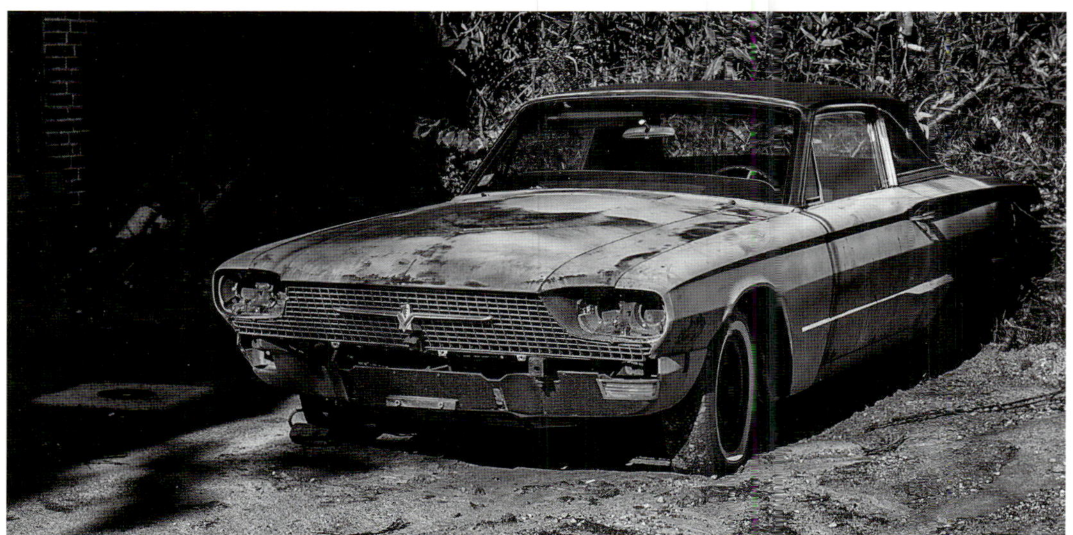

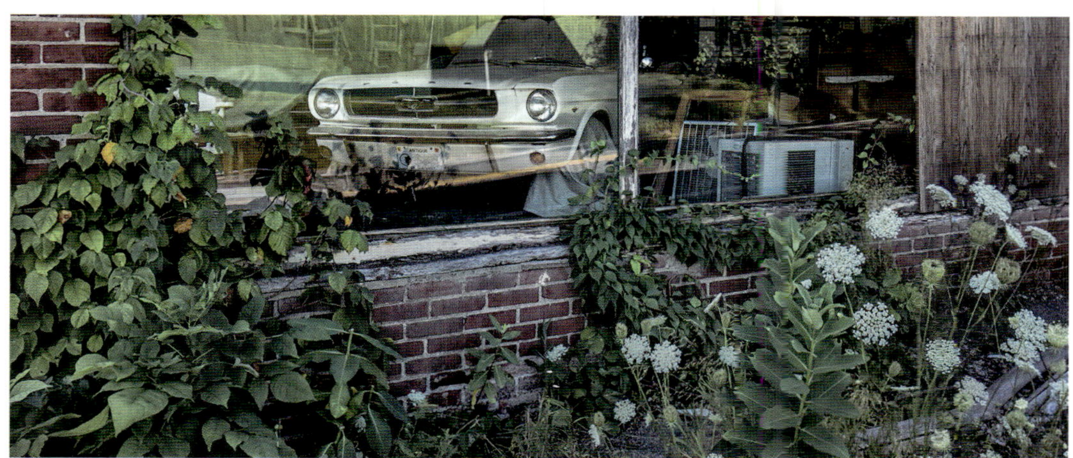

Top Left: A friend works in an auto-parts business in New Ipswich, and he took me out back to show me this 1959 Mercedes-Benz 219 (or 220S). They only deal with newer vehicles now, but somehow this car remained at the very back of the property. Perfect, as the Mercedes has special memories for me—my family owned two of them in the 1960s (inset photo—that's us, and not an outtake from *The Sopranos*). My dad was in the very un-luxurious business of roofing and siding, but somehow decided that he JUST had to have a Mercedes. To quote my very unpretentious mom, Matilda: "It felt kind of silly to drive around our neighborhood in one because nobody else we knew had a car like that." One thing I remember is that for all their touted German engineering, and reputed dependability, both cars were always breaking down. My folks finally got fed up, and replaced the second Benz with a Ford Maverick.

Middle Left: This 1966 Ford Thunderbird sits outside a legendary abandoned car dealership in Weare, just ten minutes from my home.

Bottom Left and Right: The dealership building is in rough condition, and a large back section collapsed a few years ago. This pristine 1967 Mustang Convertible is easily visible from the road through the front showroom window. My good pal, and drumming legend, who loves Mustangs and owned one in his youth, shares a story: "The only thing better than being a sixteen-year-old junior at Harrison High School, New York, in 1973 was being one with a 1967 dark blue convertible Ford Mustang with a white top, mag wheels, racked-up back, and a bad-ass 289 motor with manual shift between the bucket seats. The more I think about it, it's clear my good looks, charm and talent probably took a back seat to my Mustang when it came to girls! I also somehow managed to keep it a secret that the tranny was a 3 speed ... not a 4." *Jerry Marotta, Musician, Drummer (Peter Gabriel, Paul McCartney, Orleans, Hall & Oates, Stevie Nicks, etc.)*

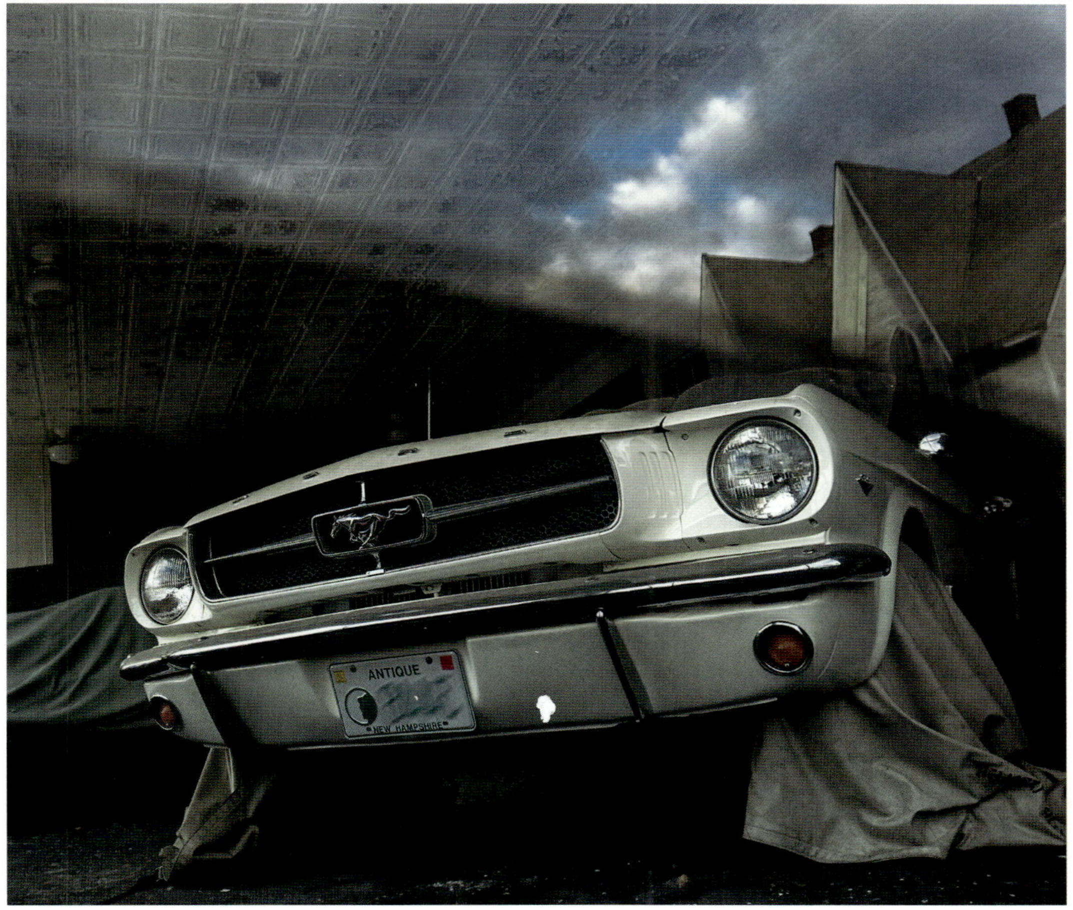

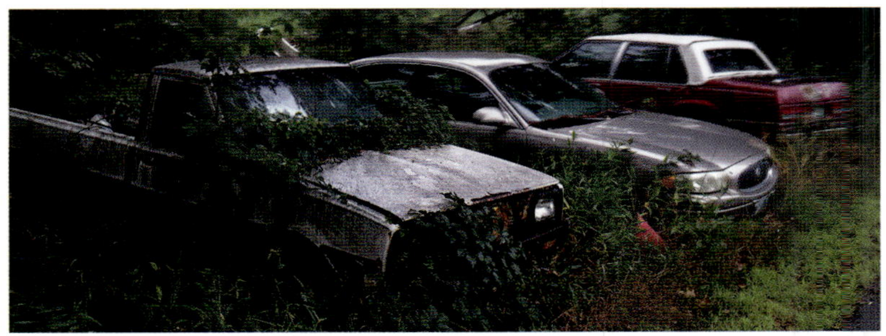

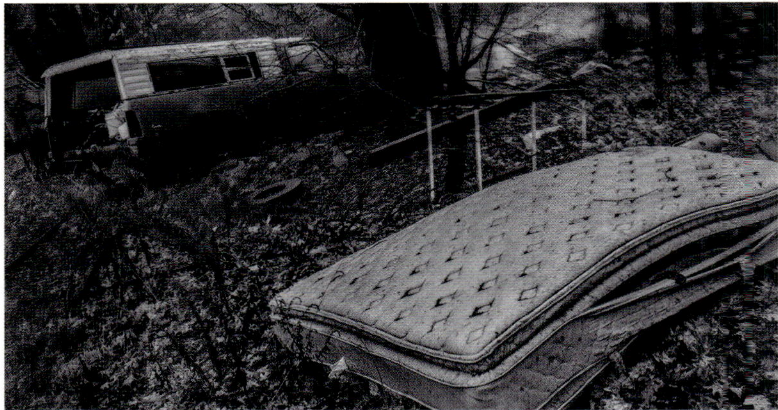

Above: In Henniker, a trio of more recent vintage cars have been sitting alongside the road in the same spot for as far as I can remember. A short distance past them, an abandoned truck sits in a forlorn area strewn with construction and farming equipment, and many other discarded items.

Top Right: Back to the abandoned car dealership in Weare for a moment, where this 1968 Lincoln Continental sits outside the brick building amongst the overgrowth and debris. The business was started in 1919 by Maurice Grant, and was known as the South Weare Garage. This building was constructed in 1930, replacing an old grist mill housing the original business that burned down. It became a chartered Ford dealership, and Henry Ford himself was said to have visited this location on a number of occasions. The owner moved the business to a larger location in the 1960s, but retained this place as storage for his personal collection, some of which may or may not be for sale. I pass by fairly often, and as of this writing there are many heavy construction vehicles on the premises, which leads me to believe that there are structural issues occurring due to its unusual perch on a hilly intersection. So far, a nice-looking retaining wall has been built along the steep drop-off at the front of the building.

Bottom Right: And finally, I'm closing out this chapter with Henniker. I've always been fascinated with miniature car replicas, and I have a few in my studio to go along with the hundreds of dinosaurs and animals populating the shelves. When I found out that longtime resident Doug Paul had an extensive collection in his garage and home, I knew I wanted to photograph them. This is just a fraction, and it's mounted on the wall at his garage entrance in plastic display boxes with a mirrored backdrop. Here's Doug's response to some questions I asked him. "I started collecting models when I was about ten, in 1954 or so. Devitts Garage (where I worked) had a display case of model cars with coin slots for each car. Old cars were metal, but the new ones were plastic. All were 1953-54 vintage, and there was a sign, 'Save today for your next new car,' so I put coins in the 1954 Chevy convertible. The first car I actually did own was a 4-cylinder 1951 red Jeepster with a black top that I paid $100 for, but my favorite classic car I had was a 1949 Ford hardtop, white over light blue. I also had a black 1981 Corvette T-top (bought it used, and had it for many years), and just sold it last summer. Oddly enough, there are no miniatures in my collection representing any that I've had, but I'm happy to have driven many that were owned by friends!" *Doug Paul, Navy, Firefighter/EMT in Hopkinton, NH, Retired Henniker Police Sergeant*

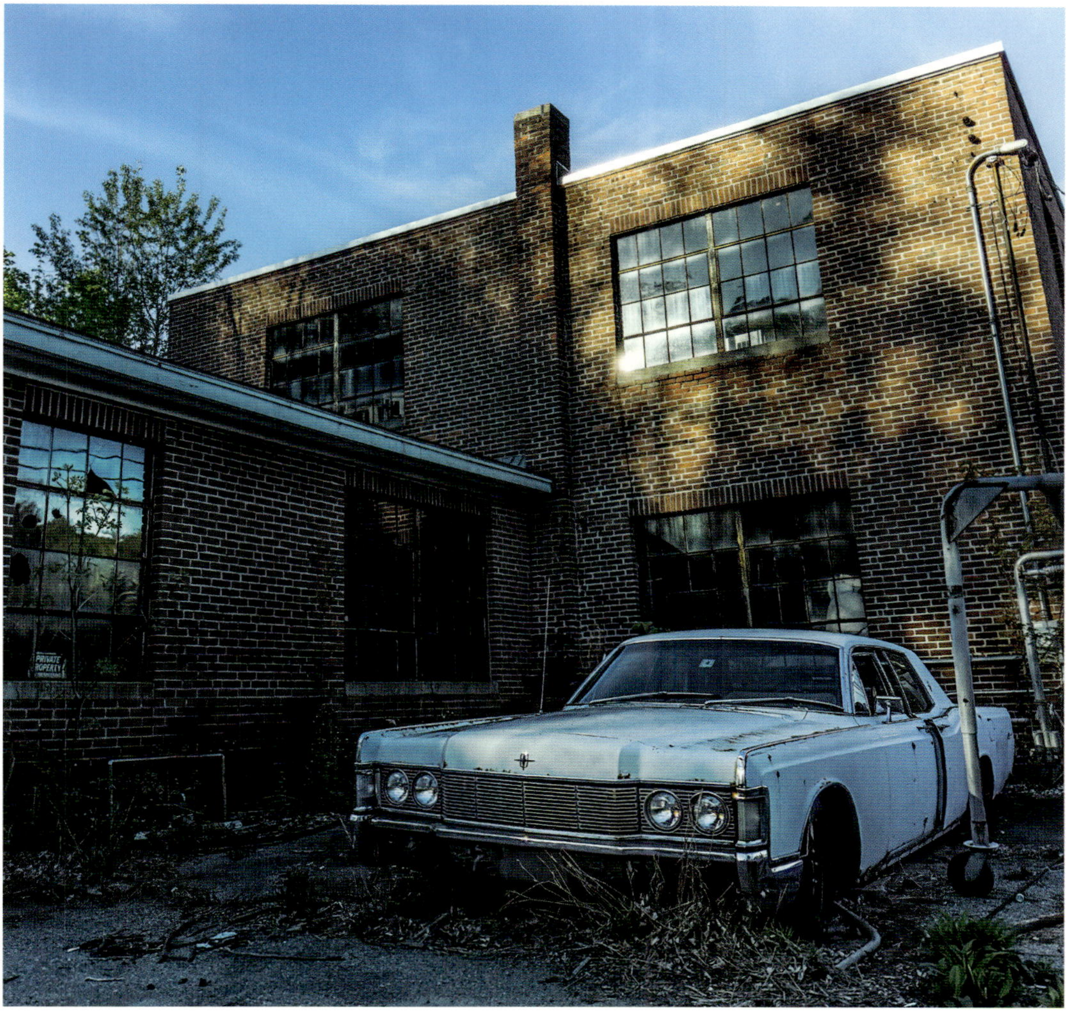

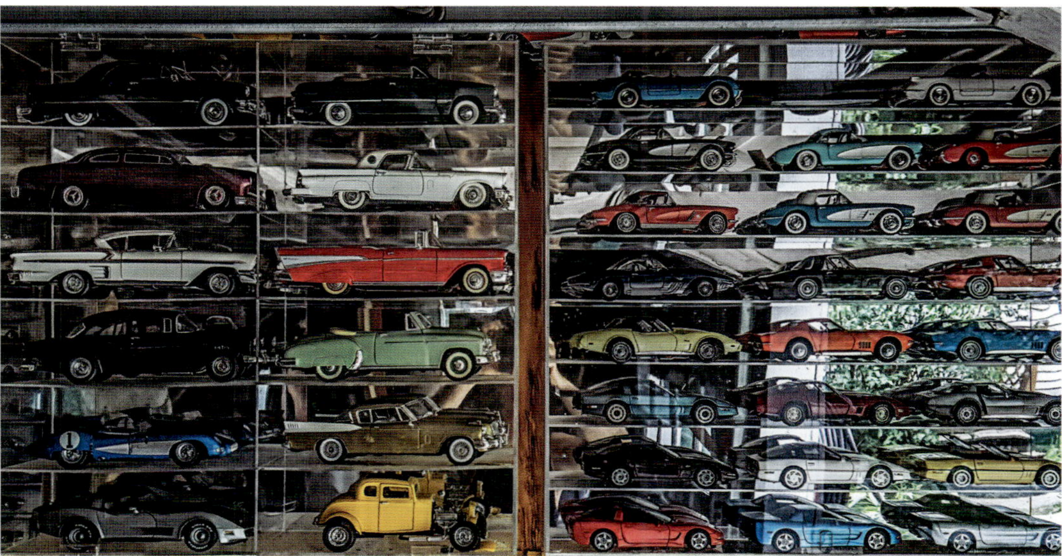

2

BLANCHARD AUTO SALVAGE

Located in Wilton, Blanchard Auto Salvage is a remarkable time capsule, and I love spending hours shooting there. Owner Wendy Blanchard has been very kind and generous, allowing me access many times with my camera on the thirty-plus acres the business encompasses. The original yard was started by her father Ken Blanchard in 1945, and it's been in operation at the present location where it was moved to in 1951. Ken was known as a very kind and generous person, and always willing to help people in need. Blanchard's was also the place where many young people would go to learn how to drive. And something close to my heart: it's nice to know that he was a performing musician, and taught his four children how to play the guitar.

Blanchard's is particularly interesting to me because of its diverse landscape. There are large open areas containing many vehicles, as well as heavy brambles, gentle hills and deciduous woods that lead to a large section with stately pines. The latter is probably my favorite, as some of the oldest cars lie here in hushed solitude, with a natural roof formed by the pines that reminds me of a cathedral. It's incredibly quiet and peaceful, and the late afternoon light that sneaks through is spectacular. Welcome to *Carassic Park!*

Right: *"20th Century Schizoid Car"* I always found this photo to be strangely compelling, and those in the musical know will understand the title reference. The palpable look of anguish brought it to mind, and I think my original LP sleeve of *In the Court of the Crimson King* has as much wear and tear on it as this old car! I also really dig it because it looks like a scary, bottom-lurking sea creature. My close friend, and a man of great faith commented on this photo; and, not surprisingly he chose something from the Bible. "' ... for dust thou art, and unto dust shalt thou return.' Genesis 3:7. This last glimmer of a soul seems wanting to tell us something before vanishing." *Mark Fredrickson, Illustrator*

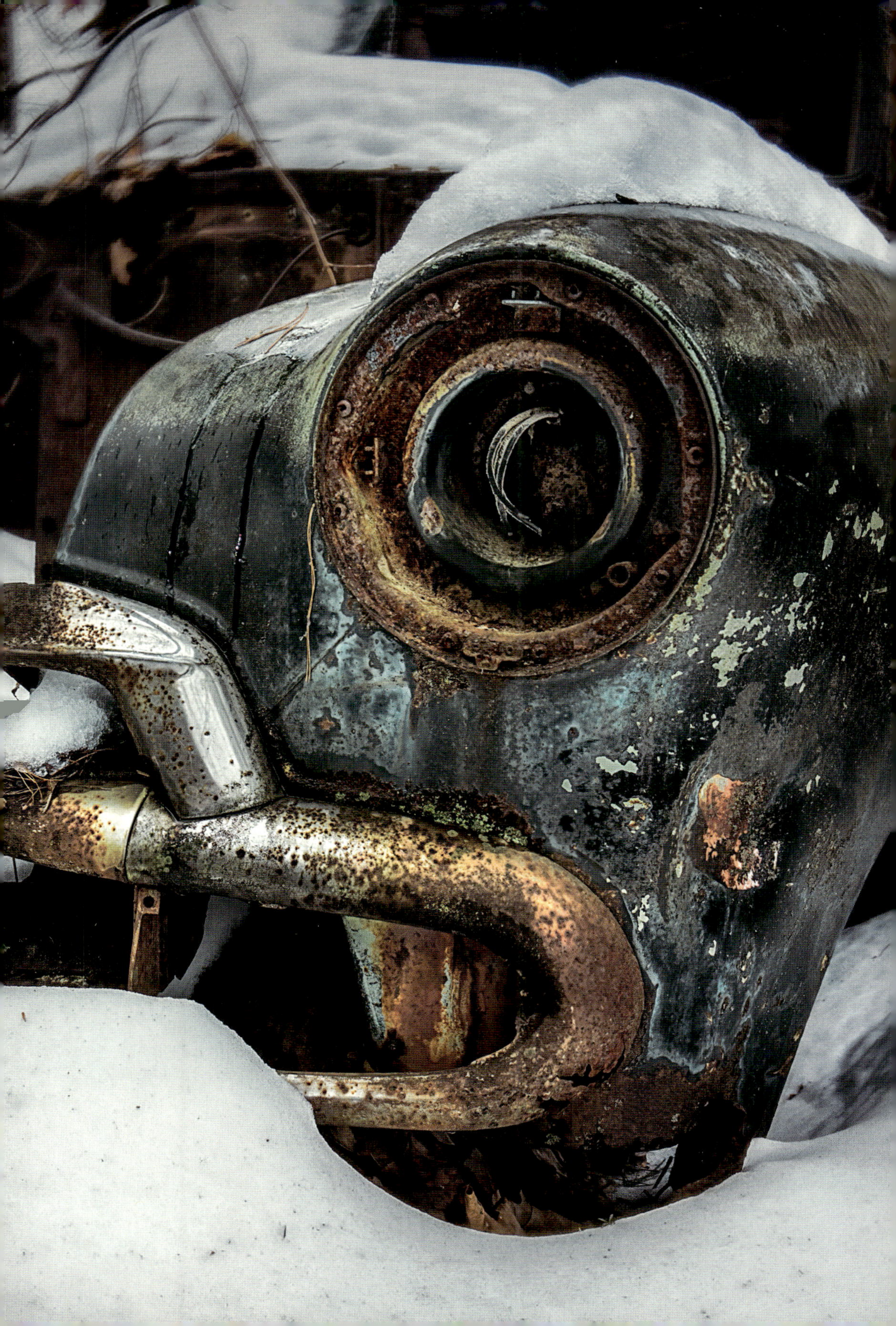

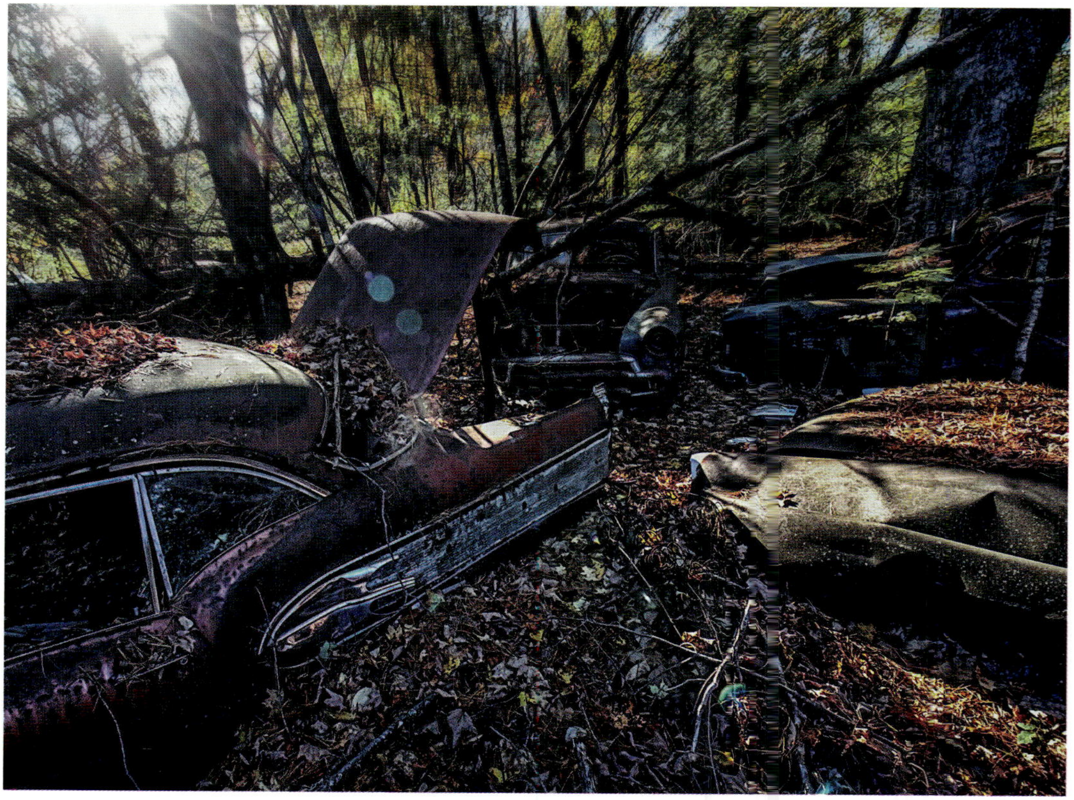

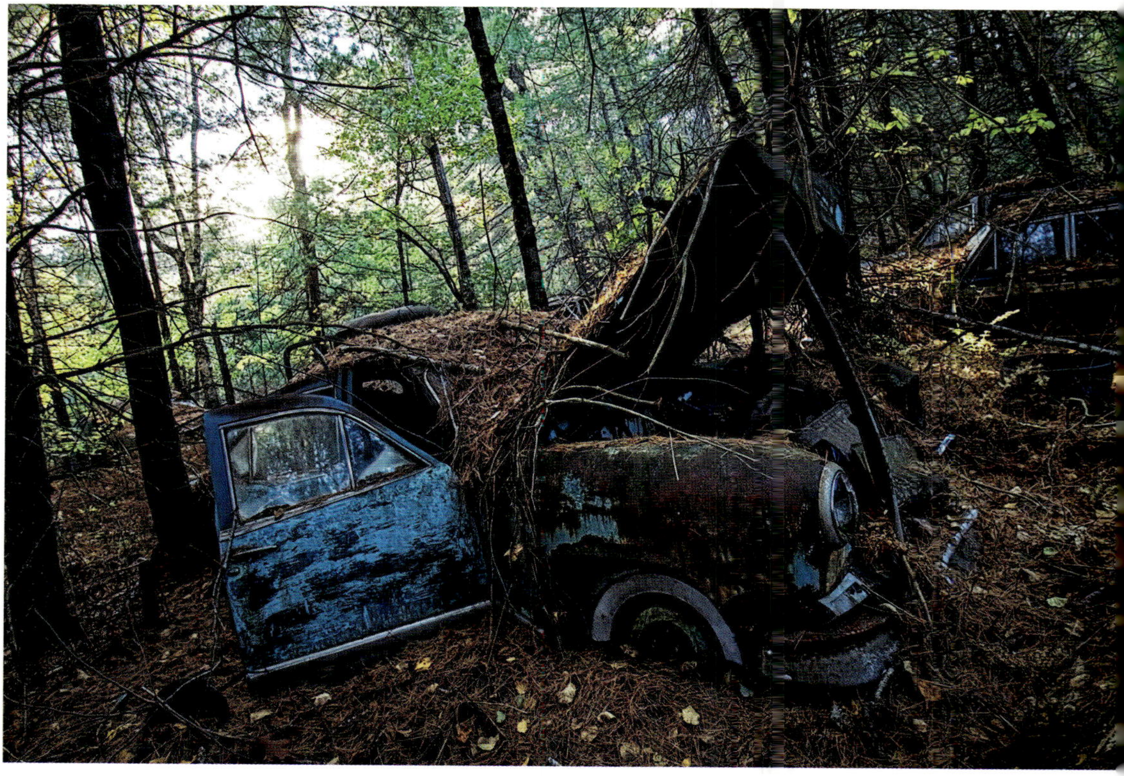

It's hard to describe just how magical Blanchard's back acres are, and how easy it is to get lost in the beauty, light, and history of this forgotten zone. Dense, with a seemingly endless array of vehicles, my thoughts are only accompanied by the sounds of birds and the occasional chattering of a squirrel. As a side note, I'm completing this book during the global pandemic of 2020, and I've been watching more old movies than usual. *American Graffiti* was fun to revisit, and I especially liked the scene with two of the characters walking through a junkyard at night. *The French Connection* has an interesting segment in a vast NYC salvage yard, and Alfred Hitchcock's *Psycho* has a prolonged scene in a car dealership. However, my wife and I are totally hooked on *The Twilight Zone*, and it's amazing to see how the thread of concepts from the early-1960s show often reflects the current world situation and state of mind. A really enjoyable episode called "The Whole Truth" is about a colorful used car salesman with a haunted jalopy on his lot, and many cool old cars make an appearance (spoiler: Soviet leader Nikita Khrushchev turns up). Many other episodes in the series showcase old vehicles, and as I watch them along with the movies, I experience a real thrill seeing the cars I've been photographing drive by in a scene, or line the streets in the seemingly normal life of a bygone era. All quiet now.

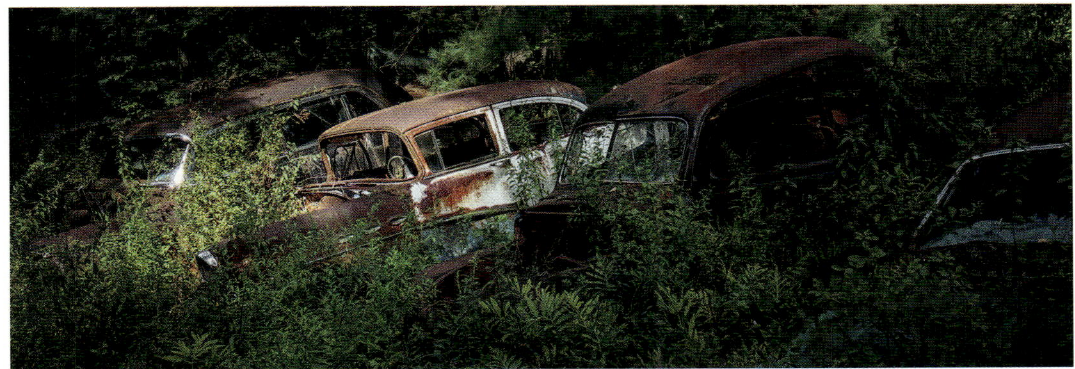

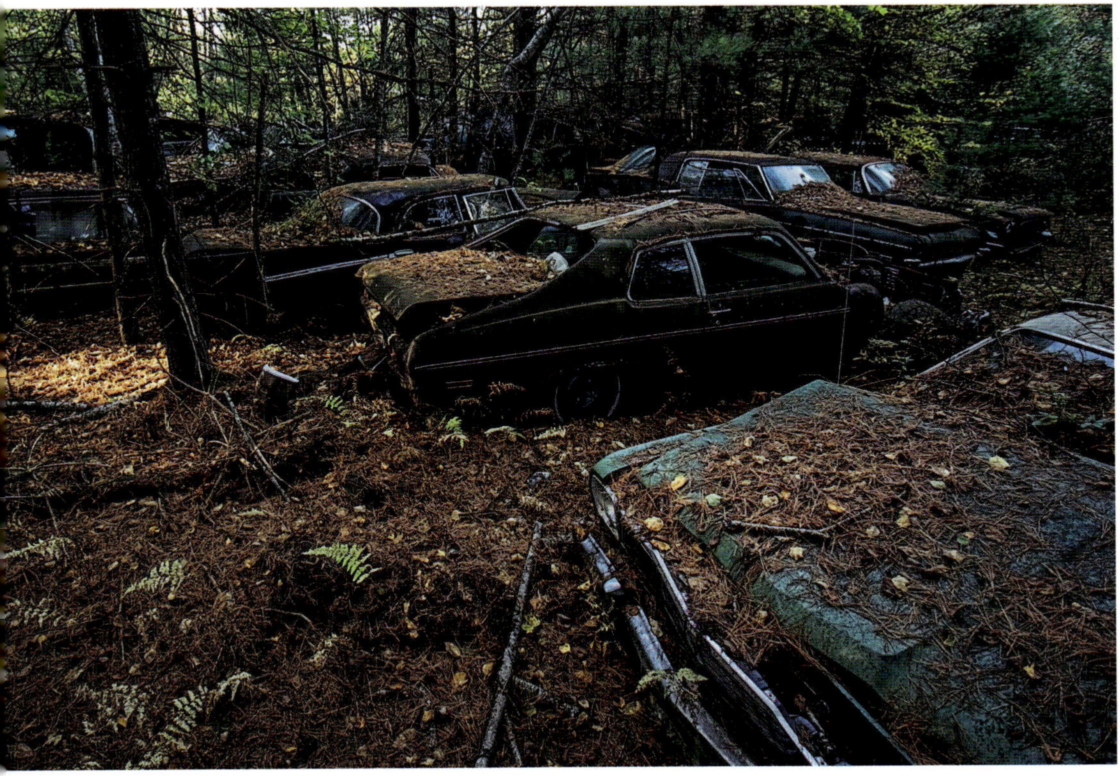

Top Right: From my very talented friend, and two-time concert performer in my studio. "The sedan in this photo reminds me of the first car I really knew—a green Dodge Dart my mom had in my early years. I wonder how it got there, and where 'there' is. Is this beside a house? Or did someone just abandon it in the middle of the forest? In California, you have to pay a 'planned non-operation' fee, but at least you won't have to get it smog checked anymore. You know, some new tires and a little Febreeze, and it might not be so bad!" *Tom Griesgraber, Musician, Chapman Stick Player*

Here's another reaction to the same photo inspired by the Bard via Kid Creole and The Coconuts. "I, Too, Have Seen the Woods" *Avraham Bank, Photographer*

"Trunk In Da Hood!" This 1961 Pontiac Bonneville Convertible is one of the most fascinating cars to be found in Blanchard's, and I love Marc's take on it. "What this photo does is simultaneously capture death and rebirth. At one point this car was treasured like a newborn baby; and, at another point in its progression, it outlived its usefulness and was cast aside. However, it now has been repurposed as a planter box for a tall and stately tree as if the forces of Nature had deemed it a proper headstone for its life." *Marc Bonilla, Musician, Guitarist (Keith Emerson Band, Ronnie Montrose, Glenn Hughes, etc.)*

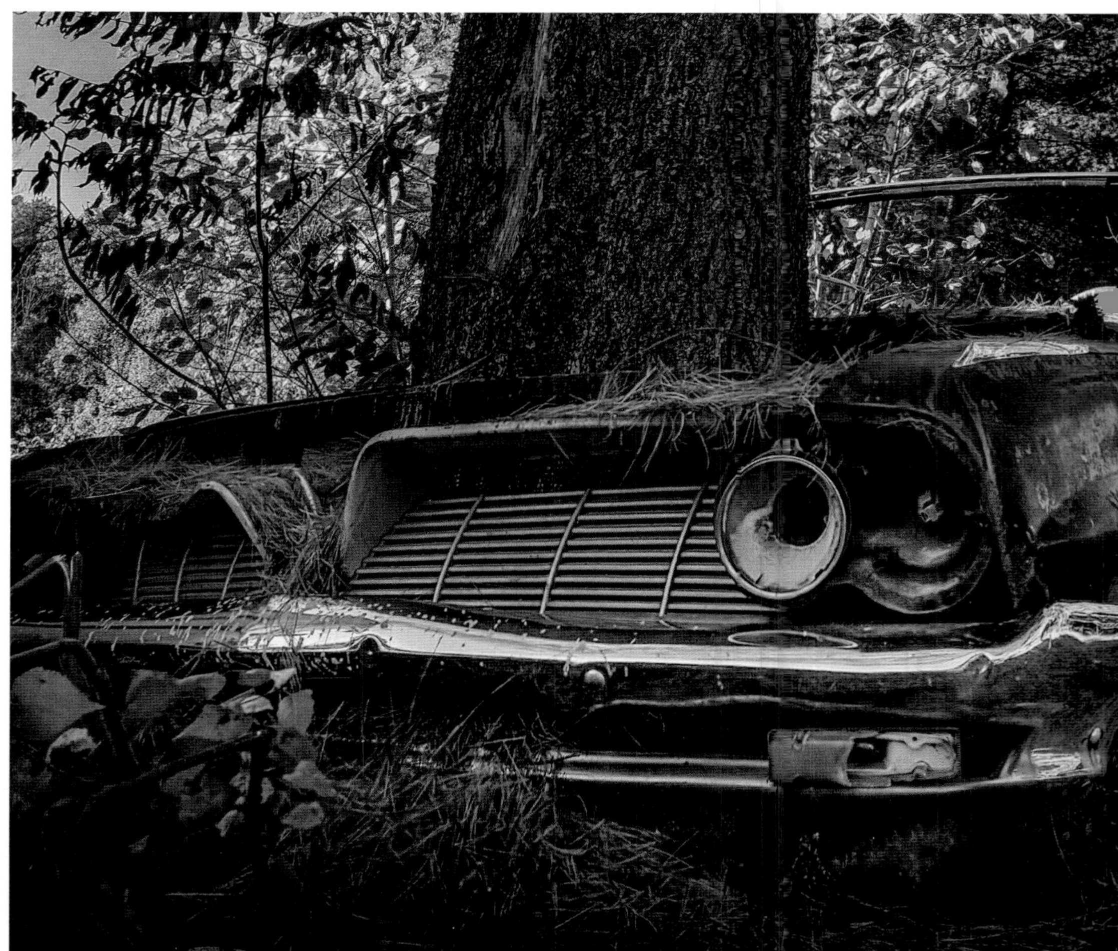

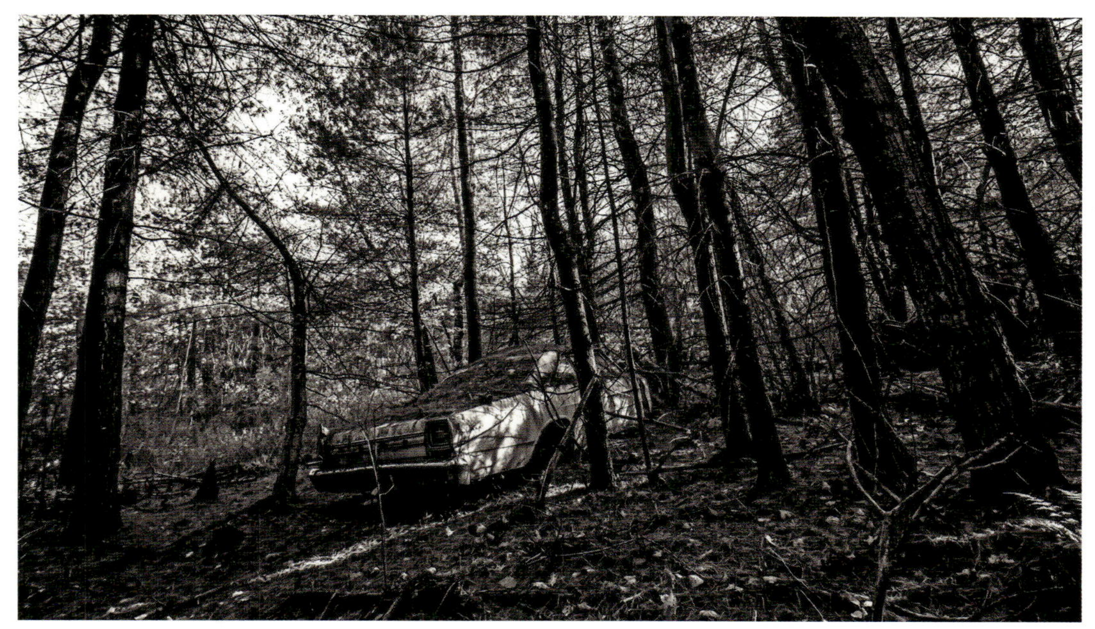

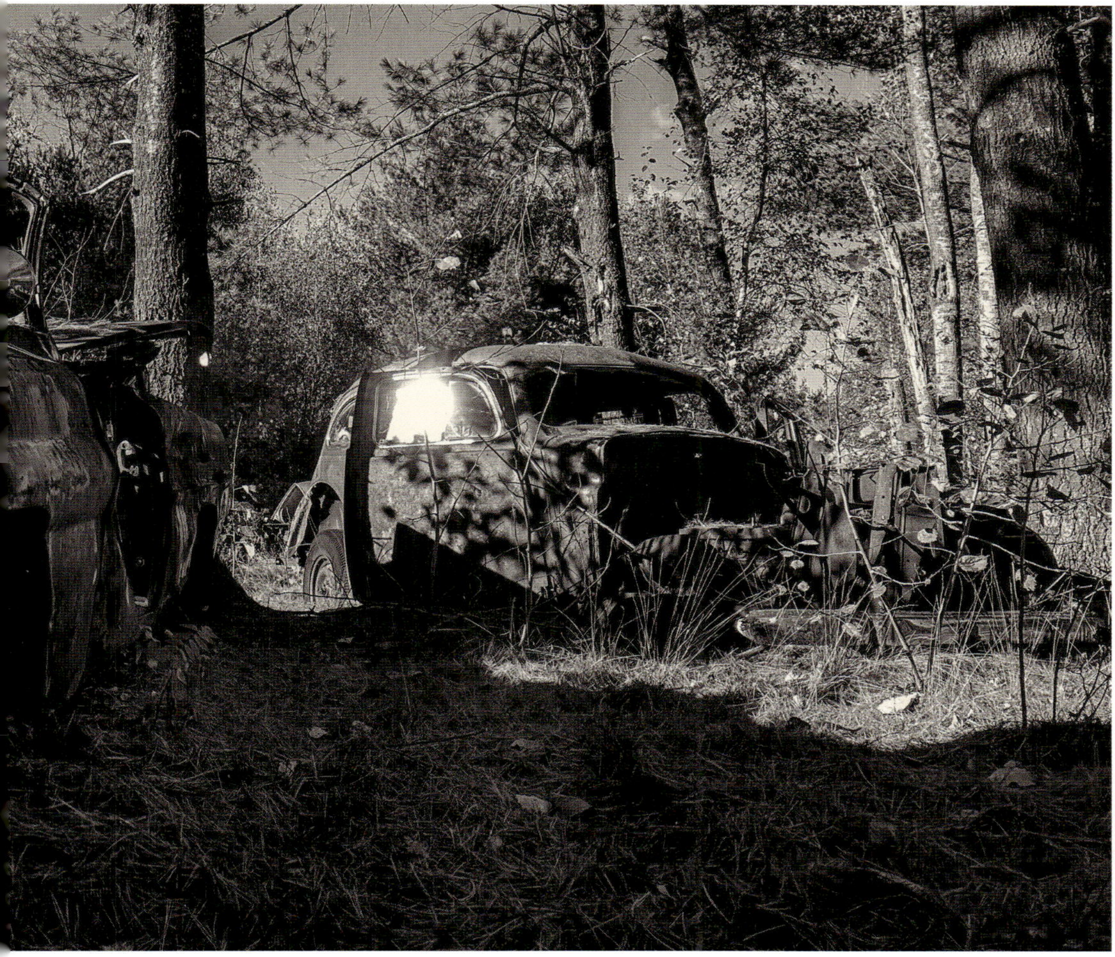

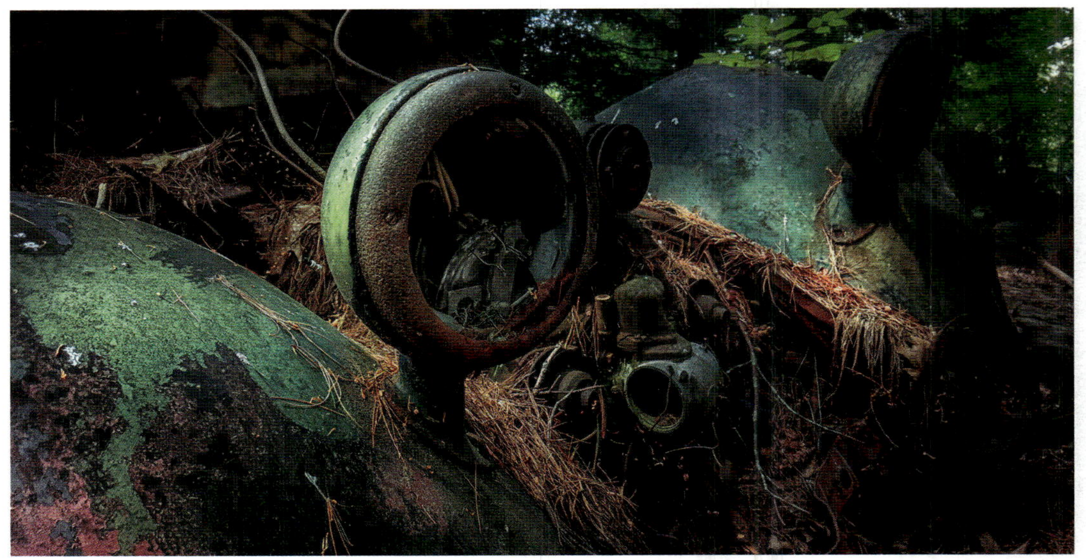

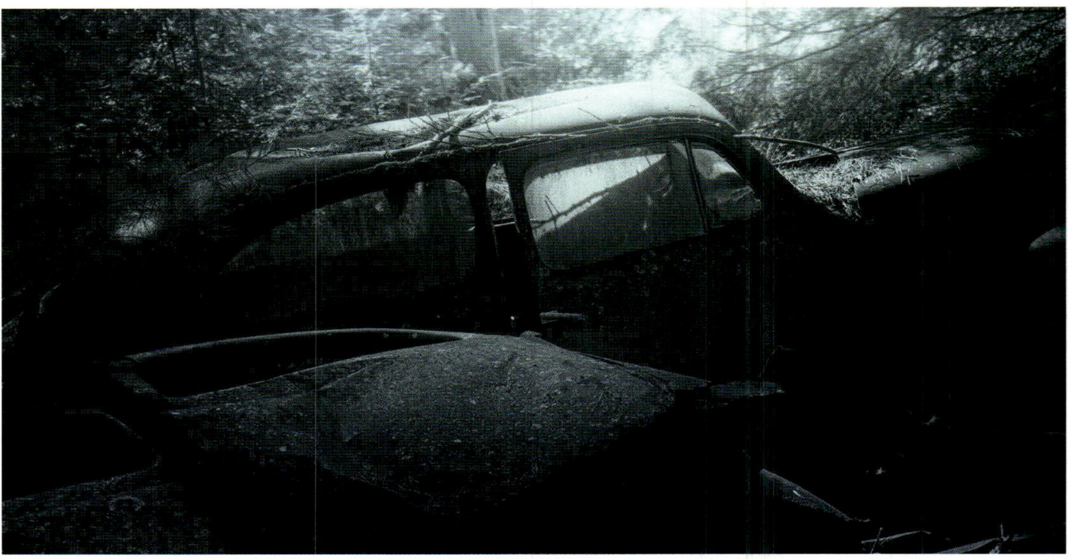

Top Left: My good friend, and one of the first artists I got to know when I moved to NH shared a poignant memory upon seeing this photo. "In 1952, my brother David (he was fifteen at the time) purchased a 1934 Oldsmobile. He spent hours on end restoring this wonderful vehicle, which was very reminiscent of one from Al Capone's era. As teenagers, we drove that tank everywhere—it was our party barge! Dave became a mechanical engineer, and really loved the continuing restoration process. He never stopped working on that car, and did so until he passed away at the age of seventy. The good news is that the 'Olds' now resides in an auto museum for all to enjoy. Oh, if that car could talk—lots of red faces!" *Bruce Holloway, Artist, Illustrator*

Bottom Left: Here's a lovely and evocative reaction from a man who paints with sound like no other. "Capturing the mystery of an underwater world while deep in a forest, this image paints wonder with light." *Tony Levin, Musician, Bass & Chapman Stick Player (Peter Gabriel, King Crimson, Pink Floyd, Stick Men, Paul Simon, John Lennon, Lou Reed, etc.)*

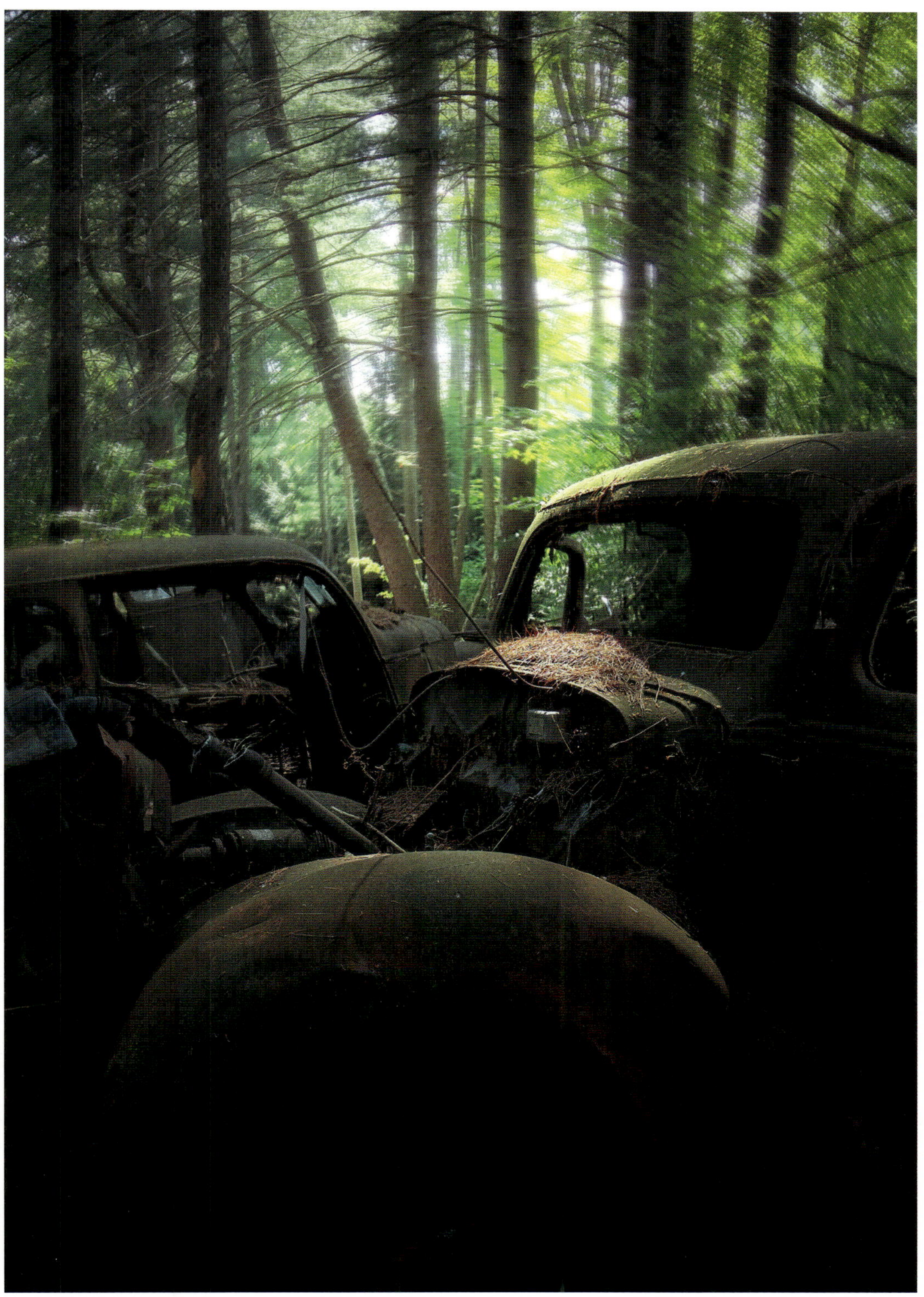

A favorite of mine, this photo (and the other two) is from the area in Blanchard's where all the oldest cars rest. Beneath this pine canopy lies a place out of time, where I contemplate and enjoy the magical light that dances across the windows and rusted fenders of automotive history.

Bottom Left: A 1951 Buick Special lies in the shadows, awash in the reflective light of a mid-November sky. Speaking of special, here's a thought from a true legend. "As a longtime car appreciator even back in England, this Buick is one of my very favorite old American cars. Take a look at the grill and imagine it restored; it looks like the car would eat you! It's a genuine piece of Americana —I love it!" *Brian Auger, Musician, Hammond B3 Keyboardist (Oblivion Express, Jimi Hendrix, Paul McCartney, Judy Garland, Tom Jones, Eric Clapton, Rod Stewart, Steve Winwood, Jimmy Page, etc.)*

Top Right: *"Welcome to the Jungle"* I love Metro vans, and even illustrated one in an ad for a dairy client some years back. This photo has an exotic flavor, and it's suggestive of a journey through the South American jungle (though not as beastly a vehicle, it reminds me of the one in William Friedkin's 1977 movie, *Sorcerer).* For that reason, I invited a student who I closely mentored that made a brave leap herself to share some thoughts. "I wonder what stories this brave little van holds. Her journey into the unknown landed her in the calm beauty of nature ... is there anything more one could ask for? Through life's bumps, wiggles, and turns, with each experience gently steering me toward my own life's purpose, a thought repeated in my head like a mantra through it all: 'Keep your eye on the prize.'" *Jessica LeClerc, Artist, Designer, Former NHIA Student*

Bottom Right: *"The Needles and The Damage Done"* This 1955 Ford Mainline Tudor Sedan appears to be swimming frantically through the pine forest.

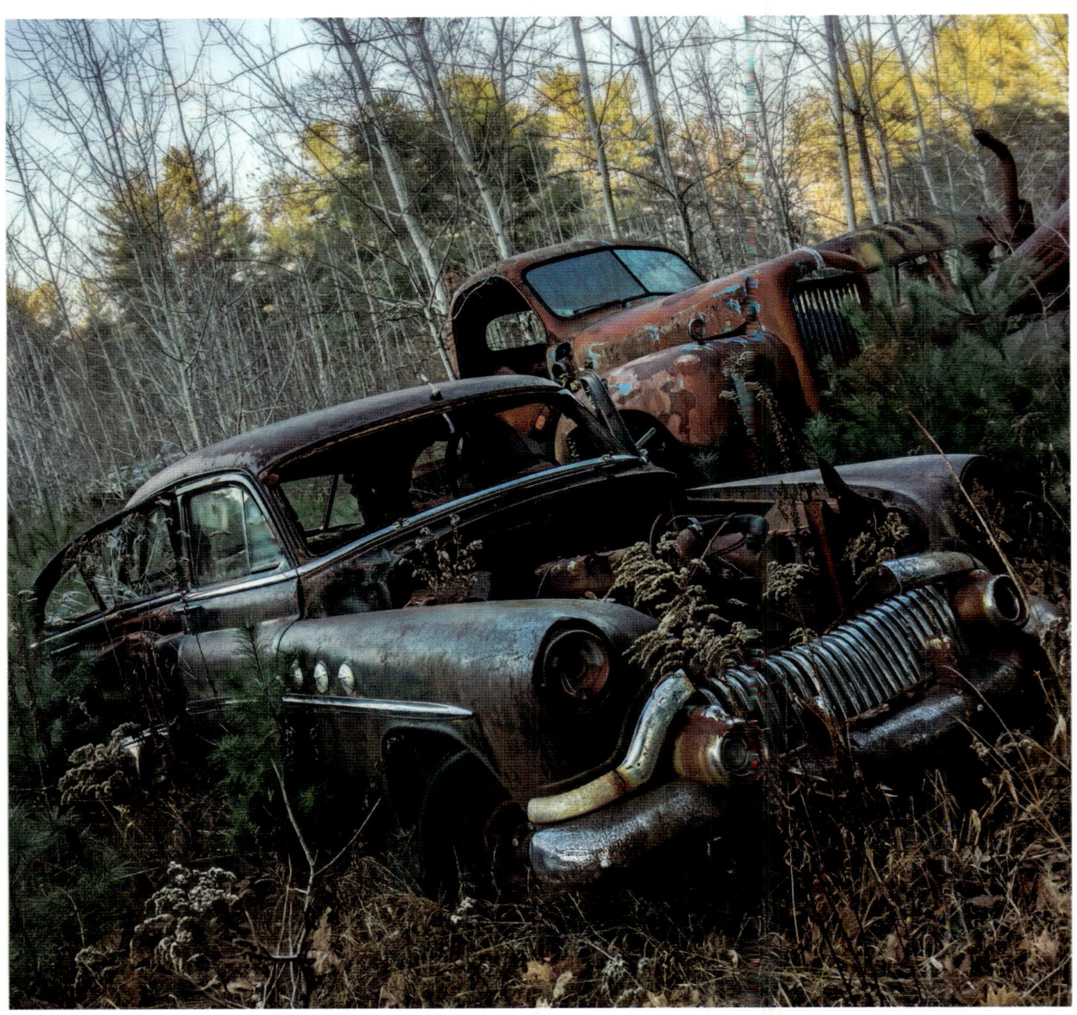

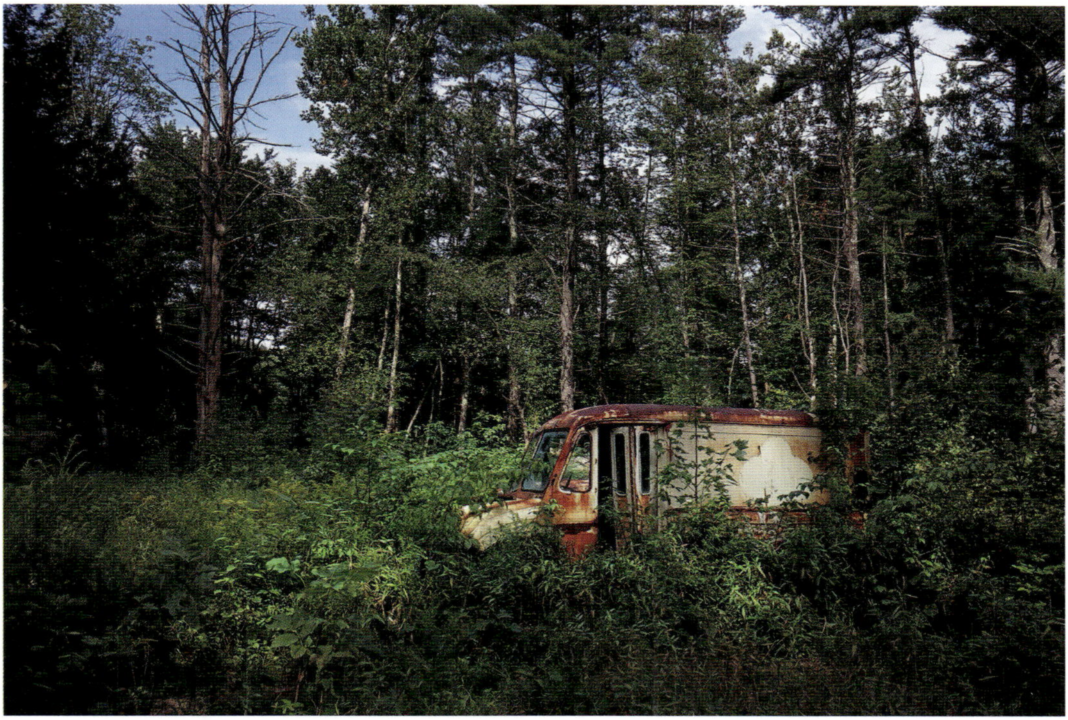

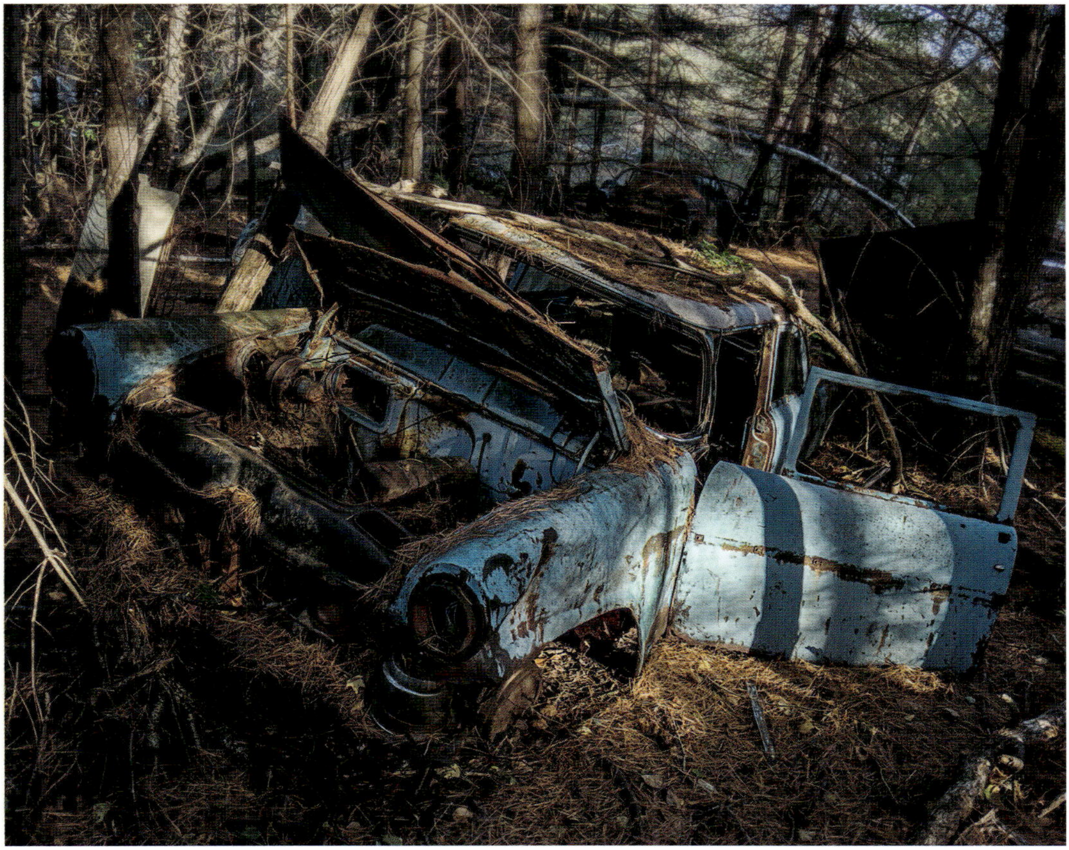

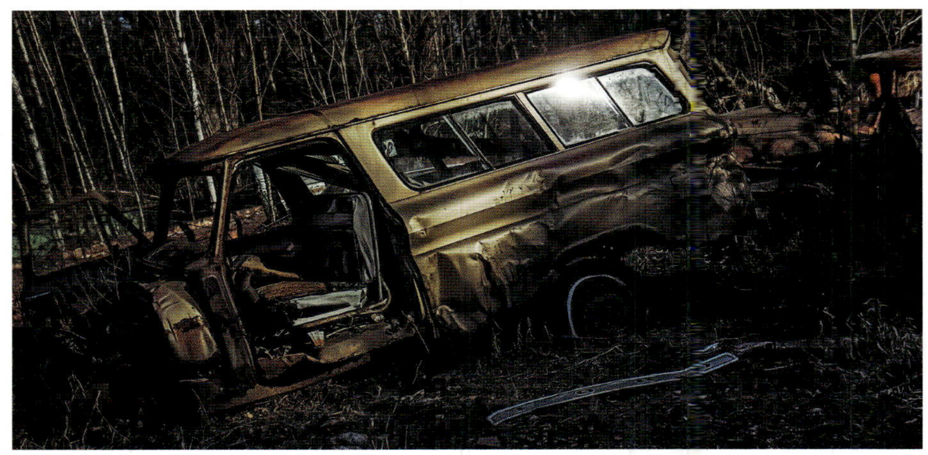

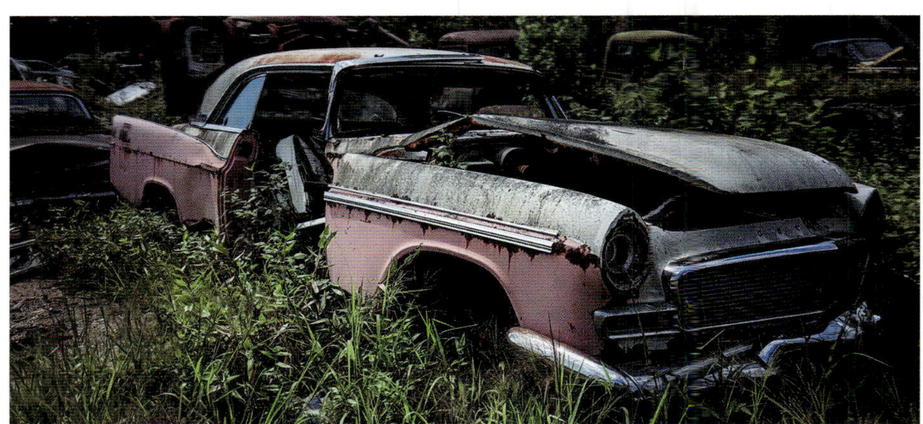

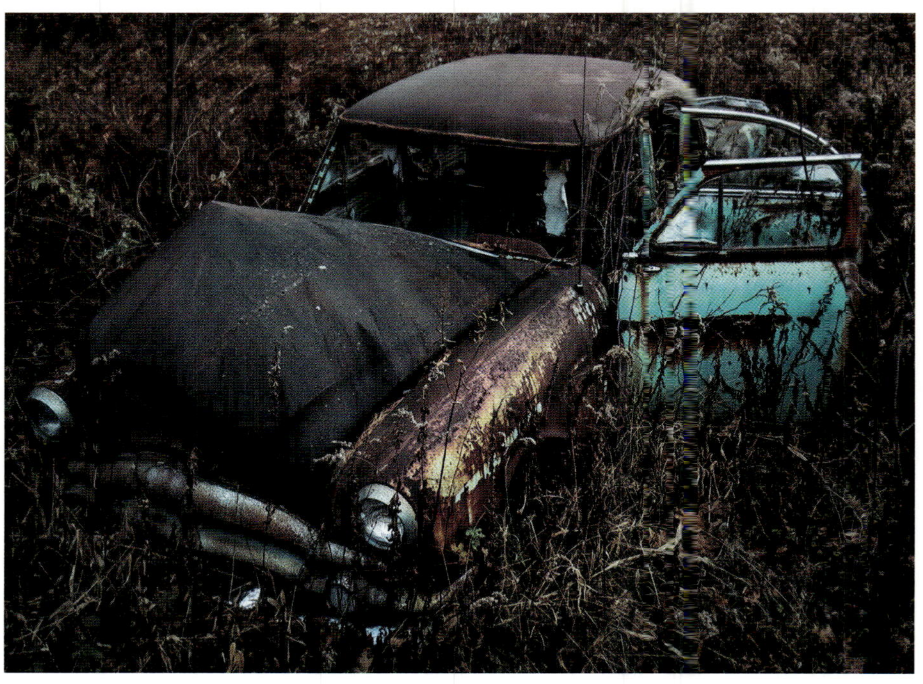

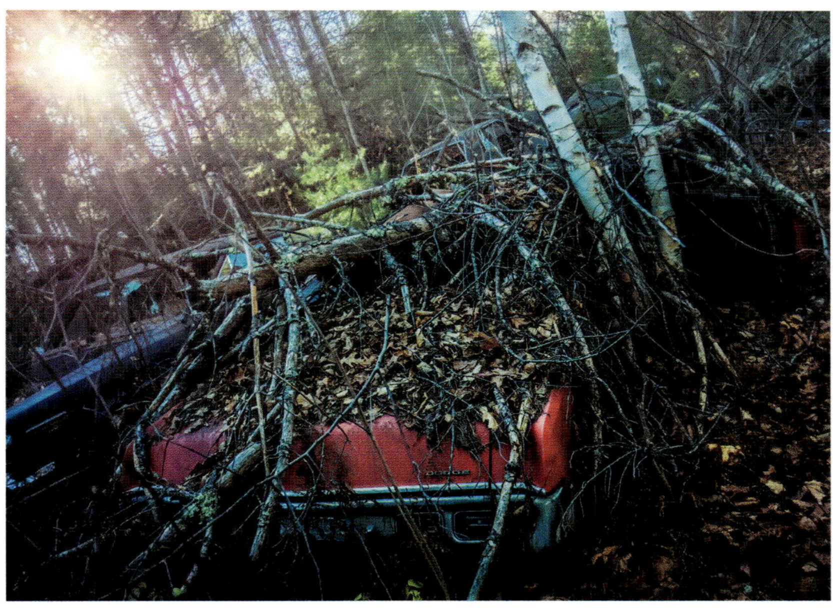

Top Left: The late afternoon sun shoots through the trees and hits this mid-1960s Chevy Suburban like a laser beam.

Middle Left: Every time I see this 1956 Chrysler Newport, it reminds me of the pink Cadillac that Willie Mays owned when he was with the Mets in 1973. Amazingly, it was parked in an area of Shea Stadium where fans could walk right up to it, gawk, and marvel at the pink rotary phone in the center console and the "Say Hey" license plates. As it turns out, Willie was given a brand-new pink Chrysler Imperial upon his official retirement in 1975.

Bottom Left: This 1955 Packard Clipper inspired a song from a fellow 1977 graduate of Farmingdale High School.
"Highway Queen
They called me Aquamarine over green,
stainless and chrome between.
A pot metal smile as I ate the miles from Detroit
to wherever my big wheels were pointed.
Anointed in thirty weight, baptized in octane.
Michigan born, loved until my shine was gone
And my seats grew too soft.
Handed down to the kids (Did they ever find that ice cream?)
they'd made in my back seat.
And then, that night when my ticking heart seized,
parked here since in my grown-in throne.
My castle thorn and thistles. My court long turned to dust.
I rust alone and my glass grows cloudy.
But you know a Queen when you see one, don't you?"
J. D. Kelly, Musician, Lead Singer of Eaglemania, High School Classmate

Top Right: *"Entangled"* The "so 70s" name of this car really cracks me up, but one thing is for sure—this 1973 Dodge Dart Swinger is no longer able go to the disco, or dodge falling branches. One of my very dearest hometown friends, as well as my West Coast music promotin' compatriot, chimes in with some very kind words. Amazingly, I sent her this photo not remembering that she owned this car! "As a former owner of a Dodge Dart Swinger (olive green), this image truly struck a chord! Jerry's art and photography has been part of my life since high school, and his keen eye and wild imagination has produced some very original, innovative, and beautiful work. I'm very honored to be part of this book." *Lauri Reimer, Musician, Singer, Music Promoter, Event Producer (Music Magique Promotions)*

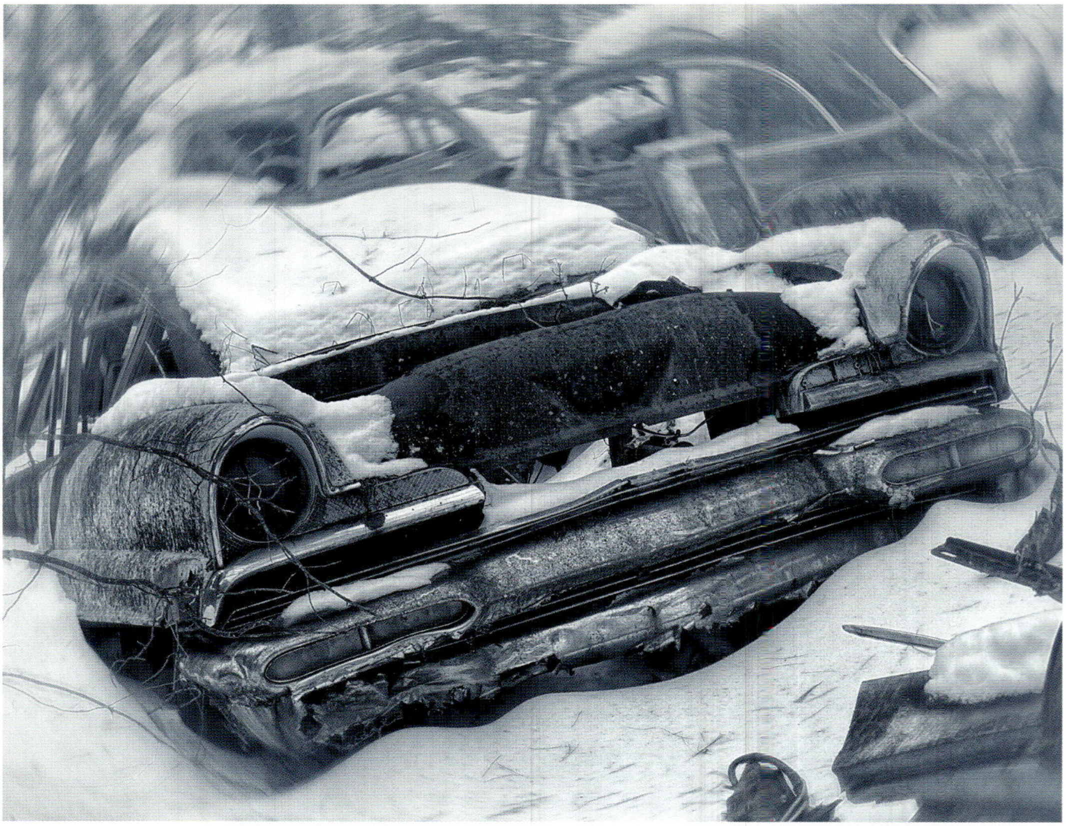

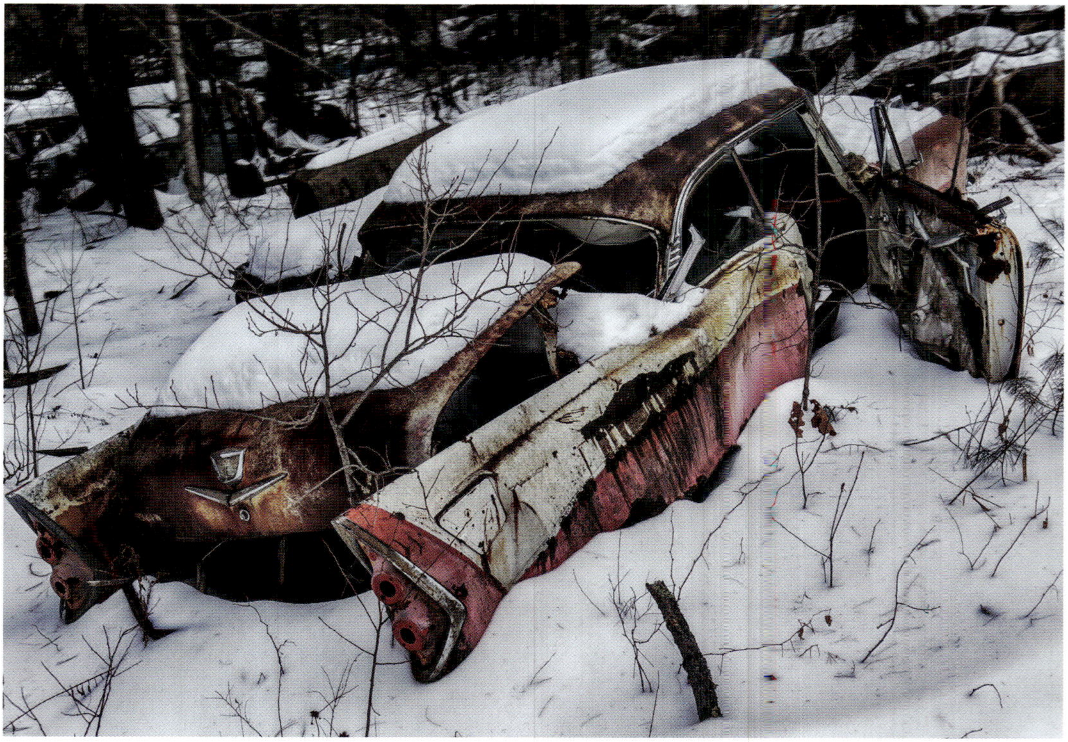

I love shooting vehicles in all seasons and weather, but winter definitely adds great atmosphere and emotion to photographs. What I learned is that only a little bit of snow is needed to be effective—kind of like icing on a cake, as too much snow can produce nondescript lumps. I asked my friend (the son of my hero Keith Emerson), who very rarely sees snow across the pond where he lives in the south of England, to come up with some possible titles. Though it's not a 1958 Plymouth Fury, *Christine* is certainly a good one for the beast on the top left. His ten-year-old son Zac piped in with *The Greasy Road.* However, I'm going with the following because it sounds like a James Bond goes to the Arctic movie: *"Snow Kill." Aaron Emerson, Musician, Keyboard Player*

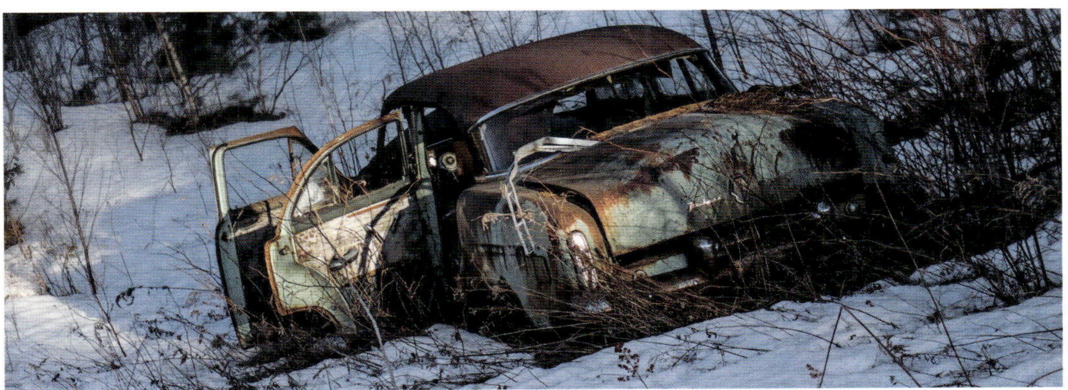

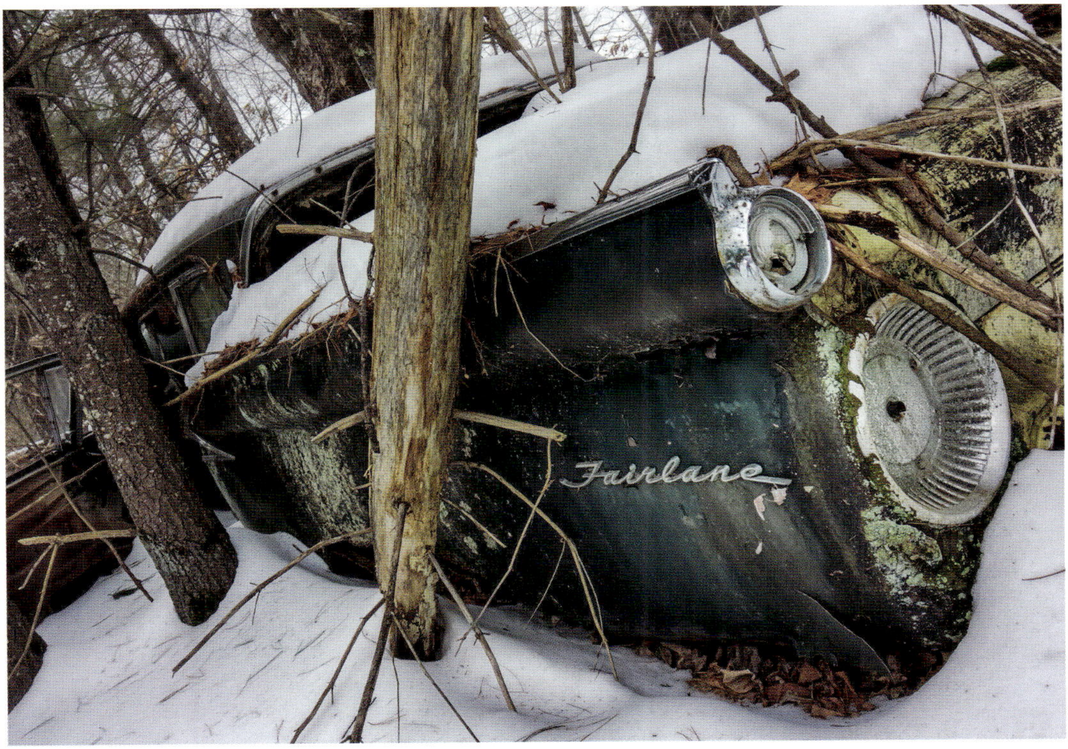

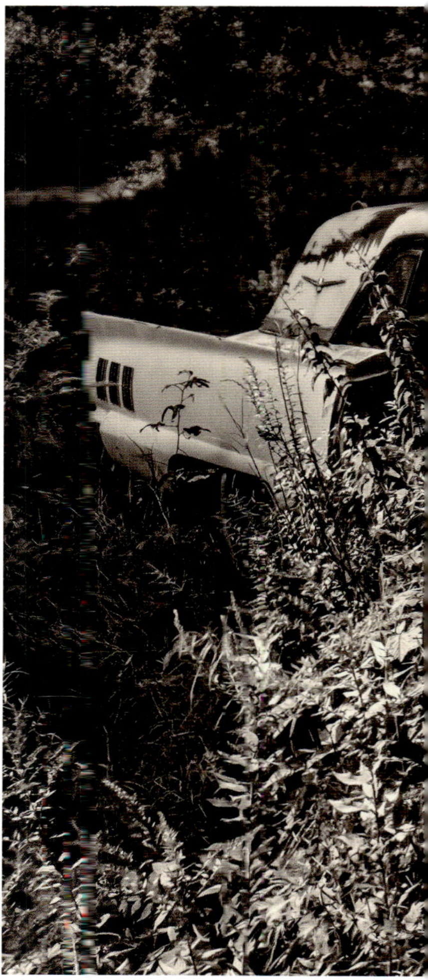

"Peggy Sue Got Married ... And Divorced!" When I first came upon this 1960 Ford Thunderbird, and the pink 1964 Chevy Impala convertible, that title was the first thing that popped into my mind. I asked the author of a well-known book I illustrated the cover for many years ago (*The Legend of Bagger Vance*) to give me a reaction. "I was seventeen in 1960 and twenty-one in '64, so these cars are my youth. And ya know what? Rusted out and abandoned as they are, they still look cool—love 'em!" *Steven Pressfield, Author, The Legend of Bagger Vance (the 2000 film was directed by Robert Redford and starred Matt Damon, Will Smith and Charlize Theron), Gates of Fire, The War of Art, etc.*

I'm also glad to have this fond memory from one of the preeminent guitarists of the last forty years, who happened to spend his childhood in the most geographically important area of automotive history—a perfect way to end this chapter! "The Thunderbird was one of my favorites. As a kid near Detroit, I would ride my bike to visit my friend, always taking a certain route just so I could see a neighbor's beautiful white Thunderbird. It had perfect lines: streamlined for its day, with that low, sleek stance. Everything today looks like a half-used bar of soap compared to the bolder lines of that era. The year this T-Bird was made, all of us kids would sit and watch the cars drive by, trying to be the first to call out the make and model of each one!" *Steve Morse, Musician, Guitarist (Dixie Dregs, Kansas, Deep Purple, Steve Morse Band, Flying Colors)*

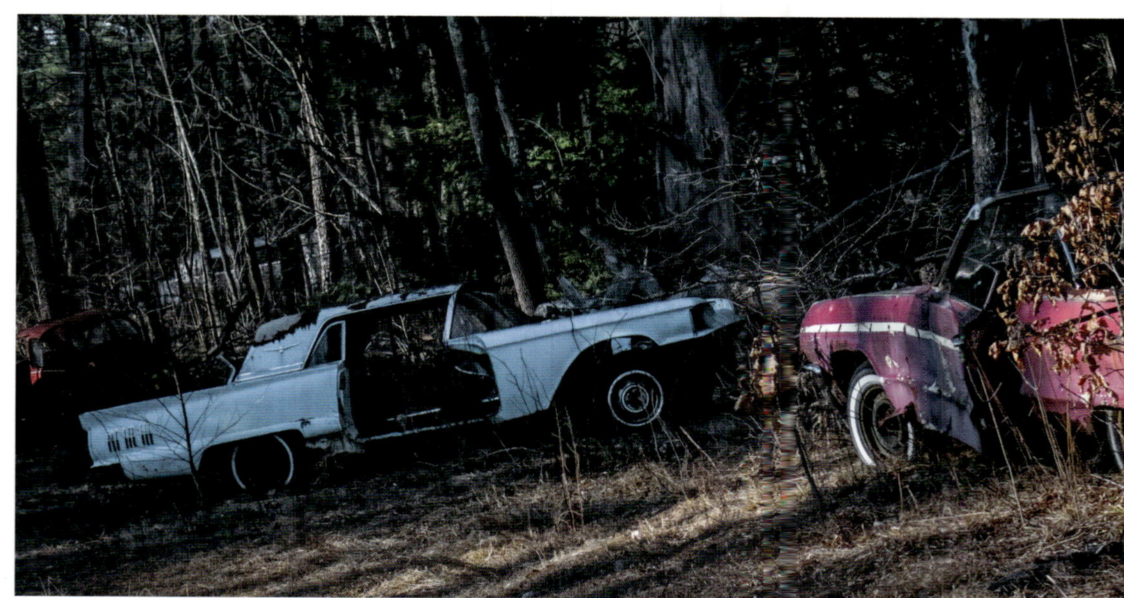

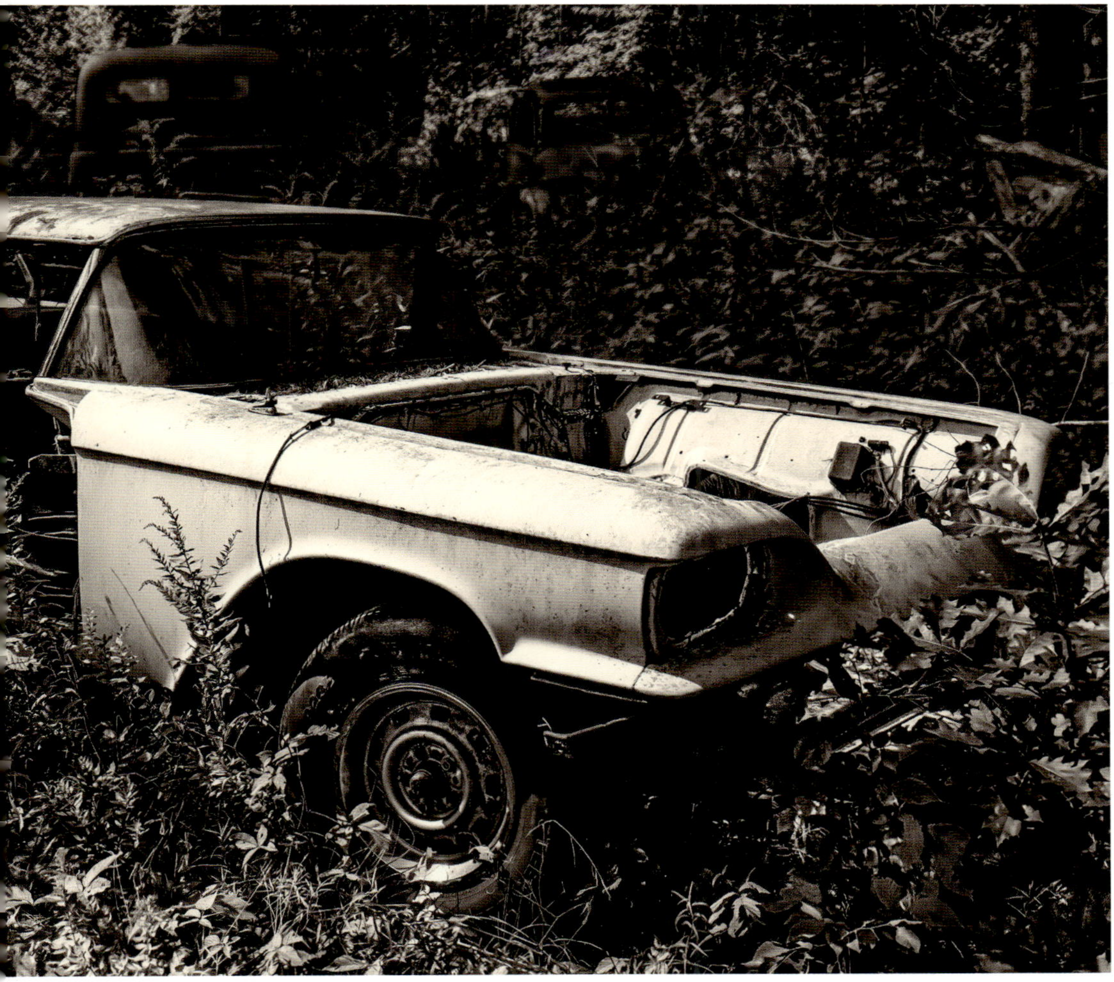

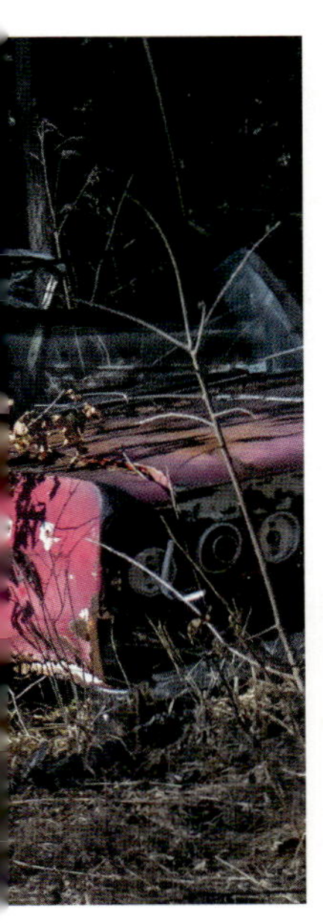

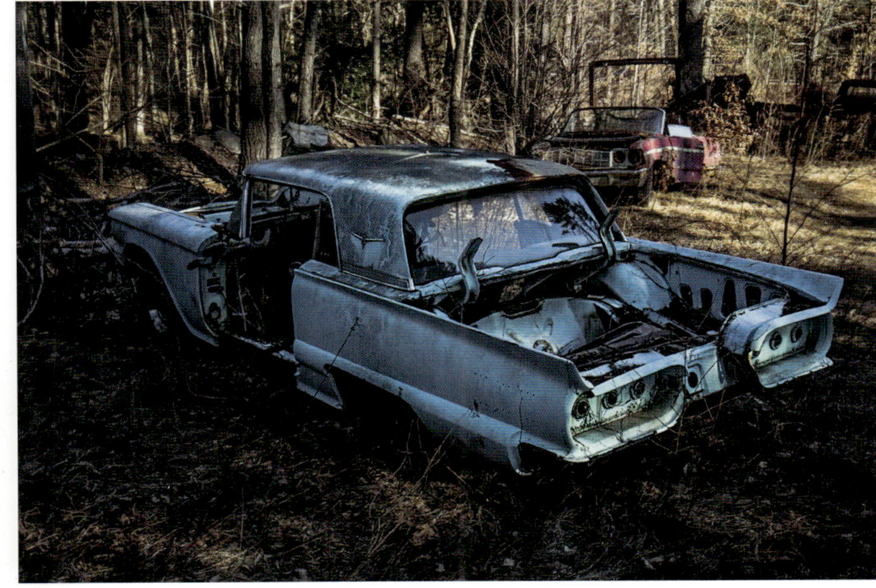

3

LANE'S GARAGE

My wife Kathleen grew up in Loudon, home of the New Hampshire Speedway, and I first started visiting her family homestead there in 1987. All those early trips had me fall in love with the state, and we finally made the big move of leaving New York City on our son Gregory's first birthday in September of 1994 to move to New Hampshire, or better yet, "out in the country." I remember many times driving past Lane's on Rt. 106 and seeing the aging sign that was actually a funny little automobile mounted up on a pole, along with an old car or two out front AND a big green carnival dragon. Though I was many, many years away from discovering my passion for photographing old cars, my curiosity about the property was certainly piqued. When I asked an acquaintance in 2019 if she knew of anyone in the area that had old cars, she immediately said go to Lane's, and "tell them I sent you." I did just that, and met with the very affable owner, Ronnie Lane, one hot August day, who gave me permission to go out back and have a good time. I was totally unprepared for how extensive and beautiful his property is, and just how many classic vehicles were out in the woods and fields. There are a lot of great stories and history about Lane's, but they will have to wait—that's another entire book!

Right: Every time I went to Lane's, I would photograph this scene, which is quite challenging for the view I hoped to accomplish successfully. Most of the time I was there when the sun was right behind the tree, which made the photos too intense and contrasty. I'm not a morning person, but I should try to get there early sometime when the light is on the opposite side. However, I was finally pleased when I captured this winter twilight shot. It actually makes me think of the early music of Genesis, which is why I'm honored to have this tremendously influential guitarist and gentleman share a short and thoughtful quote. "We are all toys of time … " *Steve Hackett, Musician, Guitarist, Songwriter (Genesis, GTR,*

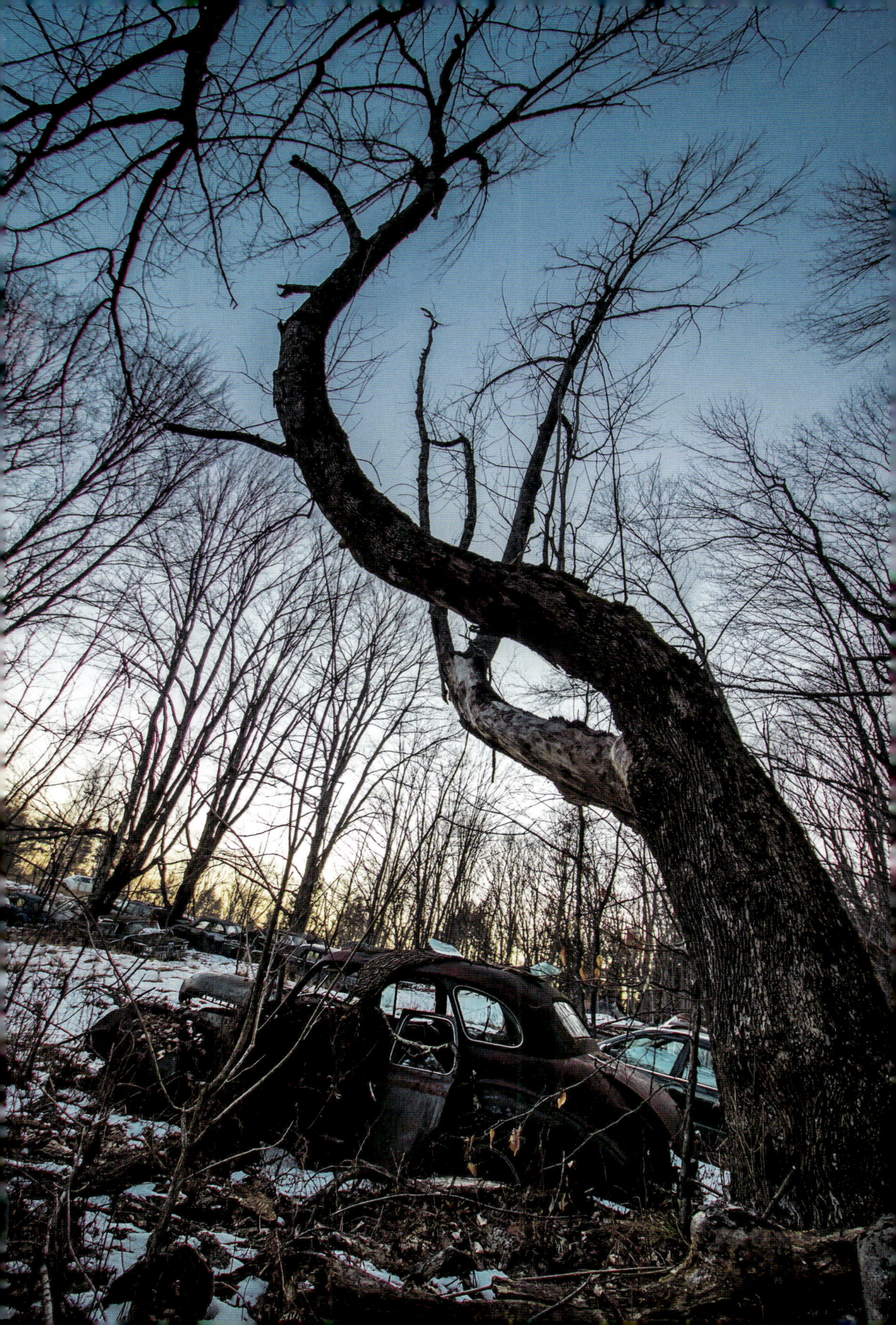

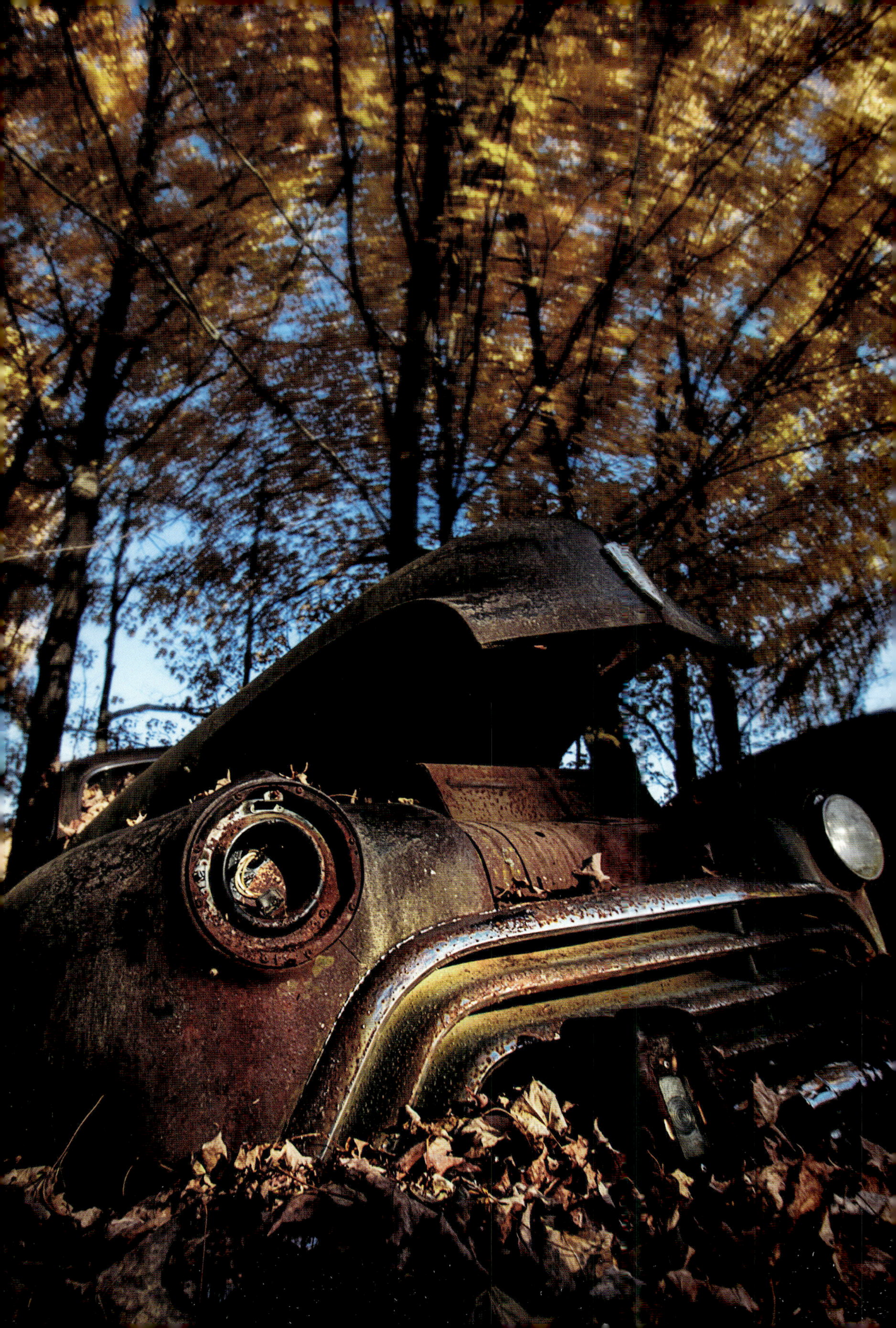

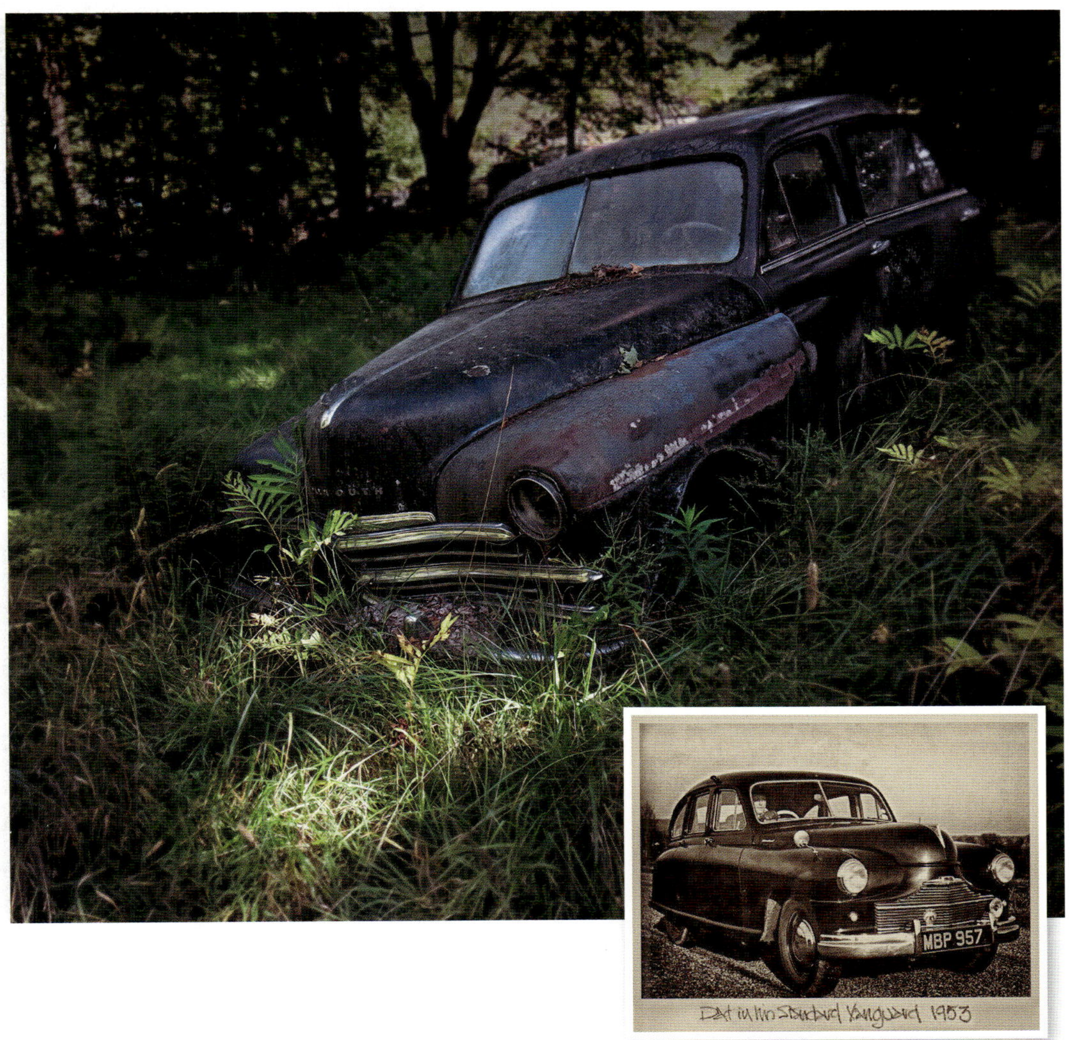

Left: This 1947 Oldsmobile is another of my favorite photos—it has such an expressive "face!" I knew this wonderful wordsmith would add an evocative thought.
"The rust borne wind carries away the miles of the past,
as the light still shines upon a bygone era."
Cy Curnin, Musician, Songwriter, Lead Singer of The Fixx

Above: *"No Particular Place to Go"* This 1949 Plymouth Special Deluxe rests very peacefully in a shady summer glade. Little did I know when I picked out this photo for my friend William to comment on, that he would have an almost duplicate British equivalent in his history; and, I just had to include the inset photo of his father in the car from 1953. "This car reminds me of my dad's old 1950s Standard Vanguard ... I loved the sound of that motor! I used to sit in it for hours on end, aided by a cushion that would help me just about peep over the dash (I would have been about five years old at the time). So, why is this lovely old motor here in the first place ... was it a short cut that went very wrong? Or maybe it was all because of Chuck Berry holding a grudge against a safety belt that wouldn't budge!"
William Neal, Artist, Illustrator (creator of the iconic album cover art for "Tarkus" and "Pictures at an Exhibition" by Emerson, Lake & Palmer)

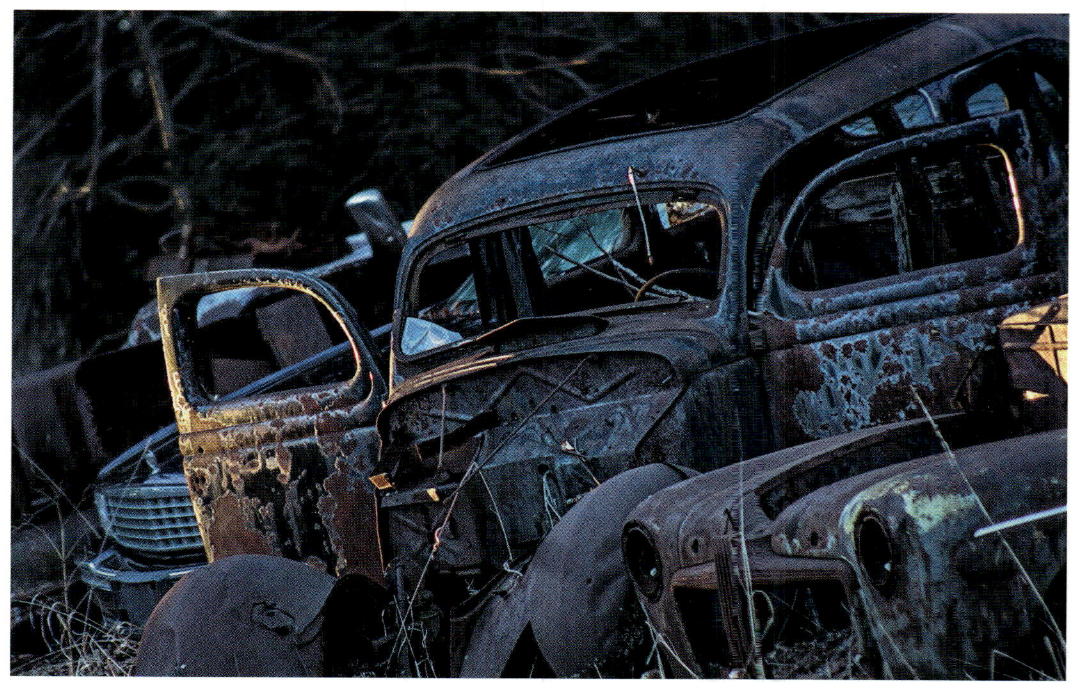

Top Left: No matter the mood of a photo, it's no surprise that this fellow would react with his quirky sense of humor. "And The Stones hit the stage one more time!" *Adrian Belew, Musician, Guitarist, Singer (Frank Zappa, David Bowie, King Crimson, Talking Heads, Nine-Inch Nails, etc.)*

Top Right: The very impressive row of classic Pontiacs that line the back boundary of Lane's property inspired a memory by my friend, and artist extraordinaire. "A ghostly reminder of the siren's song of endless summers and bygone youth, shown here in three-part harmony ... these were the type of cars we worked on and drove around in when I was a kid." *Chris Hopkins, Artist, Illustrator*

Bottom: I had a nice moment with this 1960 Chevy El Camino as I sat in the snow shooting in the gathering dusk. I love the backdrop of the weathered barn siding—so very New Hampshire! Another fun coincidence occurred when I randomly selected this photo for a musical friend to caption, not knowing that he was also a huge car buff. "Wow, an El Camino ... or 'The Way' translated to English. My first, and only 'real job' was delivering appliances when I was sixteen years old, using a 1960 El Camino with the Turbo-Thrust 348-cid V8. Definitely not great in the snow, but I have fond memories for sure." *C. J. Vanston, Musician, Keyboard Player, Producer, Film Composer (Toto, Prince, Barbara Streisand, Ringo Starr, Joe Cocker, Spinal Tap, etc.)*

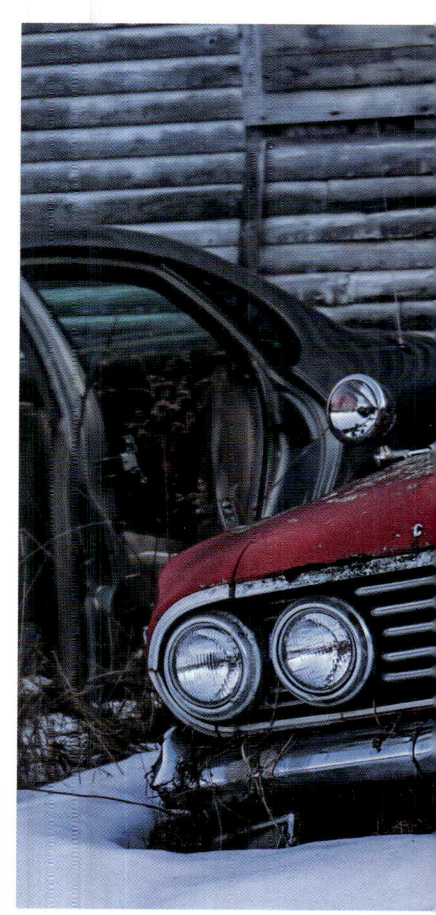

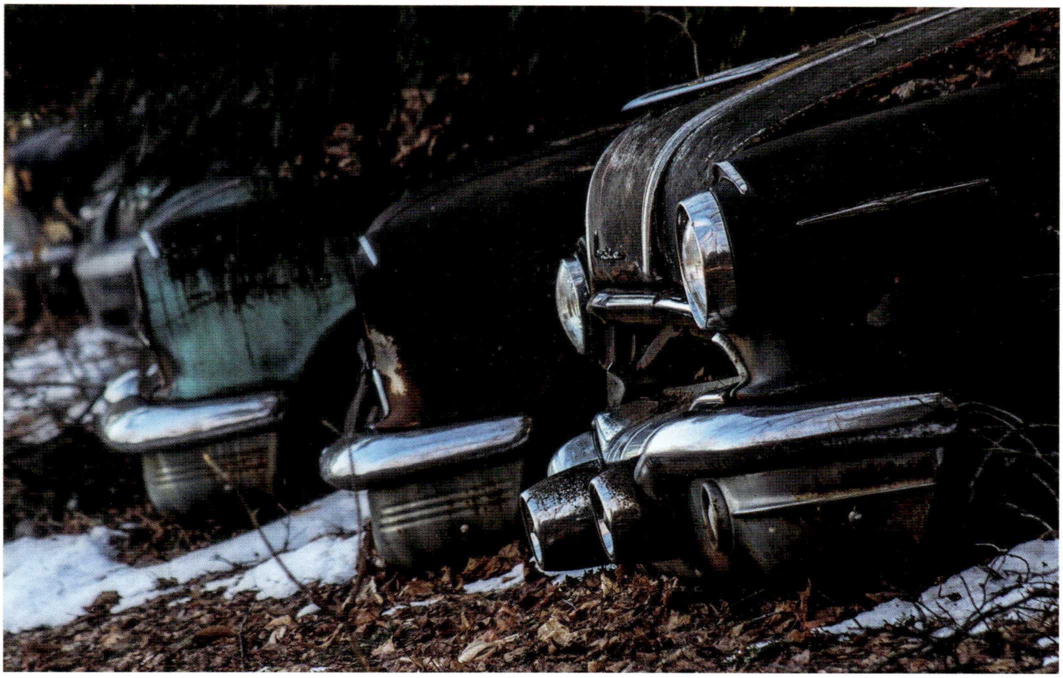

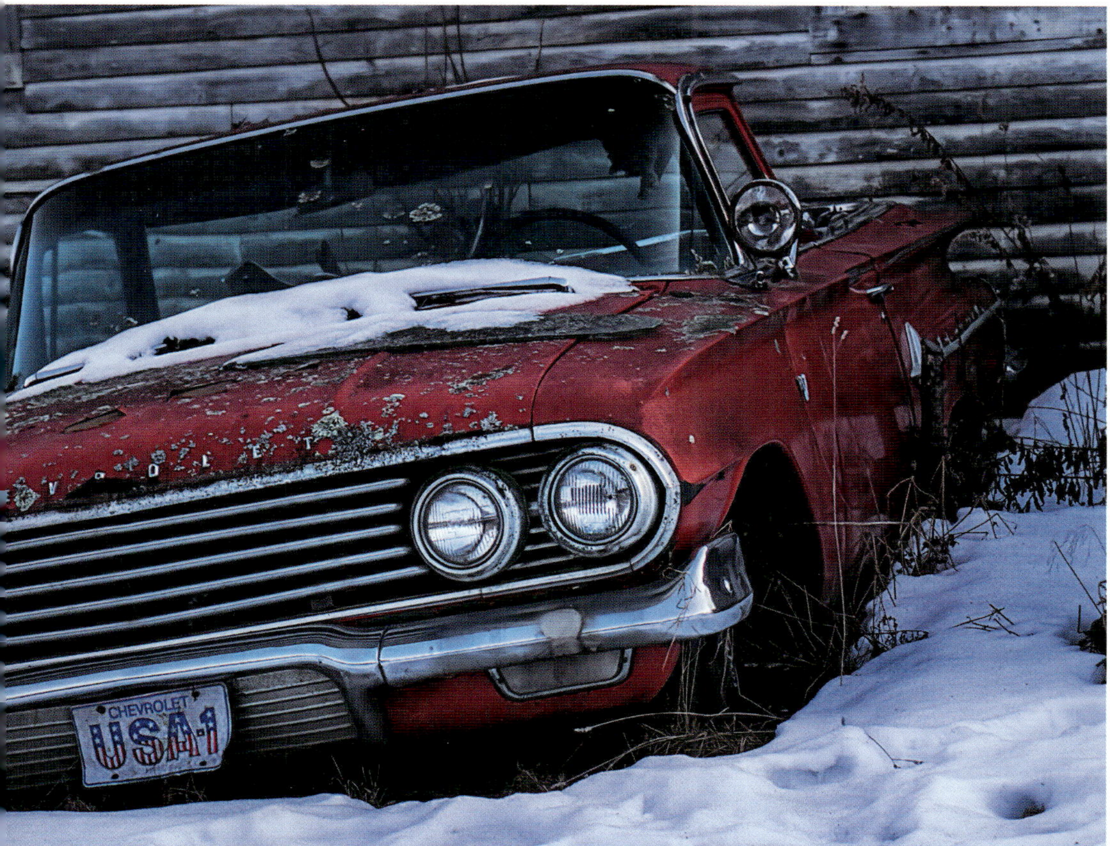

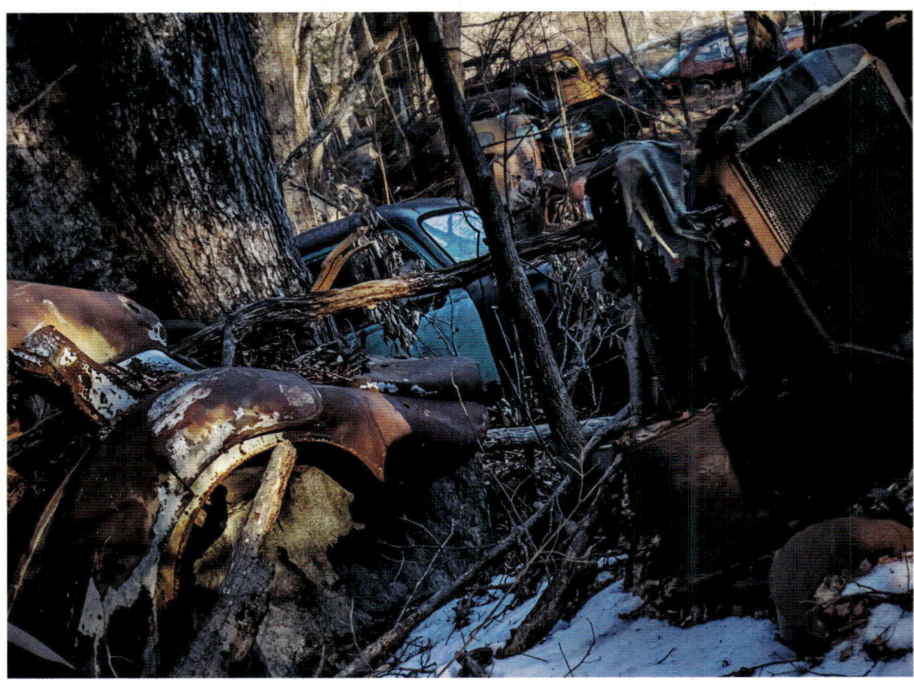

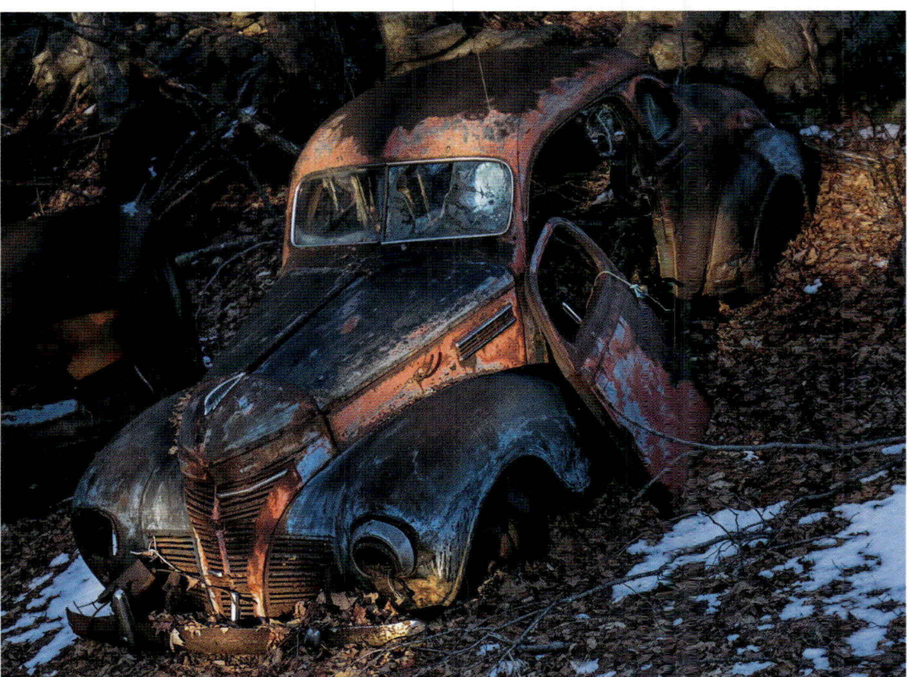

Top Left: The movement, warmth and intermixing of beautiful, subtle colors in this dense scene reminded me of the electronic music explorations of my friend. "I truly love this meditative image, as it captures the passage of time. Impermanence, yet the permanence of seasons and forest life all intertwined. The end of winter ... spring arrives. As rust turns to dust, the patient forest observes." *Andre Cholmondeley, Musician, Tour Manager, Multi-Instrument Tech (Steve Howe, Adrian Belew, Keith Emerson, Greg Lake, ELP, U.K., Al DiMeola, etc.)*

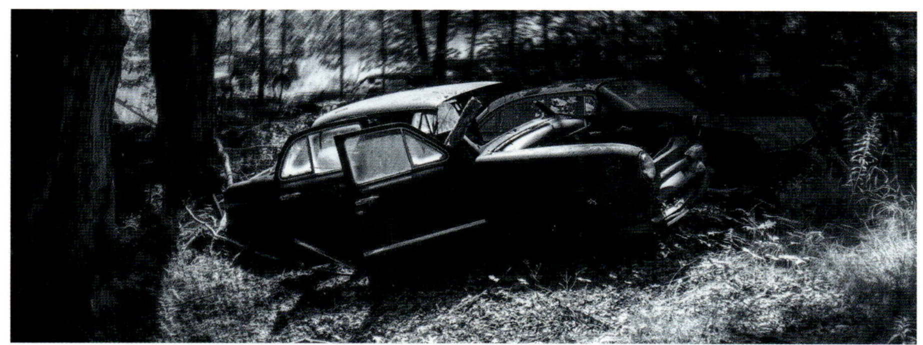

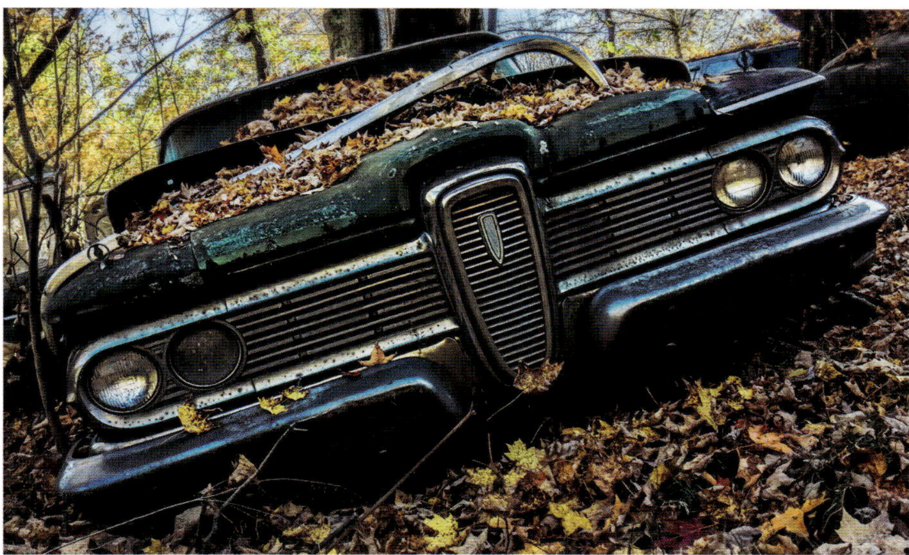

Bottom Left: Only someone from Chicago would take the following flight of fancy with this 1939 Plymouth Coupe "gangster" car. "Minutes ago, this car was involved in a high-speed chase, recklessly careening around break-neck curves attempting to out-maneuver a pursuing squad car. Then, at the last turn, the vehicle lost control and went hurtling down a steep embankment and into the undergrowth. The dazed driver stumbles and falls to the ground, and as the camera pans up from the fallen man and back along the path he ran, we hear the sounds of a police siren followed by the squad car screeching to a halt, and excited voices. 'You're under arrest!' a patrolman cries as the camera stops on this shot. The distinctive voice of Jimmy Cagney replies, 'You ain't got nothing on me, Copper—I was framed I tell ya, framed!' Suddenly, the car bursts into flames, the music swells and the words THE END superimpose on the burning wreckage." *Scott Gustafson, Illustrator, Fantasy & Fairy Tale Artist*

Top Right: A 1949 Ford Deluxe Sedan basks in a sunny spotlight beneath towering trees. My friend shared a quote from the great Irish poet W.B. Yeats (1865-1939) that encapsulates what it's like to be alive and exploring with a camera in your hand. "The world is full of magic things, patiently waiting for our senses to grow sharper." *Althea Haropulos, Photographer*

Bottom Right: A 1959 Edsel Ranger rests beneath a huge oak tree next to a stone wall. This car was Ford's ballyhooed new addition to the product line that ultimately became the company's best-known failure, and the butt of many jokes. It was actually named after Henry Ford's long deceased son Edsel, but only after many thousands of other names were considered. They even had a public contest to choose the name of this car that was supposed to be an industry game changer!

Bottom Left: A magical glow of light illuminates this 1941 Chevy Special Deluxe, imbuing it with warm elegance and dignity. Having earlier established myself as a passionate, lifelong fan of Emerson, Lake & Palmer (ok … my son's name is Gregory Emerson LoFaro), it's particularly meaningful for me to share this lovely lady's instantaneous thought channeling the beautiful and immortal words of her late husband, and another of my heroes, Greg Lake. "C'est la Vie, Have your leaves all turned to brown … "
Regina Lake, Artist, Sculptor

Top Right: This 1964 Buick Riviera has such a beautiful, retro-futuristic looking grill and headlight cover, and the photo's allegorical feeling made me think of my former New York City studio mate as the perfect choice to share a thought. "Do not weep for me; more beautiful in death am I." *Steve Youll Science Fiction and Fantasy Book Cover Illustrator (Issac Asimov's "Foundation" series, Frank Herbert's "Dune" series, etc.)*

Bottom Right: A very beefy 1957 Pontiac Super Chief inspired my New Hampshire illustrator friend.
"Left out in the woods, and anchored to the ground like a glacial erratic.
Clear eyes look out eagerly, as if it knows the roads it traveled still exist … waiting. Massive chrome juts forward, its gleaming curves exude movement, acceleration—*velocity.*
'Whop bop b-luma b-lop bam boom!'
Leaves are enough to hold it to the earth now."
Jim Roldan, Illustrator, Art Professor

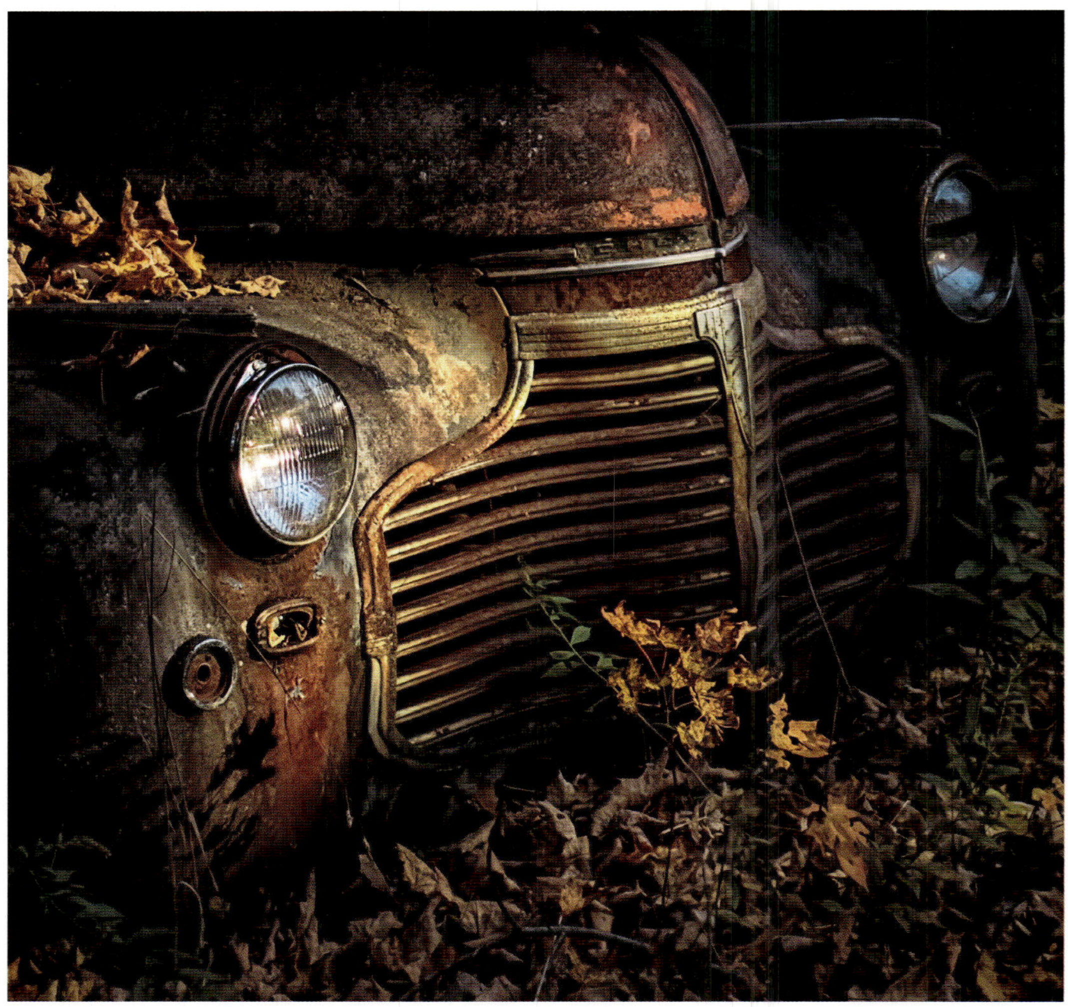

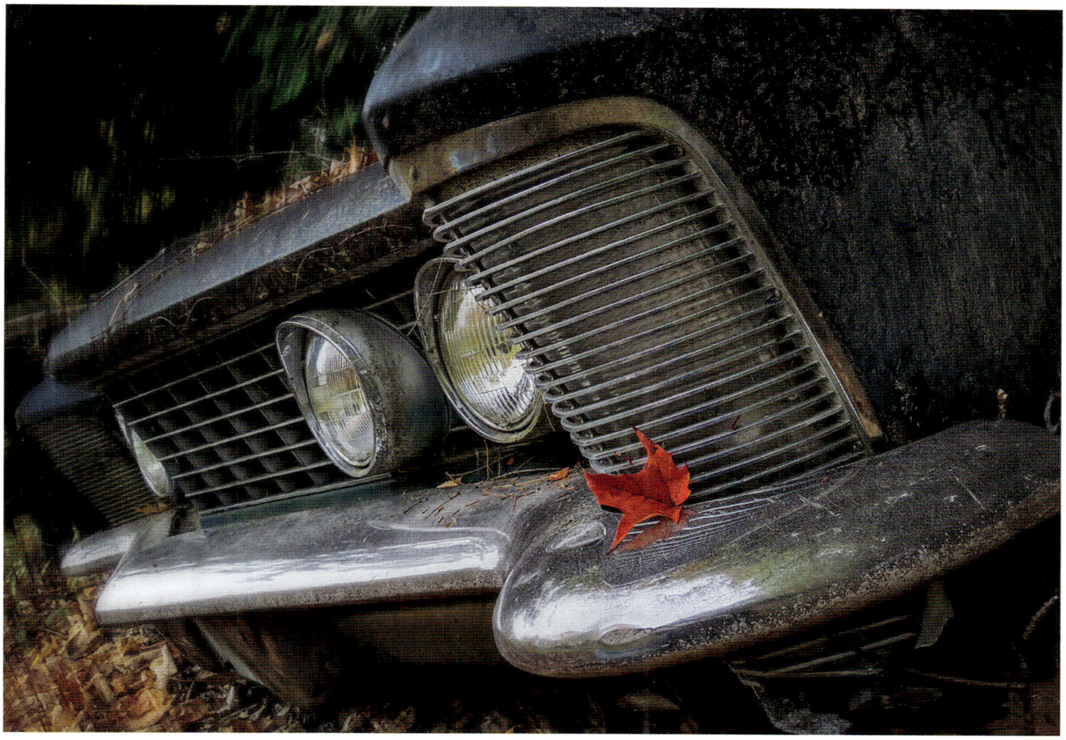

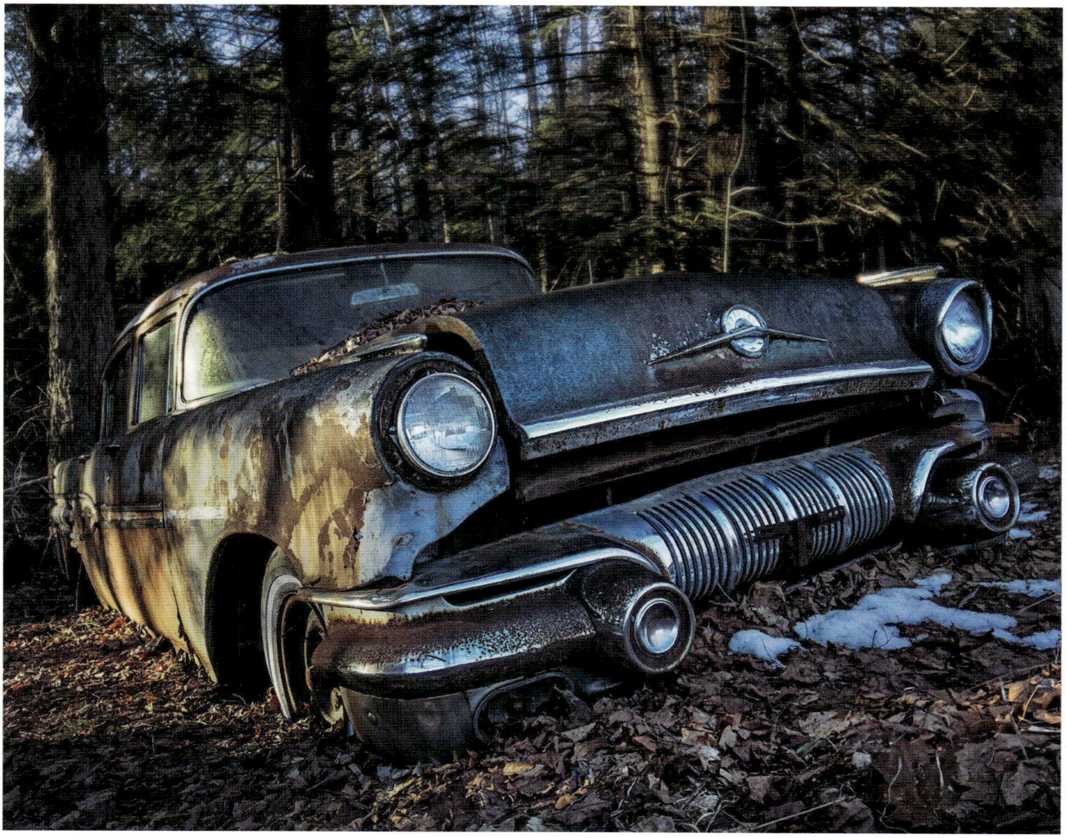

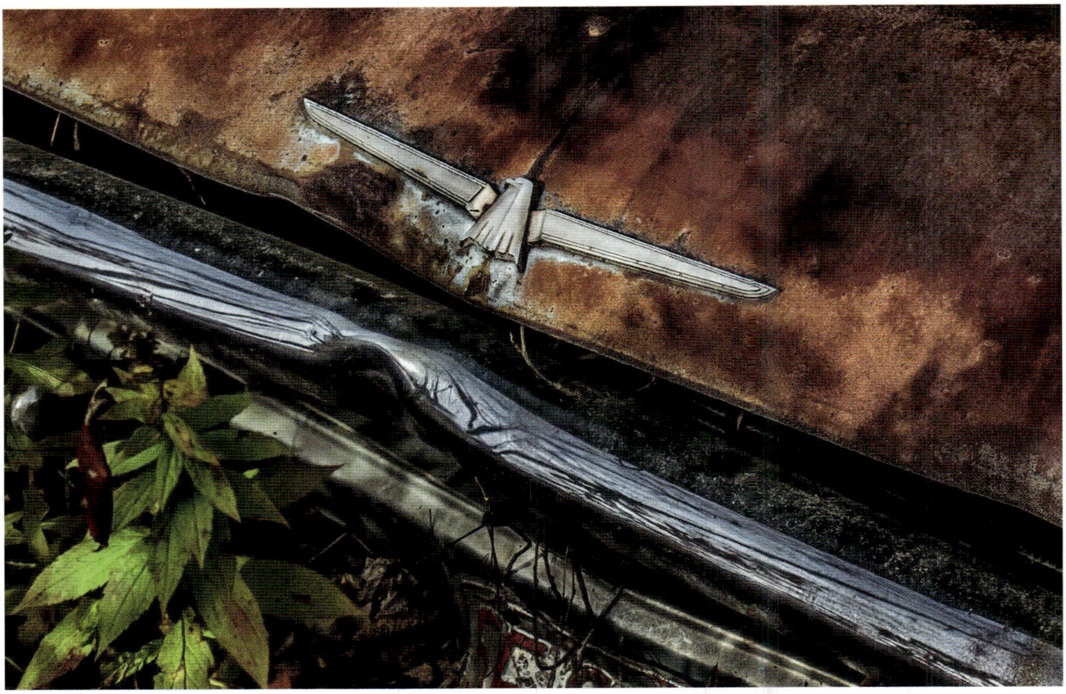

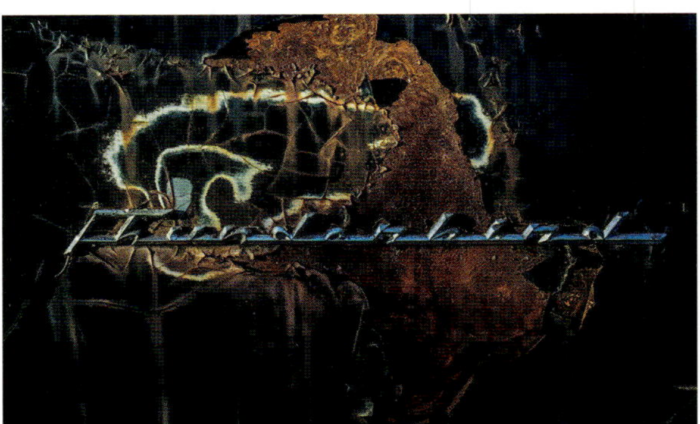

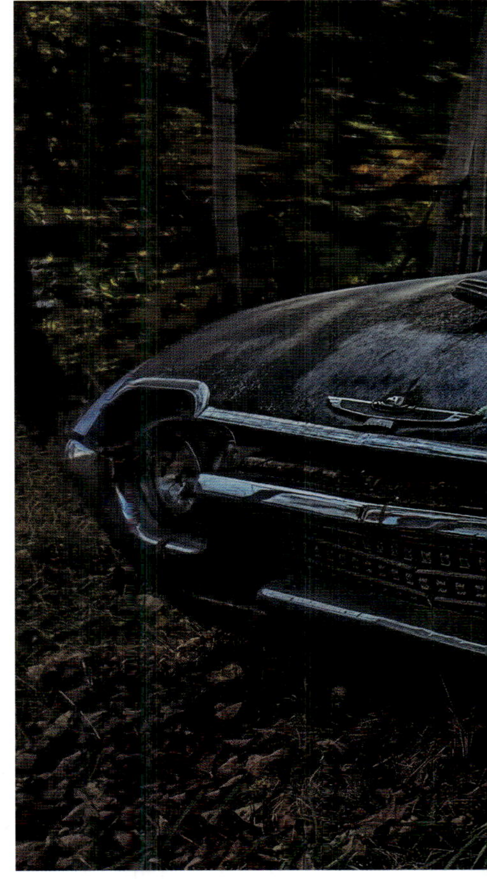

A deep, and forward-looking thought from my super-talented friend. “The relics of the past bring out such beauty and thoughts of the future. Will something as sleek and elegant as the Ford Thunderbird remain relevant fifty years from now? In all their glory, will your dreams be of more value in the future than the day they were conceived? The Thunderbird automobile, the beauty and time stamp of this image, my music ... they will last forever.”
Robert Berry, Musician, Singer, Songwriter, Producer (3 w/Keith Emerson & Carl Palmer, Ambrosia, Greg Kihn Band, Hush, etc.)

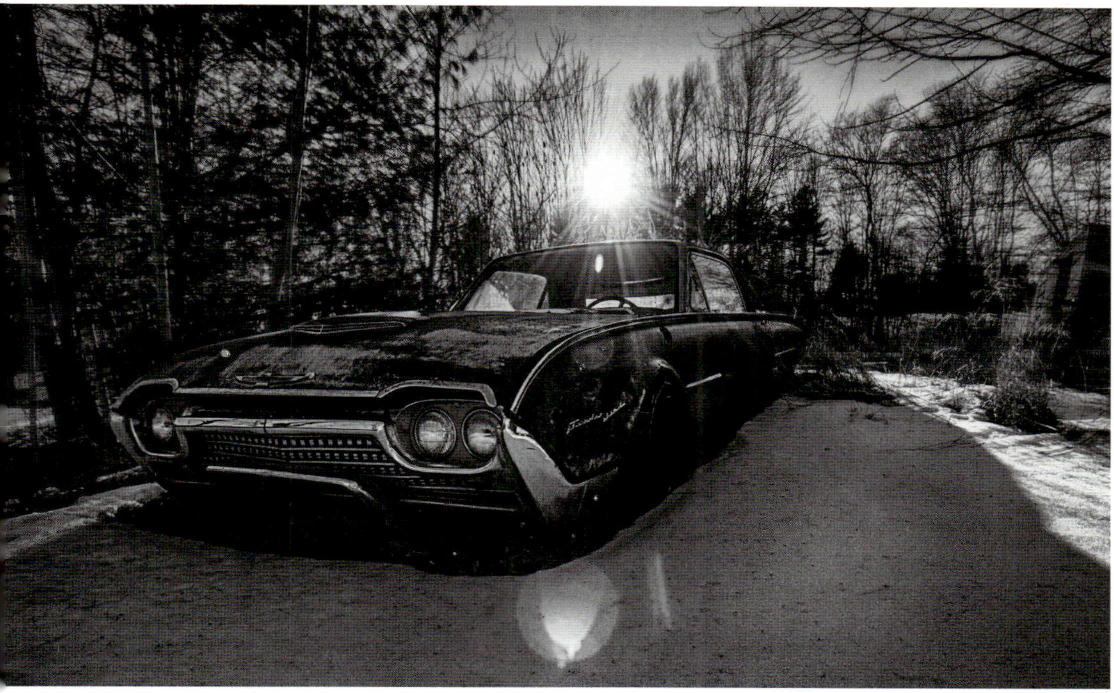

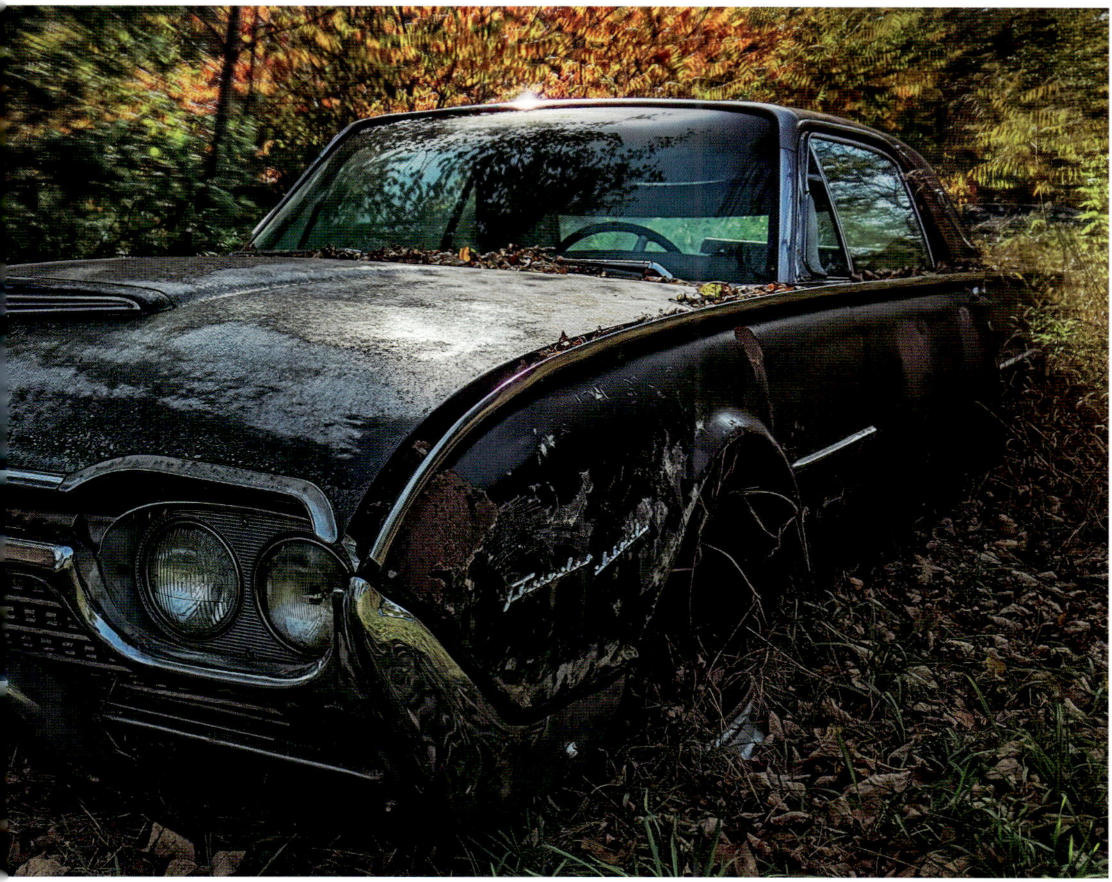

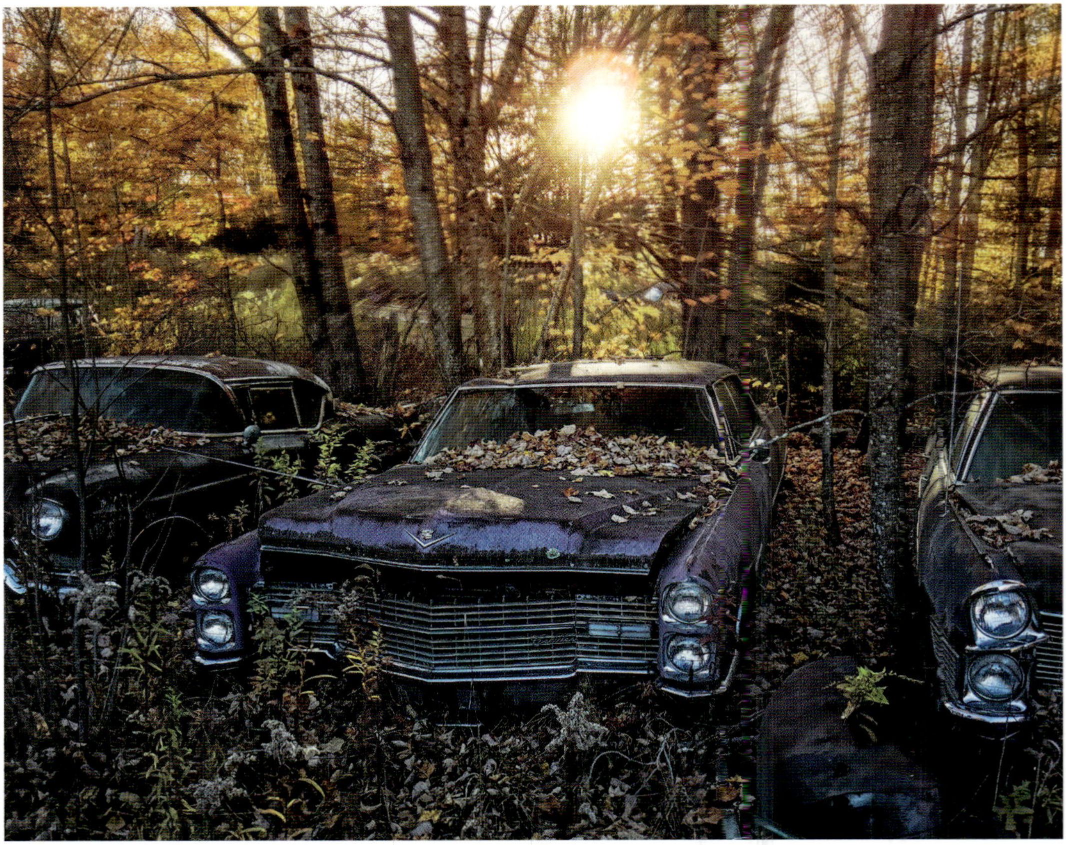

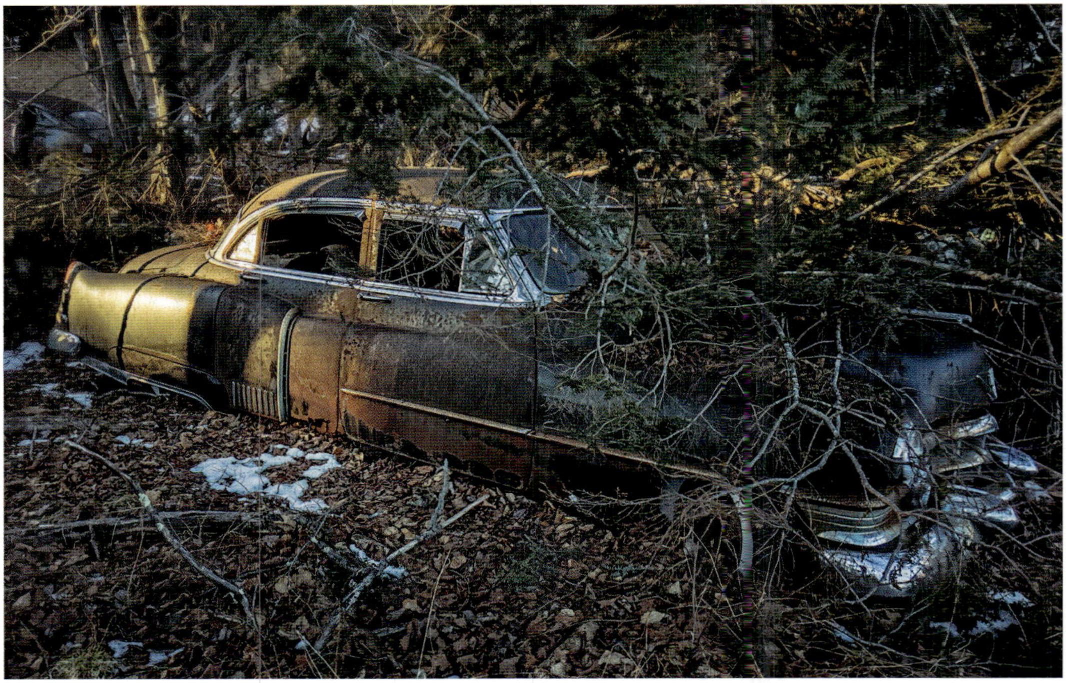

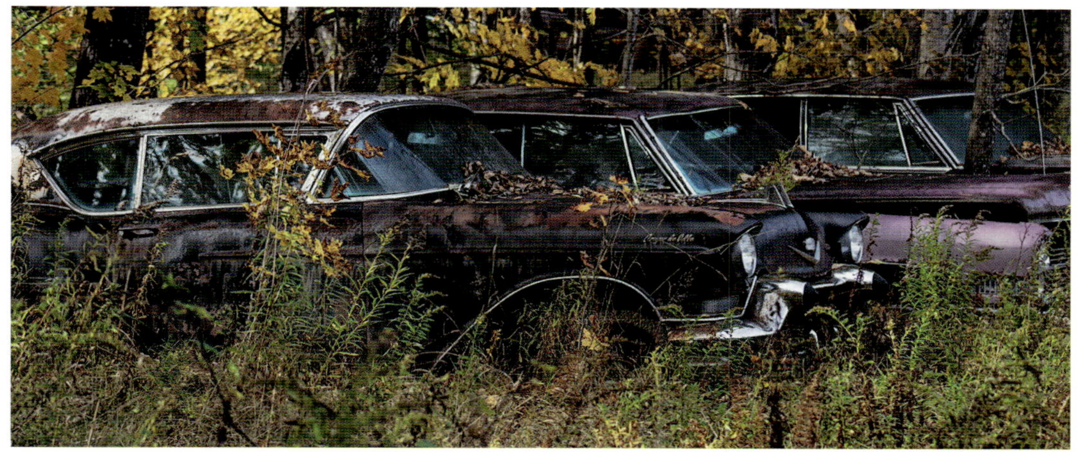

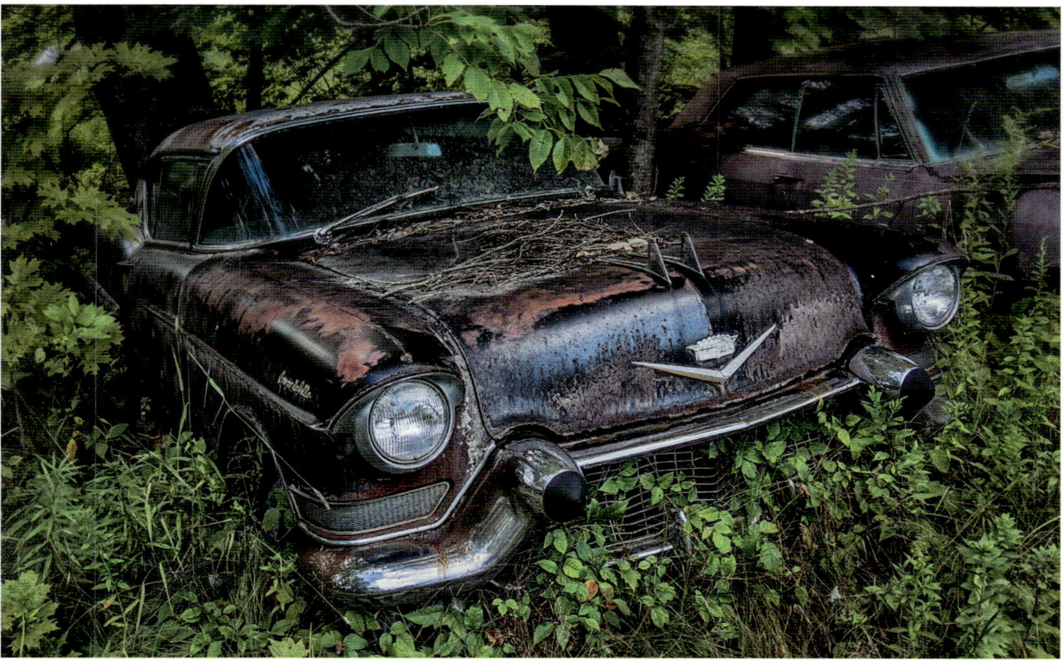

"Caddy Classics" Thoughts from my best friend, who I met in college at SUNY New Paltz in 1981. Not only have we been on a creative journey together since, but we were even each other's Best Man at our respective weddings! "If I had my way, the only car I would drive would be a Cadillac. Named for the founder of Detroit, Antoine de la Mothe Cadillac, this car was a classic right from the start, mixing comfort, reliability and horsepower. As the years went by, the brand became synonymous with luxury, status and prestige. Owners would drive them for years past their model release date, always turning heads as they drove by. The modern Cadillac's are loaded with digital systems, satellite/GPS, sound, fuel economy, and of course—improved luxury. Because of their high quality, old models were stashed away in garages, fields and junkyards hoping to be revived for a return to glory. However, it is not always meant to be, and these pages show their noble heft as they waste away. From the earth we mine the steel to produce these dream cars, and to the earth they are reclaimed." *Francis Klaess, Artist, Designer, Art Director, Art Professor*

4

THE TRUCK STOPS HERE

I find the remains of trucks and construction equipment to be particularly impressive—veritable prehistoric, heavy-metal monsters! Mack, dump, flat-beds, fire, tow and others galore, these are the vehicles that get things done and are a continuing and essential part of development and commerce around the world.

We hate trucks when they loom too close to us in our rearview mirror, or when we get stuck behind one on a road with no, or risky passing. However, we sure love them when they deliver goodies to our doorstep, or carry away our garbage! For me, I like seeing them retired in peaceful solitude after a lifetime of hard work. I also find it gently comforting when I encounter one of the most quintessential of American icons, the vintage pick-up truck, rusting away in countless fields and along roadsides in every state. It's nice to consider that maybe their purpose is to make us slow down, and gently remind us of a simpler, less chaotic time in our country.

Right: I asked artist James Gurney, who I worked with creating art for a style guide to accompany his *Dinotopia* TV series many years ago, to comment on this photo because a) it made me think of a dinosaur, and b) it also reminded me of a painting he did of a giant yellow robot! James also shares my passion for abandoned vehicles, and even hosted a "Dead Vehicle Challenge" —a plein-air painting competition via his Gurney Journey Facebook Events. "This old truck sits in an above-ground grave, its passenger door flung open, and a dent in its forehead. It's a Mack cabover with no sleeper, so it probably didn't do long hauls. But what kind of rainy or snowy weather did those wipers contend with? We'll never know, as it settles into its afterlife, hub-deep in the grass at the edge of the wild woods." *James Gurney, Artist, Illustrator, Author, Creator of Dinotopia*

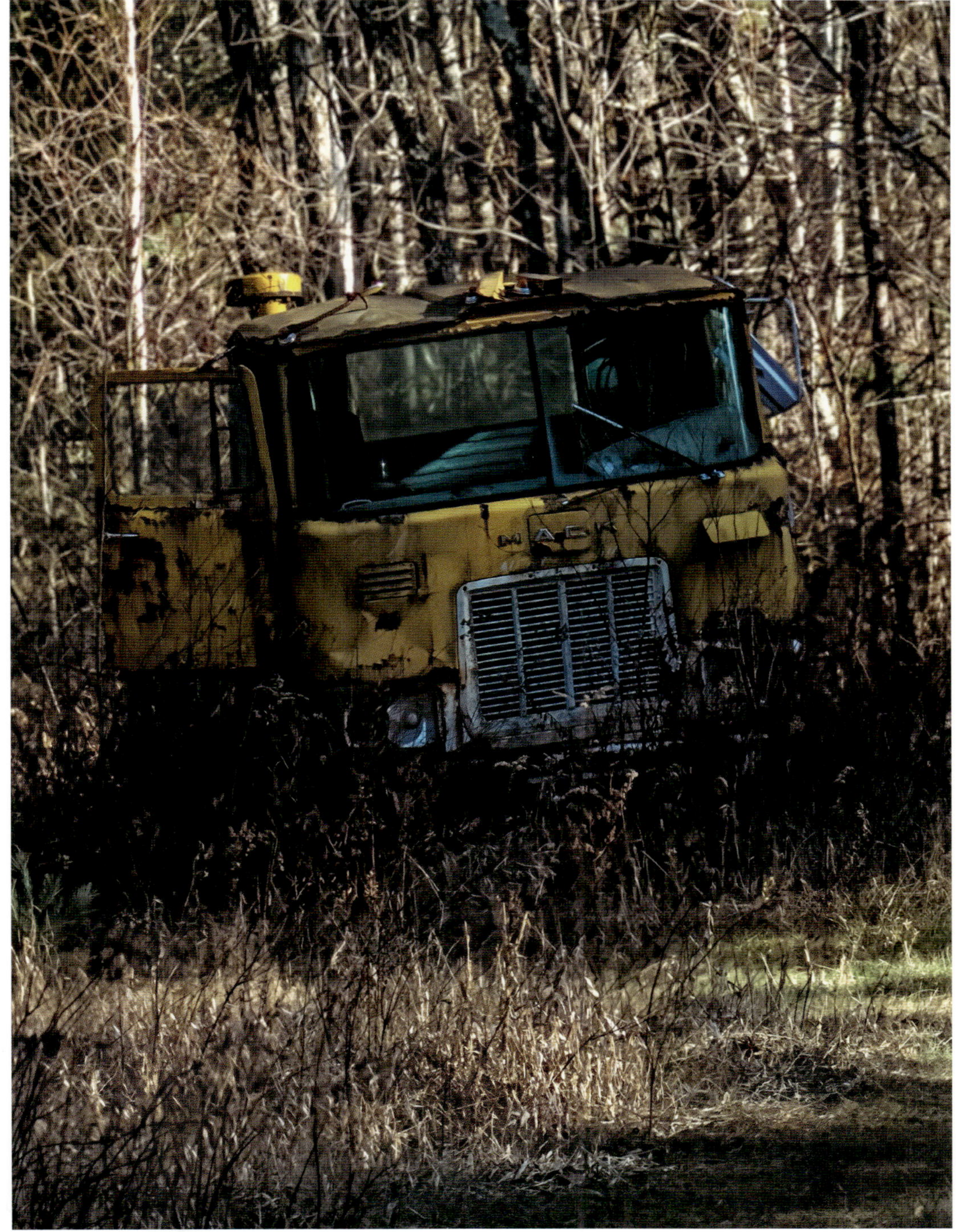
MACK

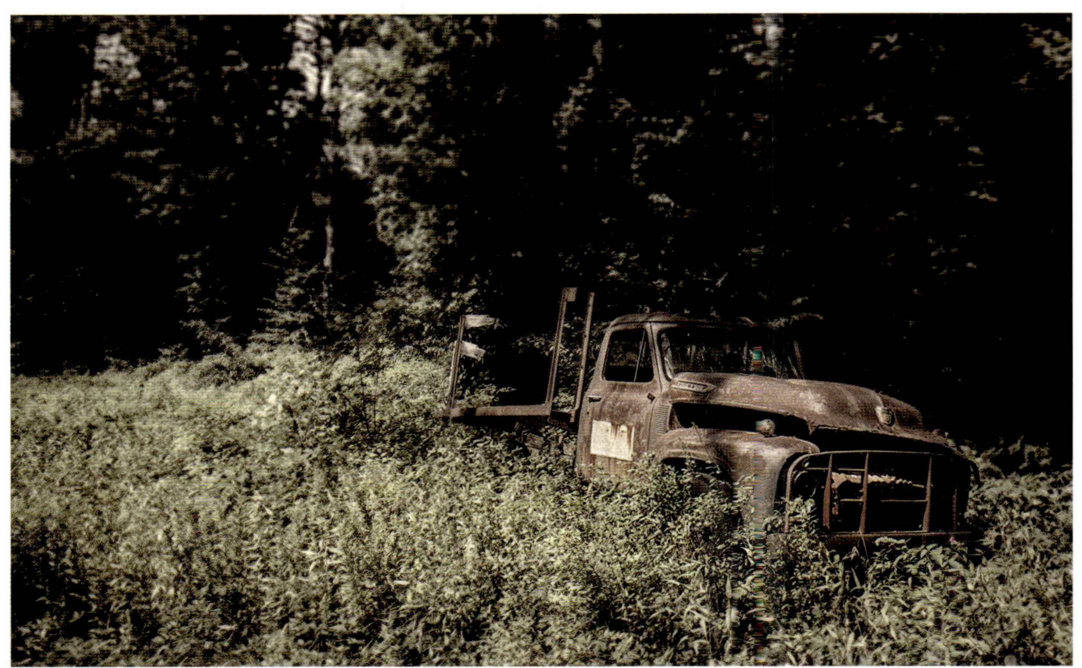

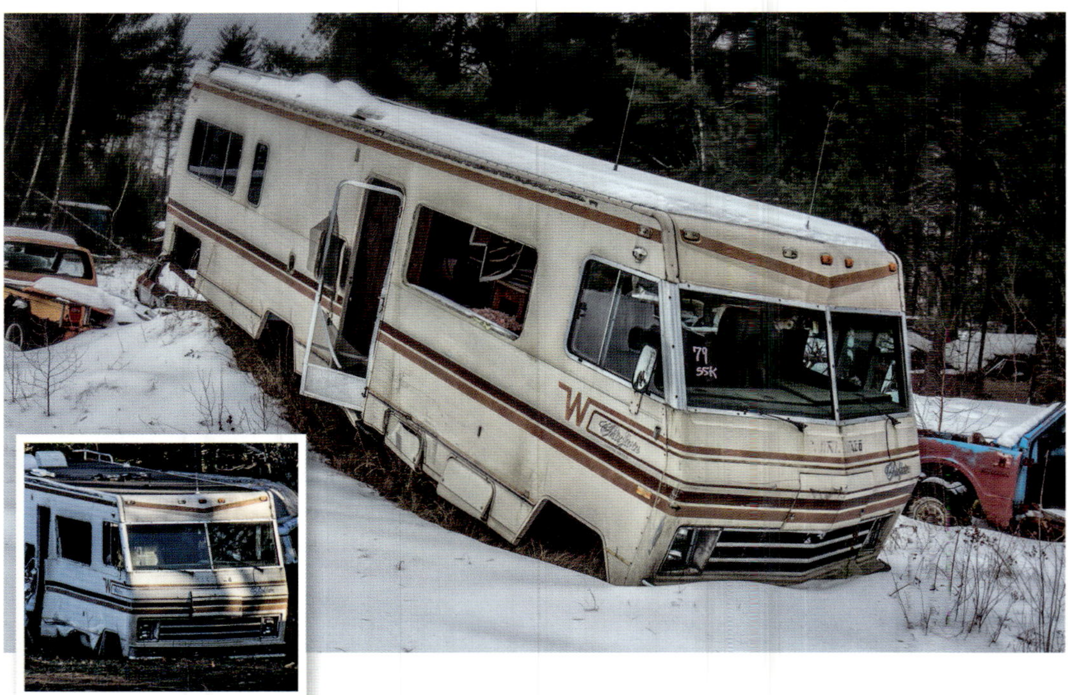

Top Left: "Sailing in The Sea of Green" I handed this off to my friend and peer, who has an Americana flavor to so much of his beautiful work. "Waiting. Waiting. Truck and tall summer grass become one." *Robert Crawford, Illustrator, Fine Artist*

Bottom Left: My talented paisan's immediate reaction. "Who the hell left the door open—what, were you raised in a house or somethin!" *Flav Martin, Musician, Singer, Songwriter (David Crosby, Al Stewart, Steve Morse, etc.)*

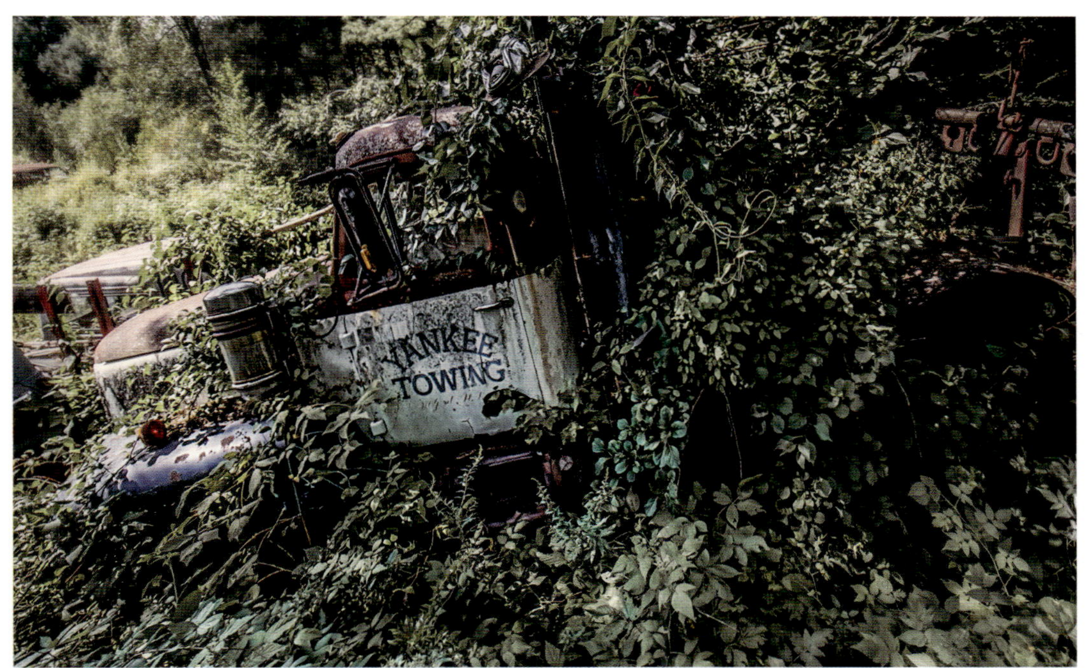

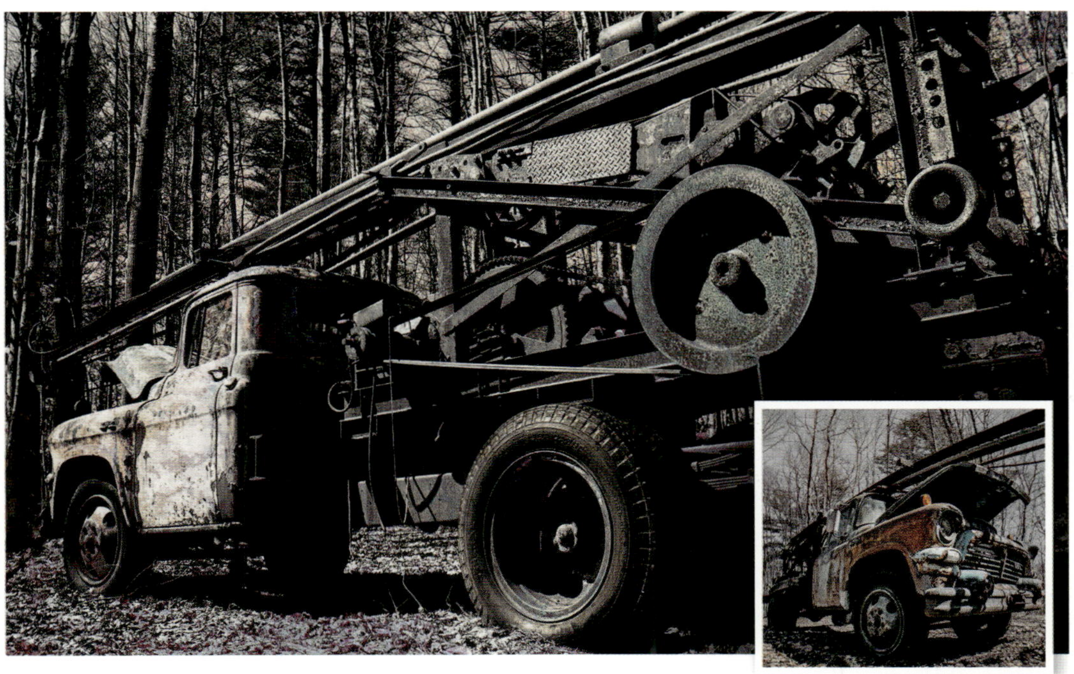

Top Right: A simple observation by my right-hand man in concert hosting. "Vintage tow truck. Needs work."
Elliot Gould, Photographer, Videographer

Bottom Right: A very handsome rusting beast, this 1957 GMC 300 flatbed truck was converted into deep-well drilling rig, and sits out of commission a pretty good distance from the road in the woods of Loudon.

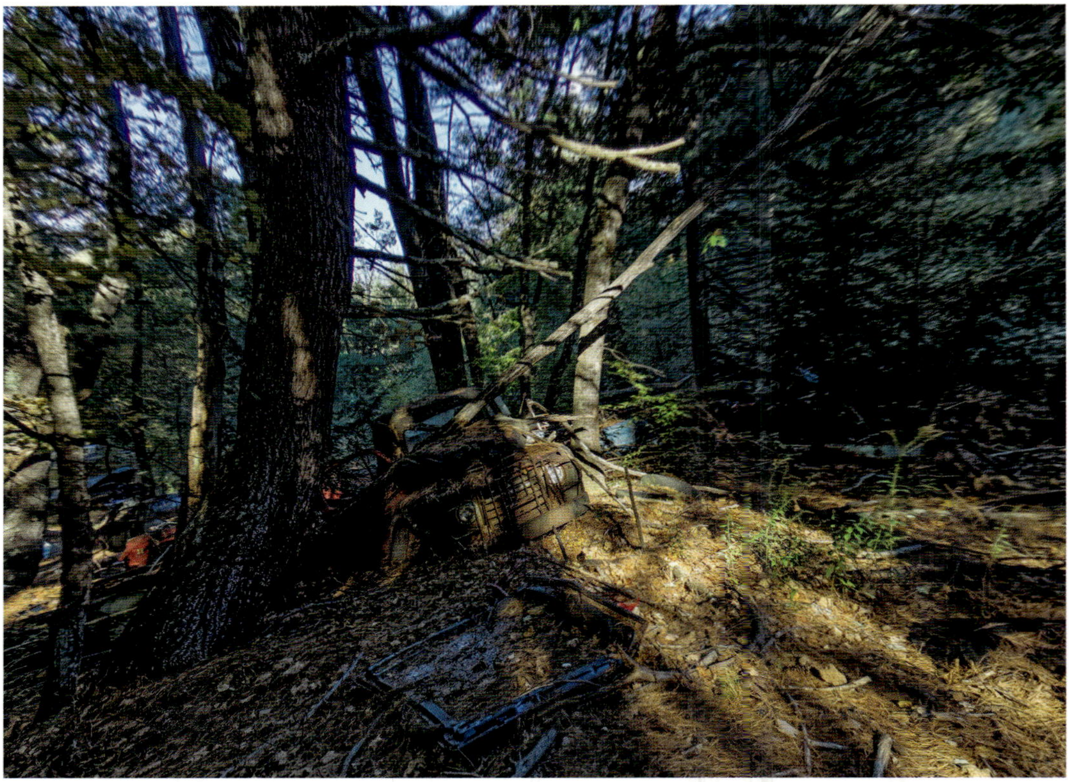

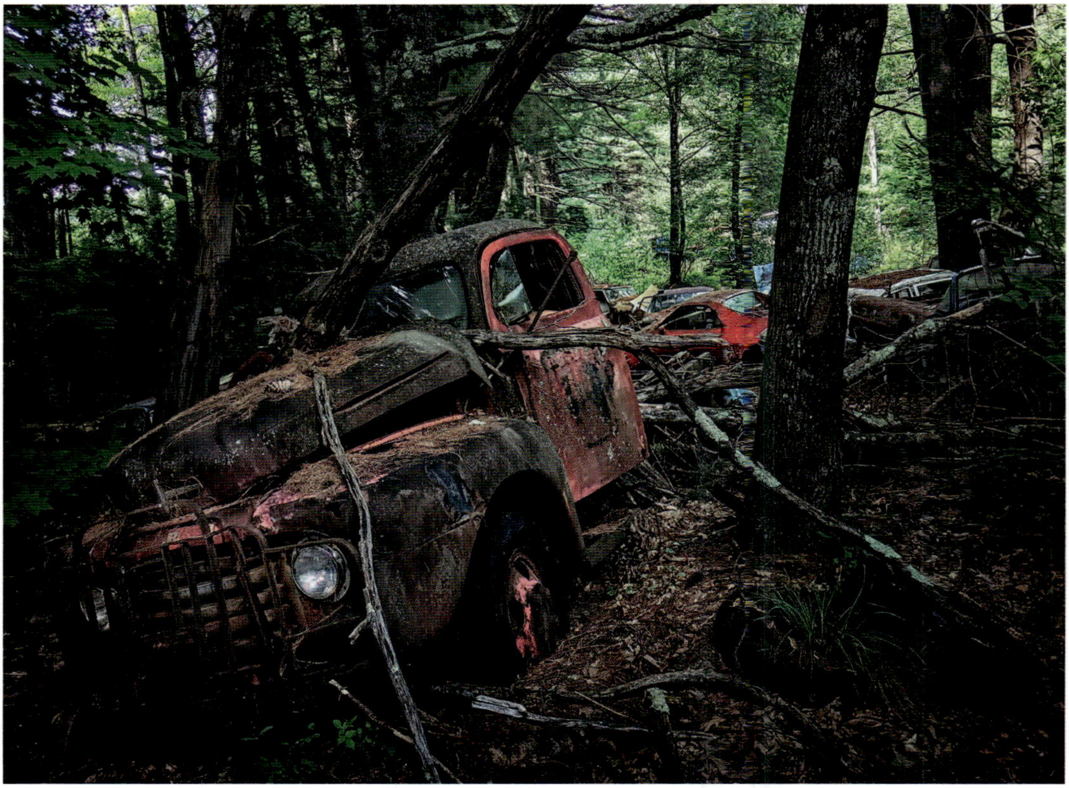

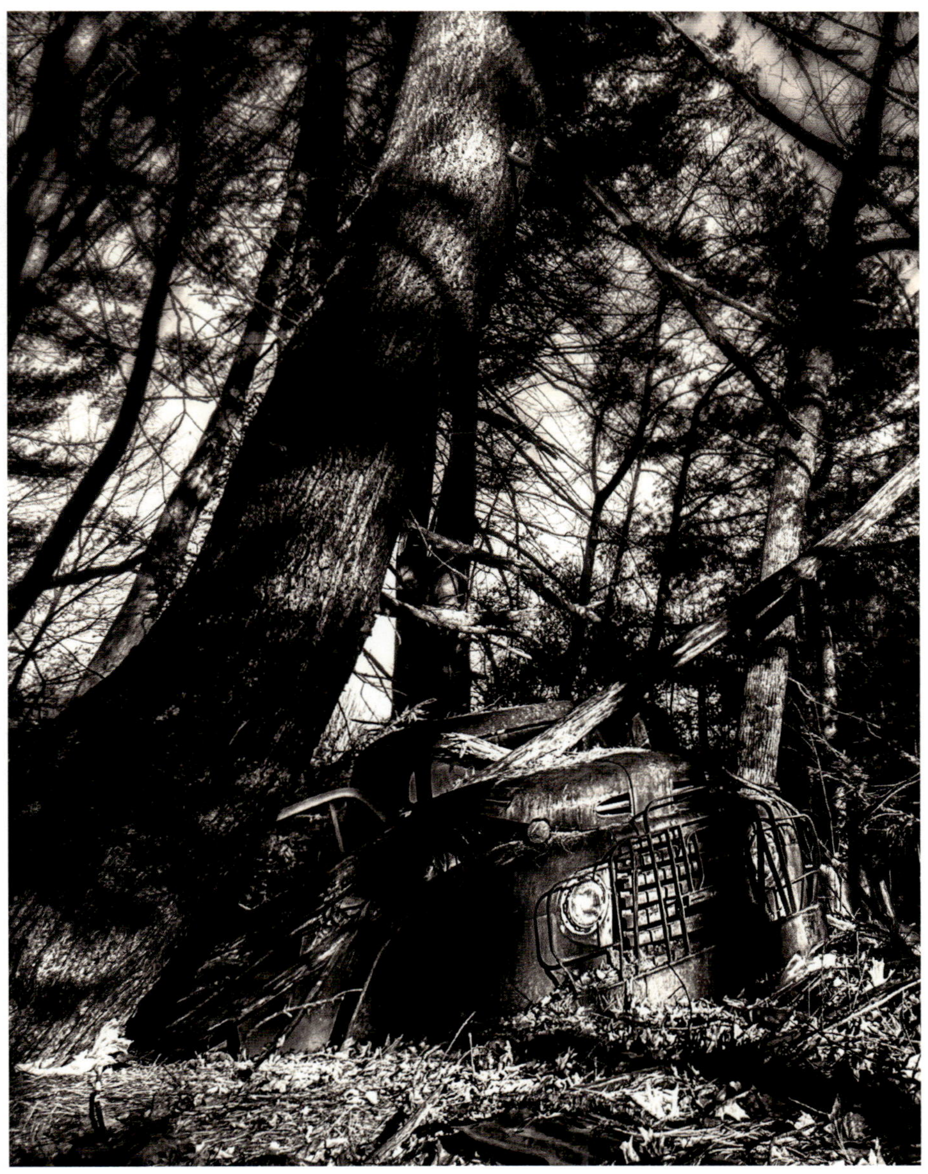

"Welcome to Carassic Park" This Ford truck rests dramatically next to a huge pine in Blanchard's, and has been the target of falling branches over the years. I've photographed it many times, and its deep-forest, primal energy is what inspired the title. It is because of this energy, and so many big "sticks" at different angles, it felt right to ask a masterful drummer to comment. Serendipitously, it turns out that he had family memories unlocked by these photos. "My dad's got a bunch of burned-out vehicles where he lives up in The Plumas Forest (Northeast California) ... grease, water, and fire trucks along with a couple of old U.S. Army Jeeps from the 1940s known as Willys. Everything is in disrepair on the lot, and there are trees and fungus growing inside most of them. These photos actually look like they could have been taken on his property, and in fact he even had the same Ford truck. My dad was the oldest of five, and I heard stories of him driving trucks, bulldozers and tractors when he was fourteen or fifteen (maybe even as young as twelve), and he was driving logging trucks by the time he was eighteen." *Pat Mastelotto, Musician, Drummer (King Crimson, Mr. Mister, Stick Men, XTC, etc.)*

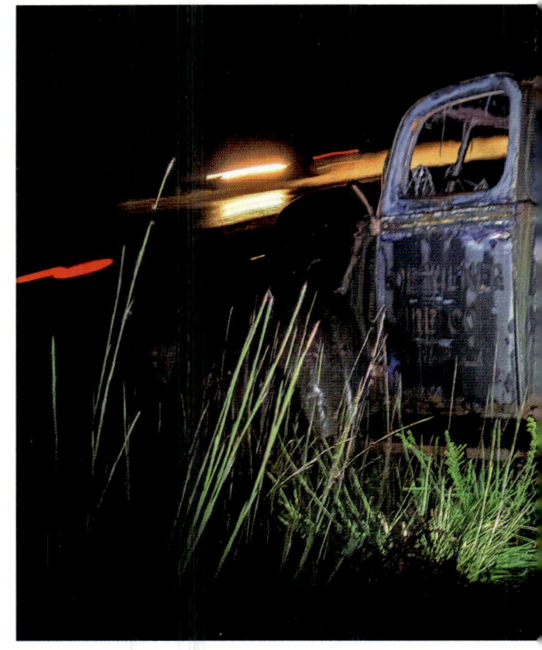

This Ford truck poses right off of Route 9/202 in Stoddard, and is another that I frequently shoot. My friend, and two-time performer in my studio, wasn't totally sure what to write, but the strange moods of the photos brought to his mind the *The Last Flowers,* by the great Russian Romantic era poet Alexander S. Pushkin.

Rich the first flower's graces be,
But dearer far the last to me;
My spirit feels renewal sweet,
Of all my dreams hope or desire--
The hours of parting oft inspire
More than the moments when we meet!

Bert Lams, Musician, Guitarist (California Guitar Trio)

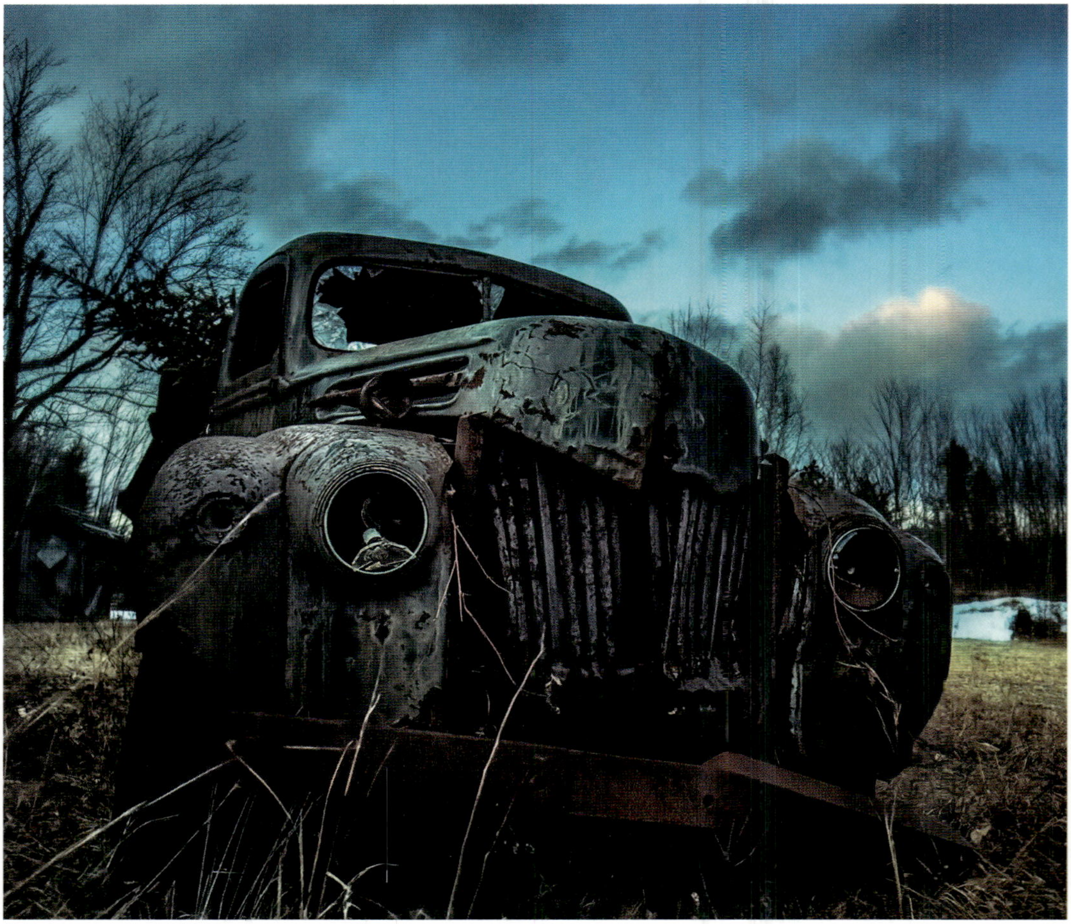

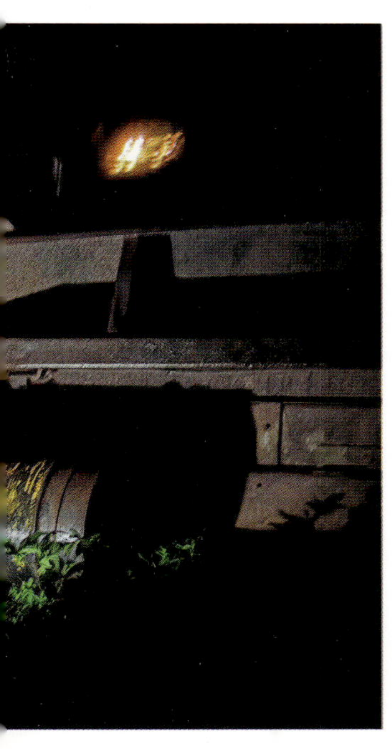

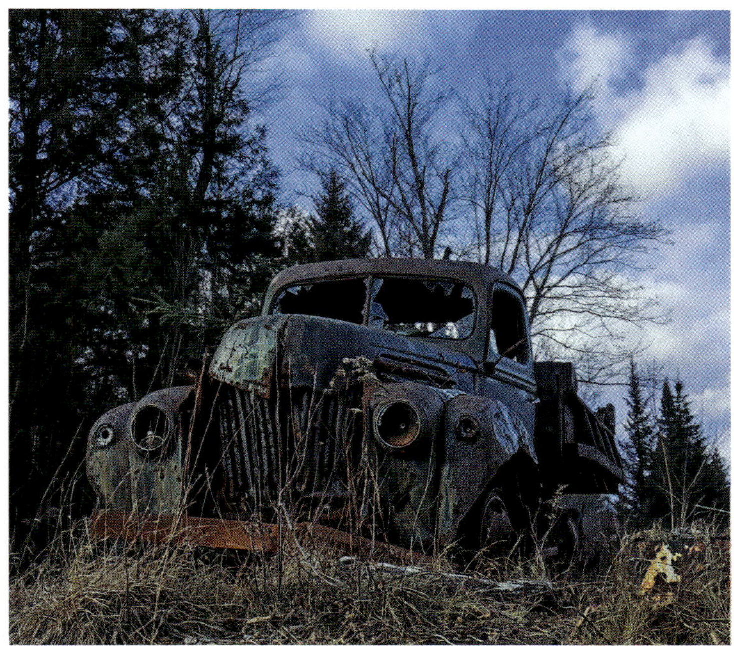

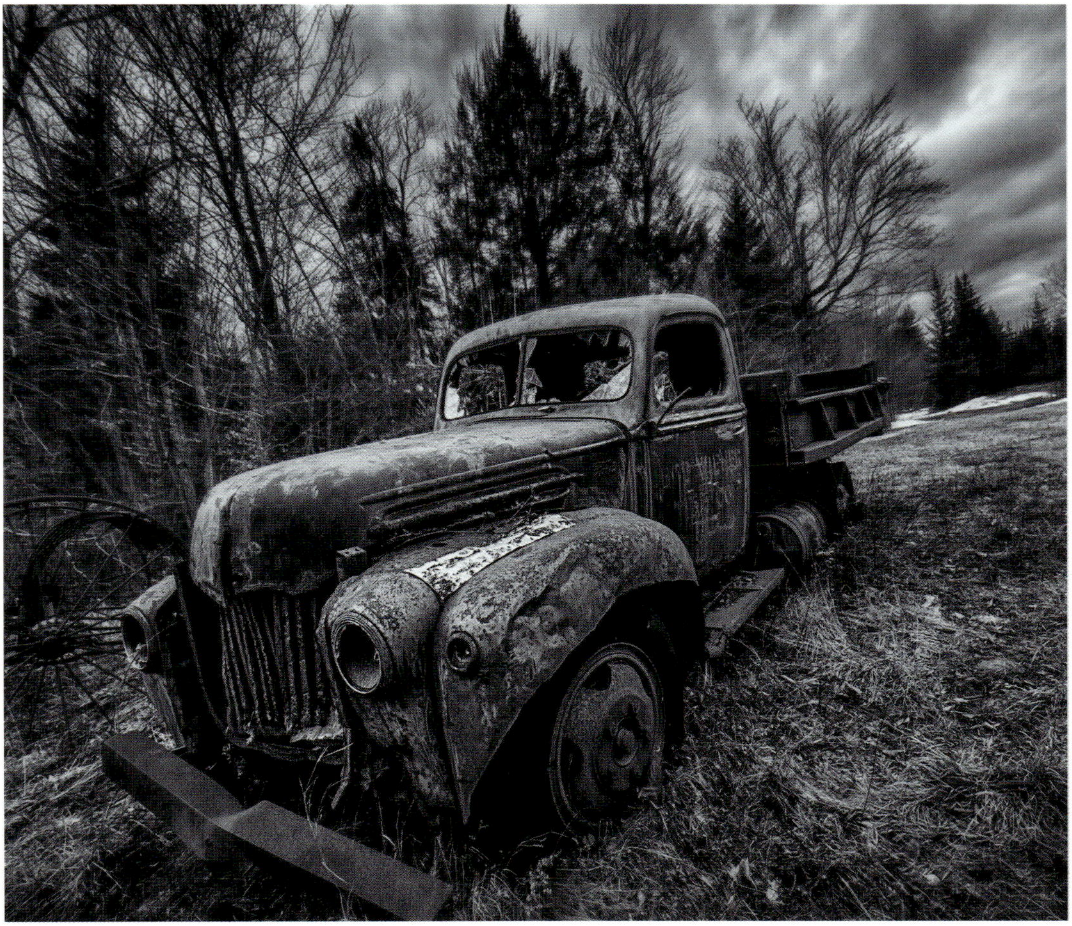

Bottom Left: My longtime illustration peer and prehistoric pal shares a poetic thought about this truck, which I gave a little extra TLC in Photoshop to. "The ancient traveling-machine locks its rusted stare onto the ceaselessly shifting clouds, dreaming of its nimble past." *Joe DeVito, Illustrator, Artist, Author (King Kong of Skull Island)*

Top Right: This early 1950s Seagrave open cab fire truck sits behind the abandoned car dealership in Weare, keeping a watchful eye on a discarded engine. As previously mentioned, I drive by this place fairly often, and I've taken many photos of the building along with the other vehicles scattered about.

Bottom Right: Sometimes my timing is perfect, and this wash of sunlight and shadows adds a beautiful dimension to the fire engine.

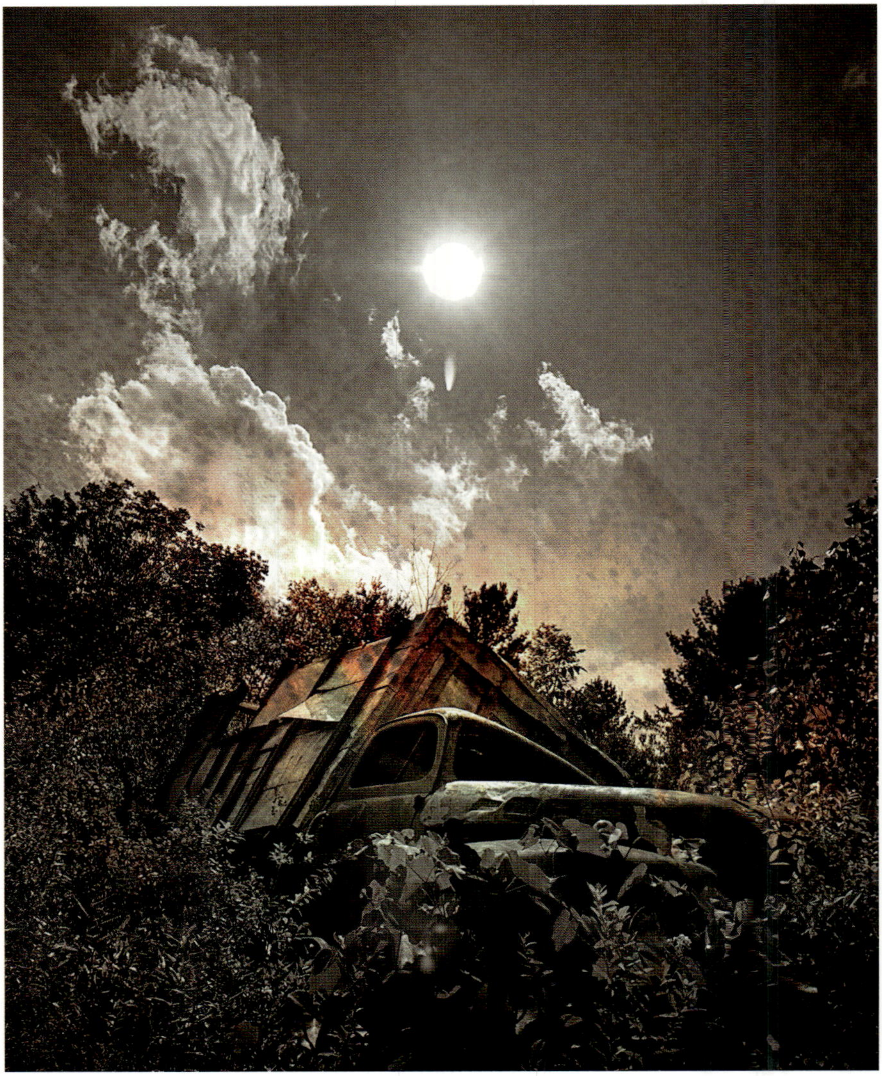

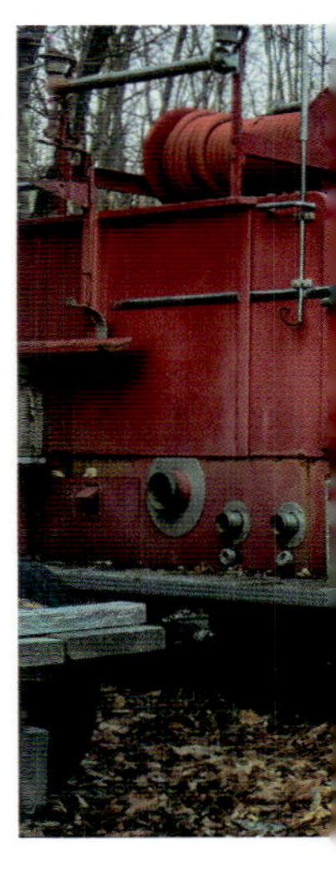

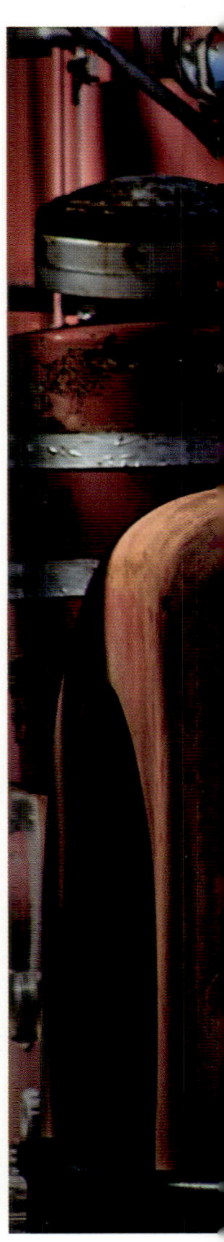

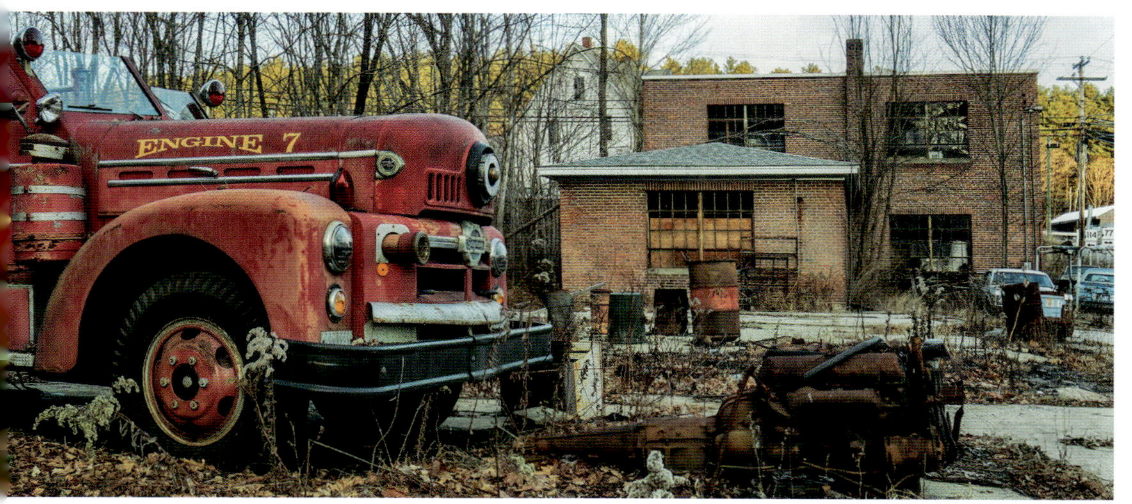
ENGINE 7

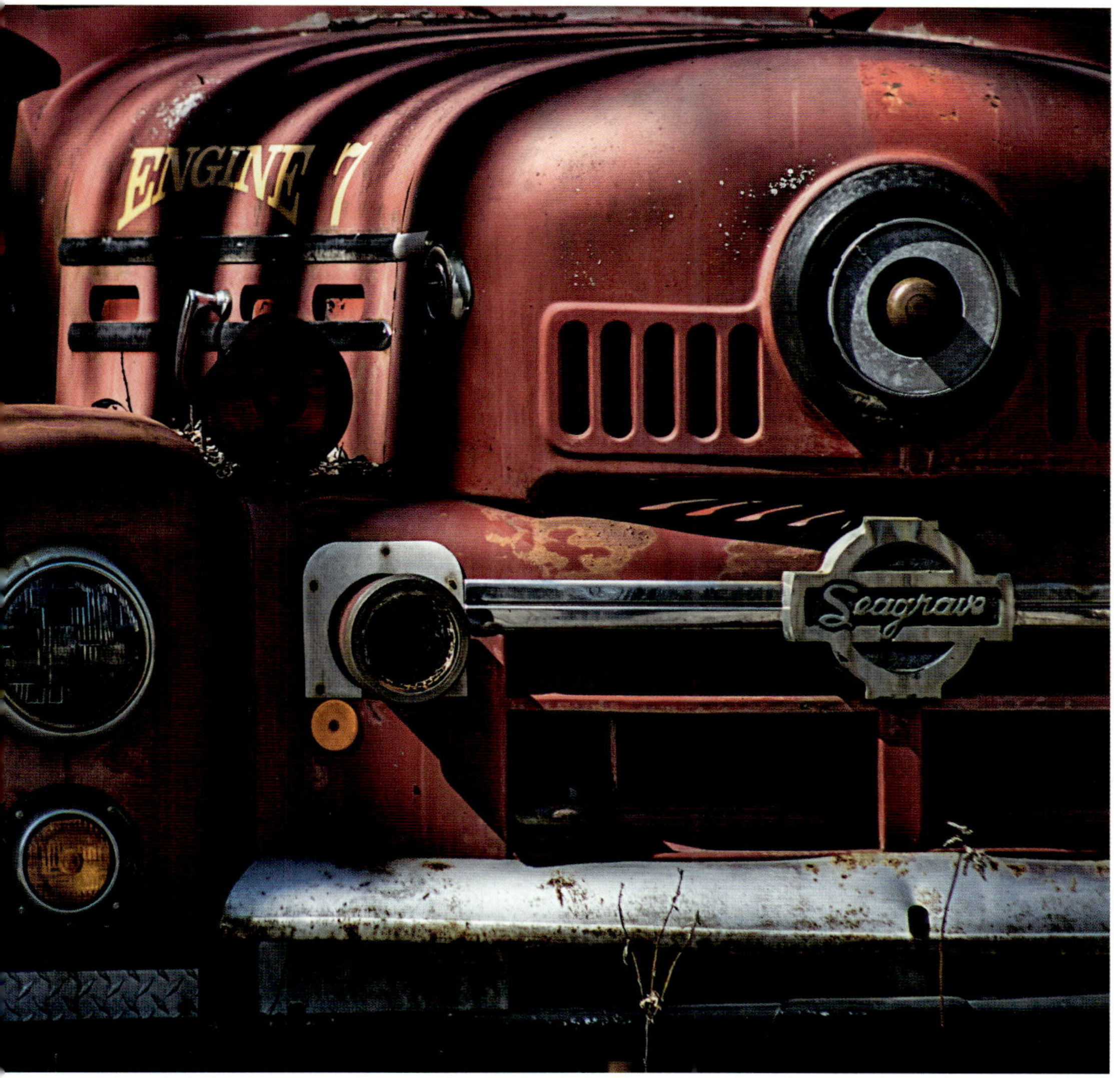

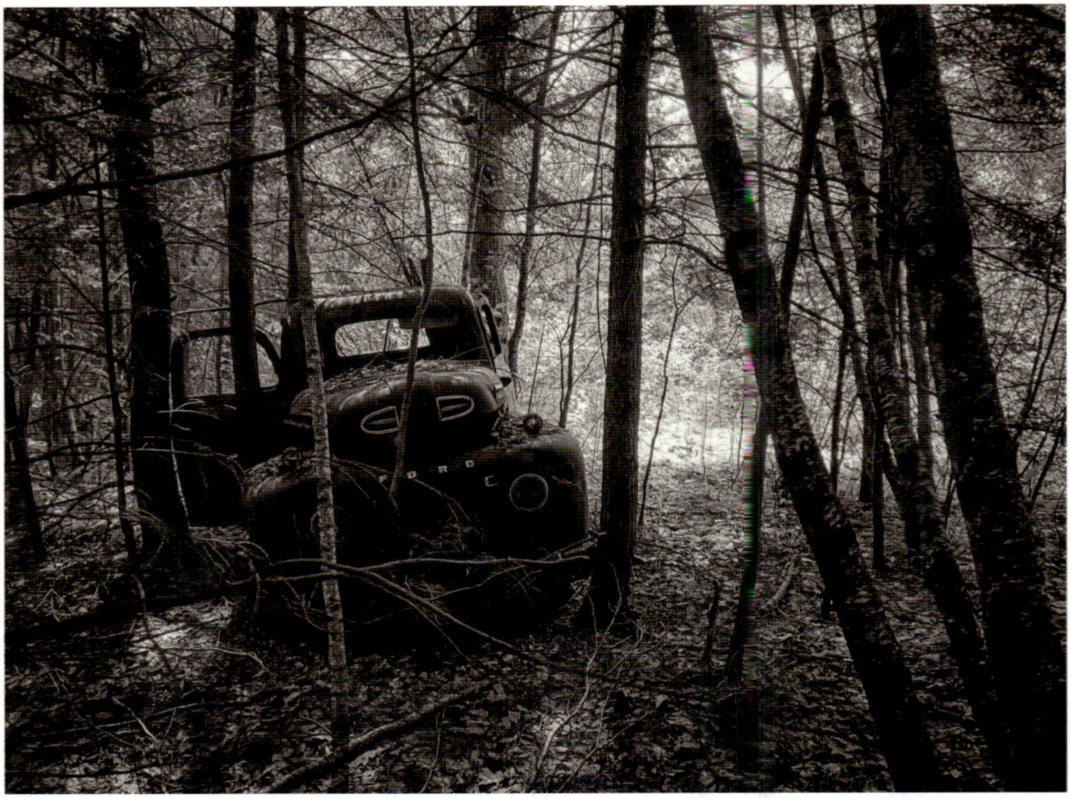

This Page: *"The Ghost of Gulf Road"* I first encountered this Ford truck on a neighbor's property in 1997, shortly after we purchased our home just up the road from them. I thought it was pretty cool, but it somehow didn't even occur to me to photograph it at the time. However, when the rusty bug finally bit me all these years later, I went out on a hot spring day in 2018 to find it still quietly tucked away, though much further out in the woods than I remembered.

Right: With new people occupying the property in 2019, I introduced myself and asked for permission to photograph the truck. With a December super moon aloft, I hedged my bets … "Would you mind if I crawl around your property late tonight?" Happily, no problem, and I bundled up and returned with a few assorted lights and flashlights around 10:30 pm for a really fun shoot.

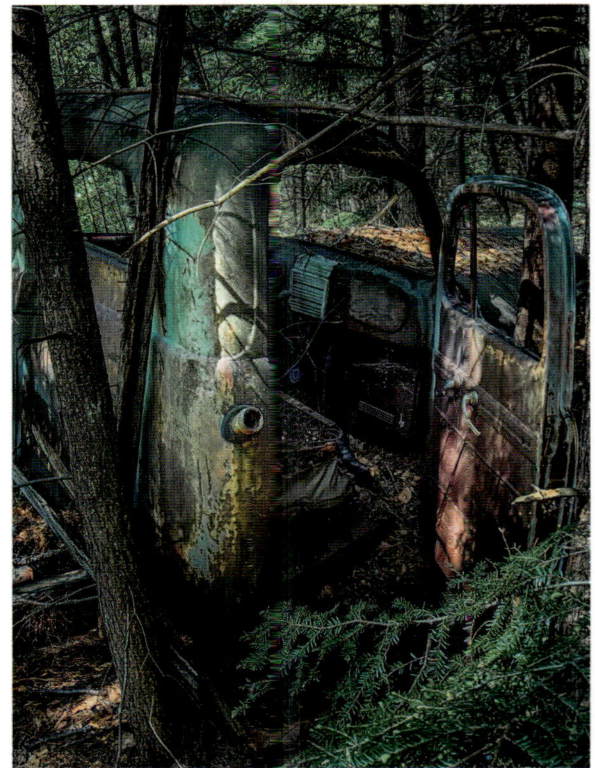

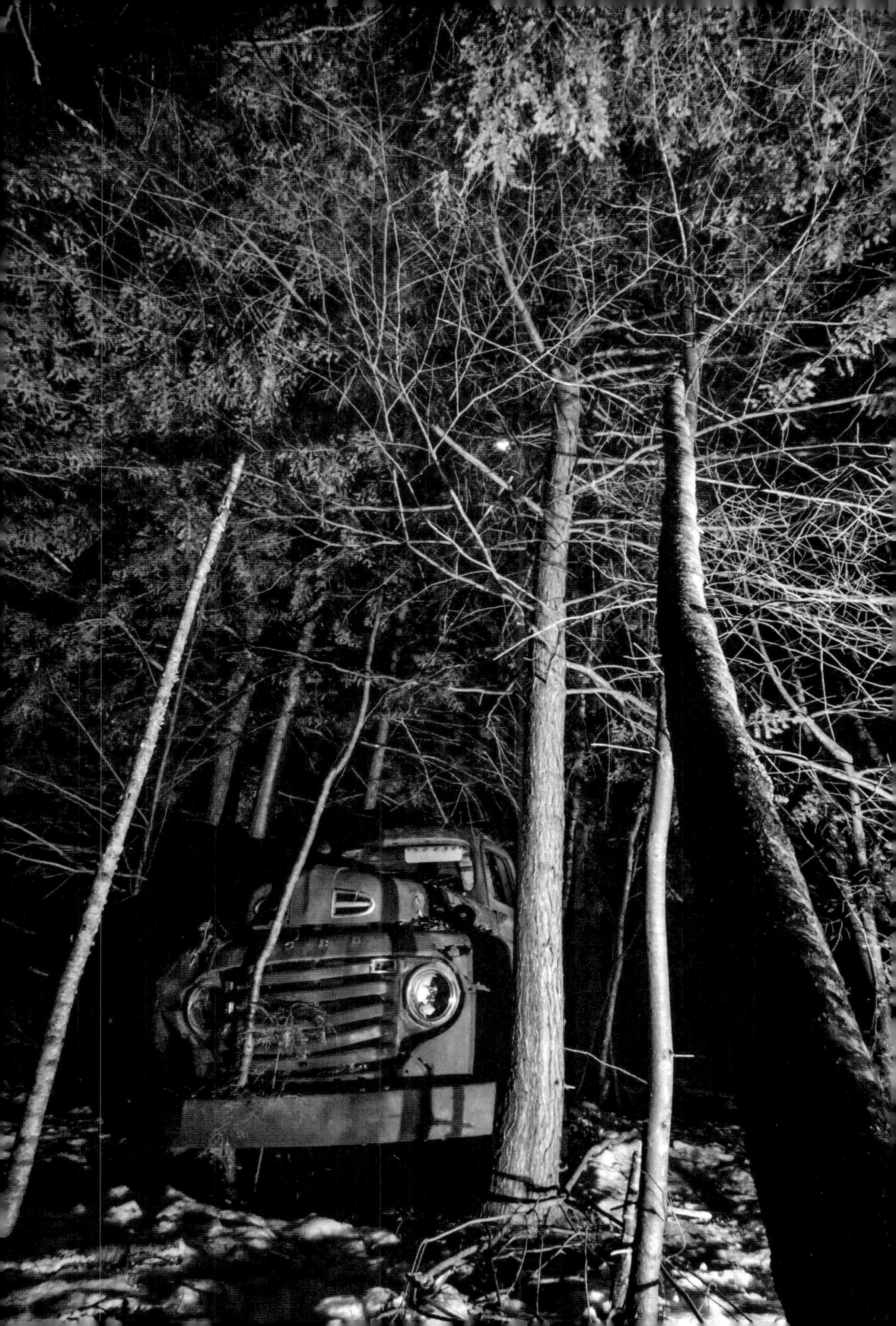

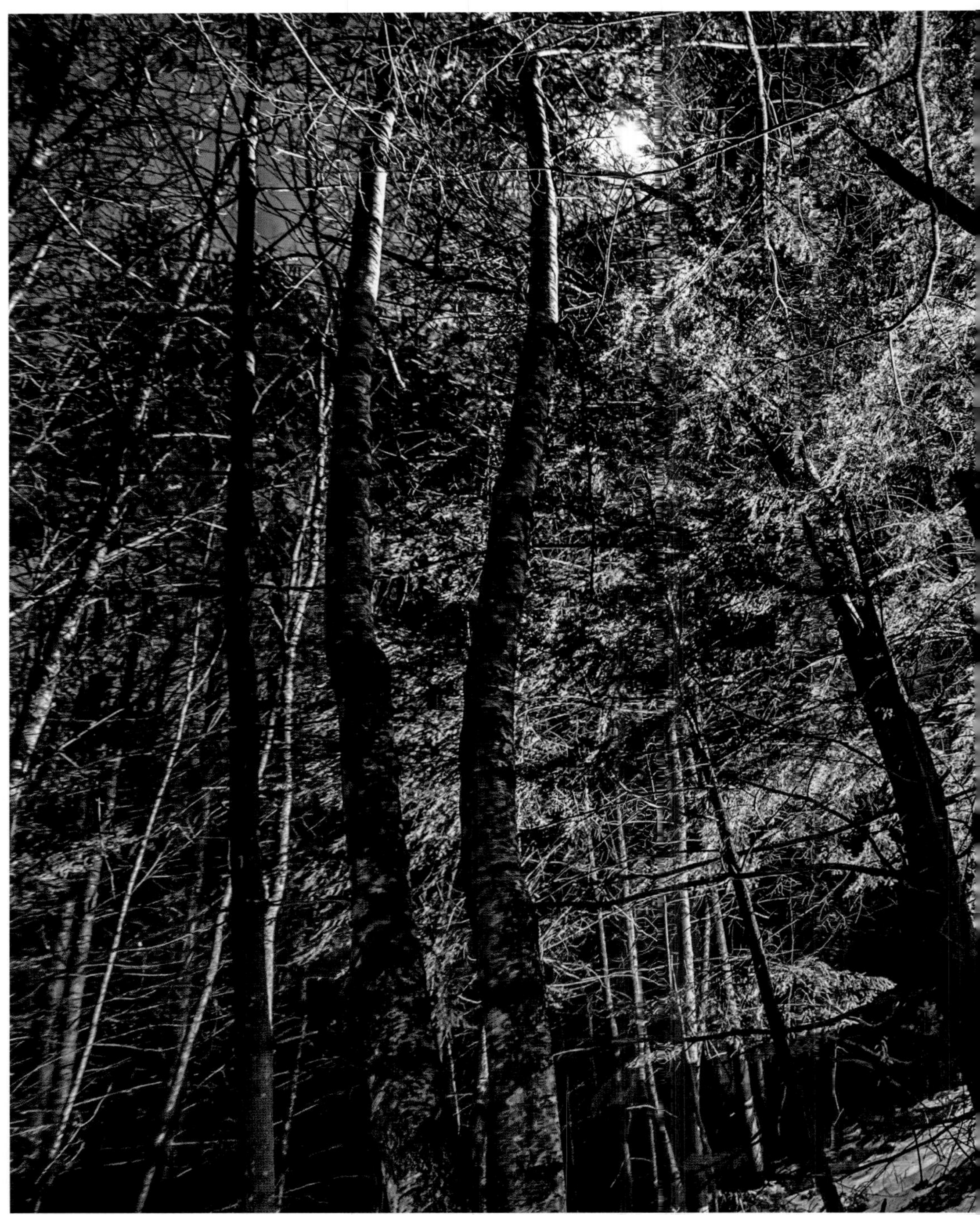

With this relic being so far out in the woods, it was actually kind of scary—especially for someone with a wild imagination like mine! There was just a bit of snow on the ground, and not even the slightest breeze, and I found myself enveloped in an eerie, muffled silence. However, to be out there all by myself was mentally invigorating, and I loved having those two hours to relax with my cameras. With a full moon above, coupled with backlighting below, the end result was a shimmering, crystalline scene, punctuated by staccato angles and vibrant energy. These qualities made me think of my dear friend and partner in creativity, who happens to be one of the most accomplished keyboard players in rock history … he totally nails it!

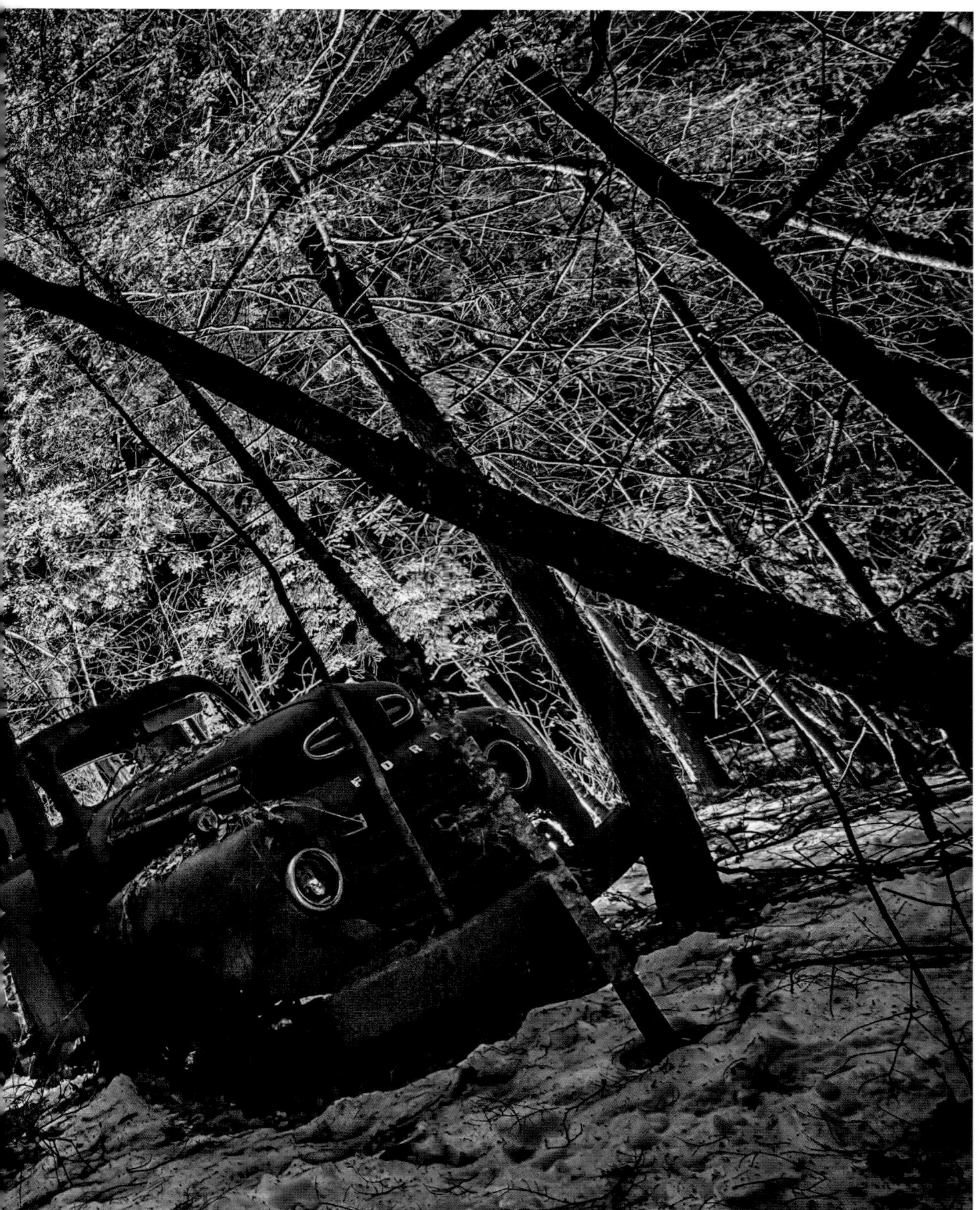

"Empty stillness and a moment frozen in time.
Entering a dream, I walk through the hidden gates and my imagination bursts into the unknown.
Magic and beauty, sadness and separation.
My thoughts are alive."
Jordan Rudess, Musician, Keyboard Player (Dream Theater, Liquid Tension Experiment, Dixie Dregs)

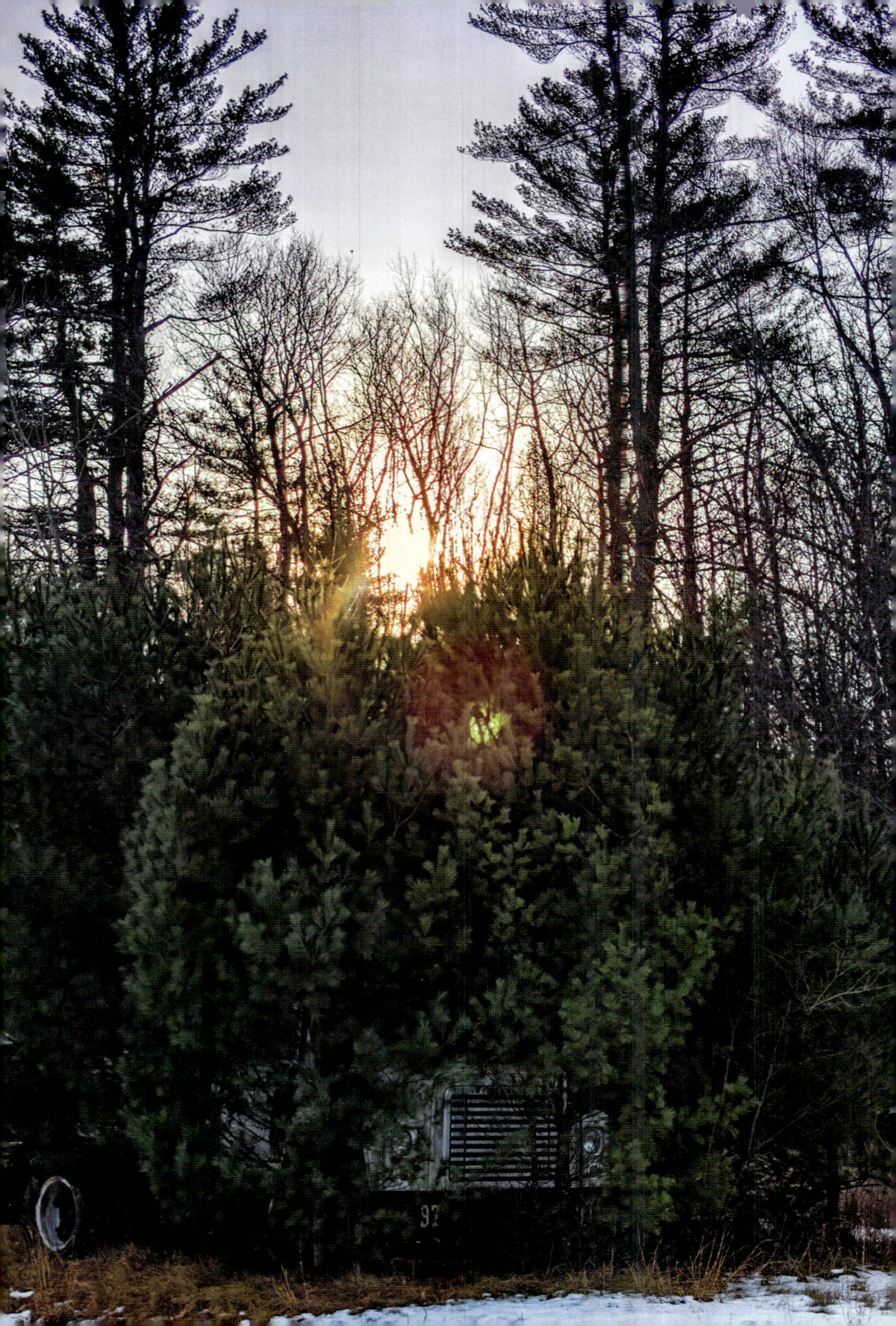

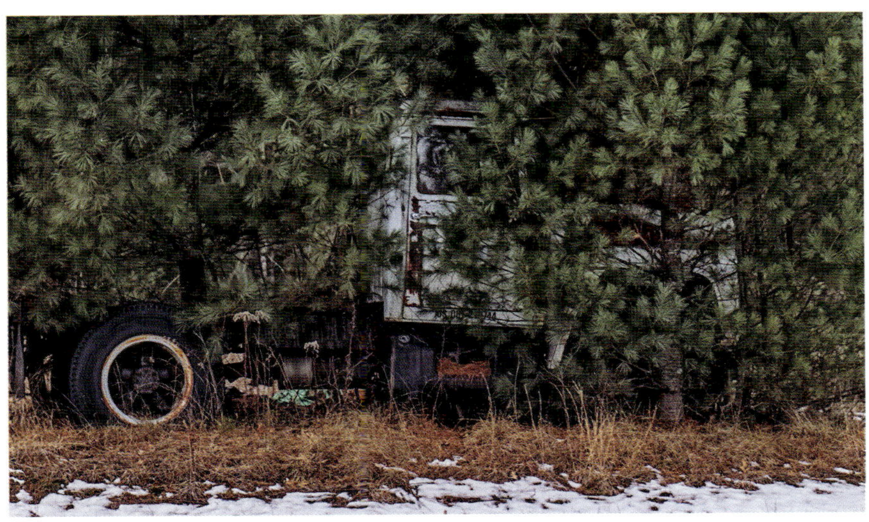

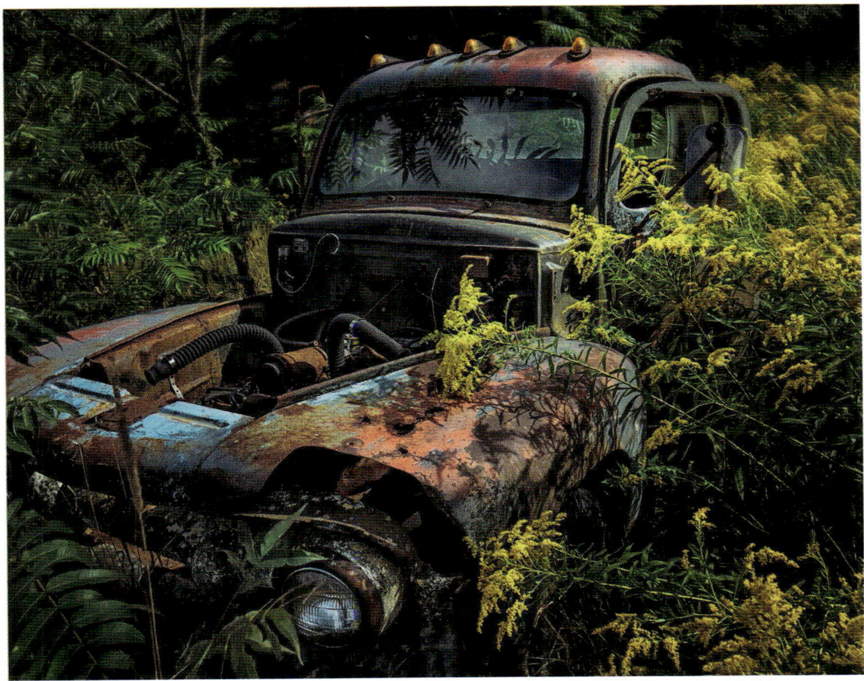

Left & Top Right: *"Gimme Shelter"* As I was on my way to a promising location in the backwoods of Warner, I saw this Chevy International truck completely engulfed by pine trees. I slammed on the brakes, pulled into the driveway of the nearby farmhouse and knocked on the door to ask permission to photograph. I entered after someone yelled to come in, and found an elderly man in a hospital bed in the living room watching a Patriot's game. It turns out he was recovering from back surgery, and I had a lovely conversation with him and his wife, both of whom were very amused at my interest in the truck! Here's a quick thought by my funny-man British friend. "I talk to the trees, and so they locked me away!" *Jim Davidson, Comedian, Actor, TV Show Host, Celebrity Big Brother UK Winner 2014*

Bottom Right: The serene and beautiful mix of colors had me share this photo with an art director I worked with a lot. "How happy I'd be to spend an eternity amongst the goldenrod!" *Kim Kaufman, Art Director, Designer, Department Manager (The Mountain)*

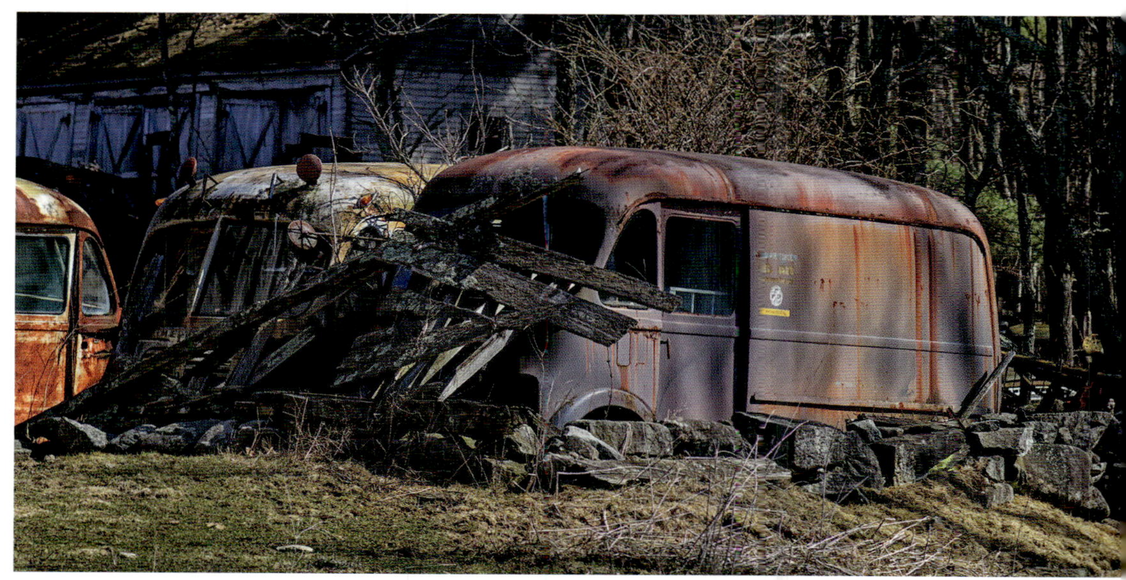

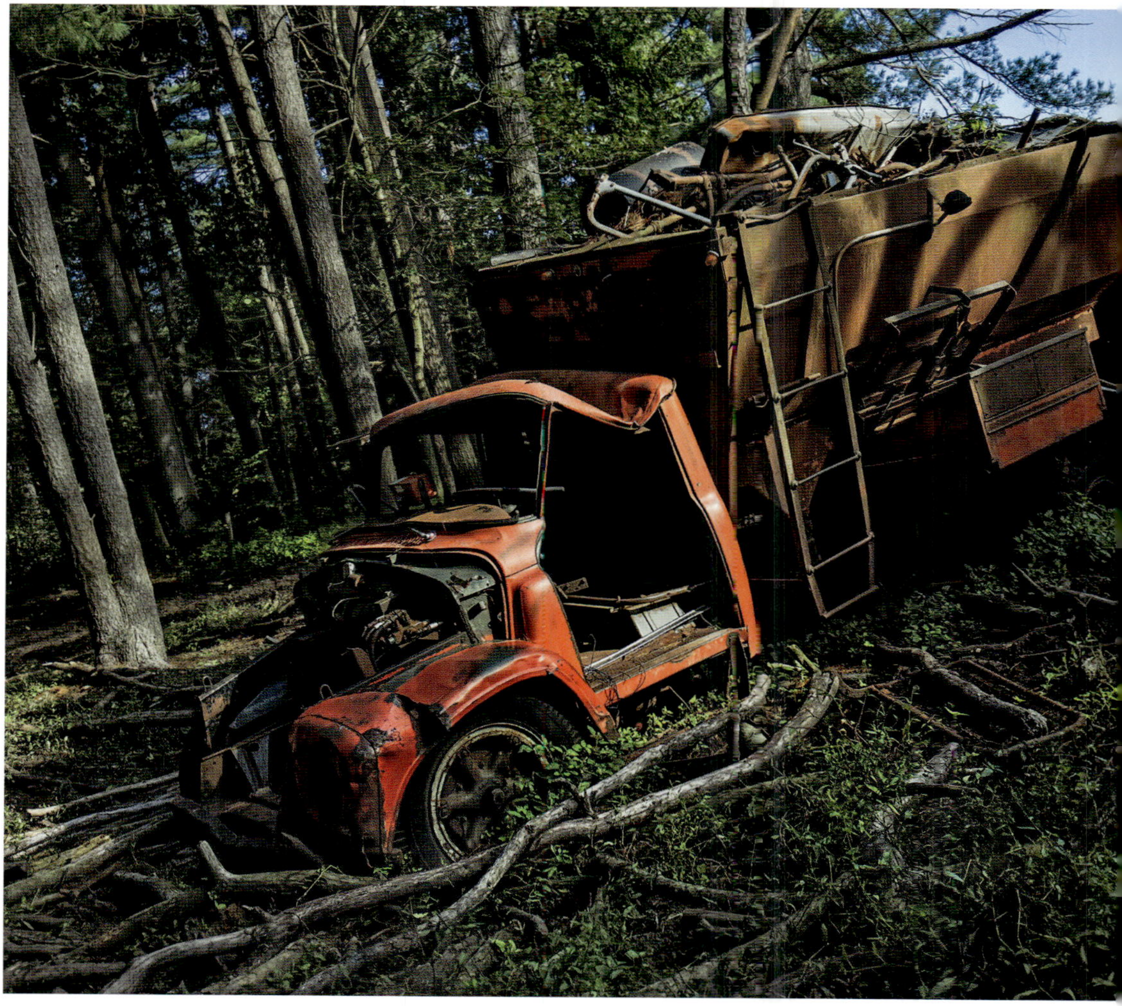

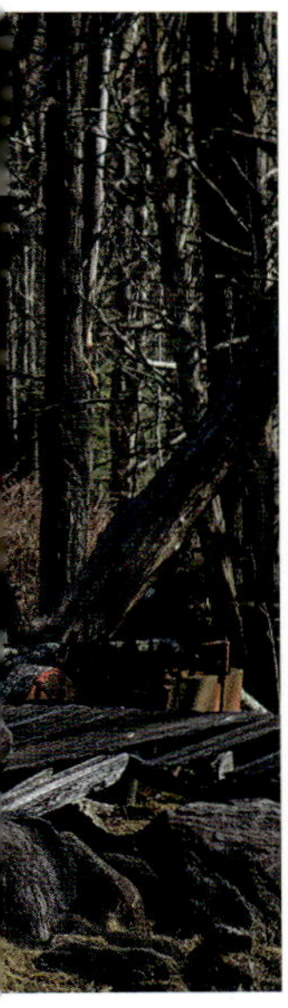

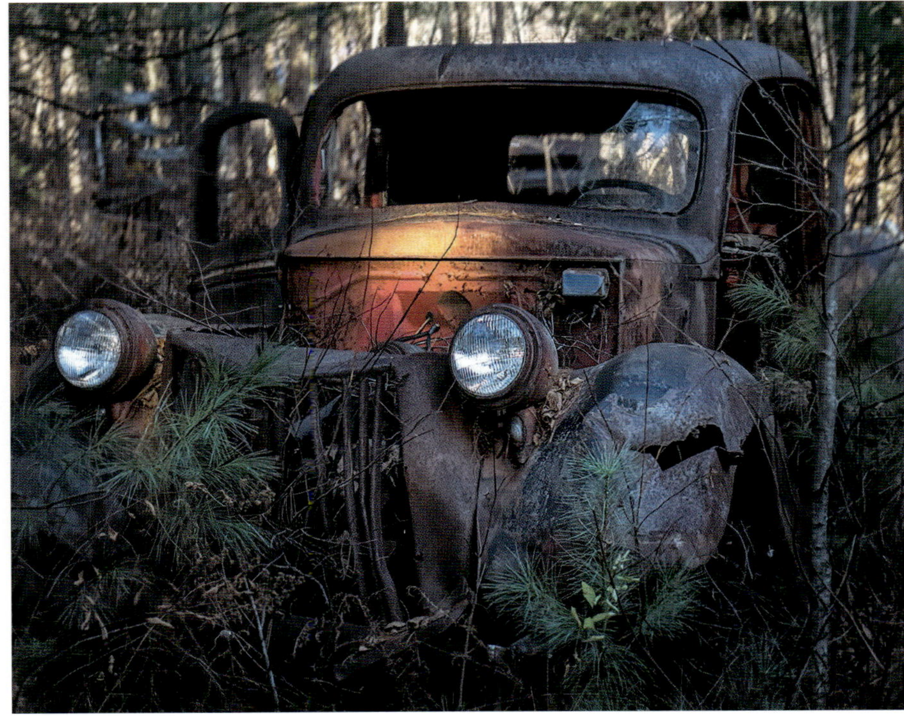

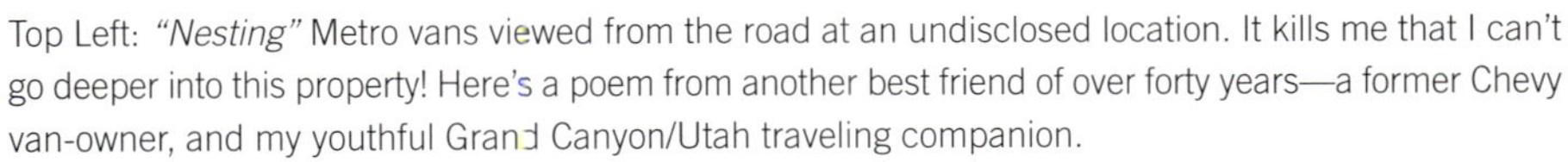

Top Left: *"Nesting"* Metro vans viewed from the road at an undisclosed location. It kills me that I can't go deeper into this property! Here's a poem from another best friend of over forty years—a former Chevy van-owner, and my youthful Grand Canyon/Utah traveling companion.

"Can you see summers past,
not everything was meant to last.
Dreams shattered into dust,
or lie in fields and turn to rust."
Andrew Levine, Photographer

Bottom Left: I can't even imagine what happened to this farm truck in Concord. Here's a thoughtful rumination from a fellow who I remember many years ago when he was a just a mere intern at The Society of Illustrators of New York, and has long since become one of the top illustrators in his genre. "As we come to our final resting place, few of us are able to shuck off the lifetime of baggage we carry with us. Those who enter peacefully into the end do not necessarily clean out their haul, but arrive at their destination in a blissful state of acceptance." *Donato Giancola, Science Fiction and Fantasy Illustrator*

Top Right: This 1940 Ford 3/4 Ton flatbed truck displays a beautiful range of color in the late afternoon light. When I asked my old friend and illustration peer to contribute a thought, he found himself encountering a complete writer's block—nada, nothing, zilch (he wasn't the only one). However, he did go on to say a number of flattering things about my long creative journey, and I thought I'd include this kind and funny thought. "After many years of illustration, Jerry has turned his eye toward photography, and again—excellence. King Midas has nothing on him, as anything he touches turns to gold. Even rust is golden when Jerry shoots it!" *Ken Westphal, Illustrator, Designer, Airbrush Workshop Teaching Partner*

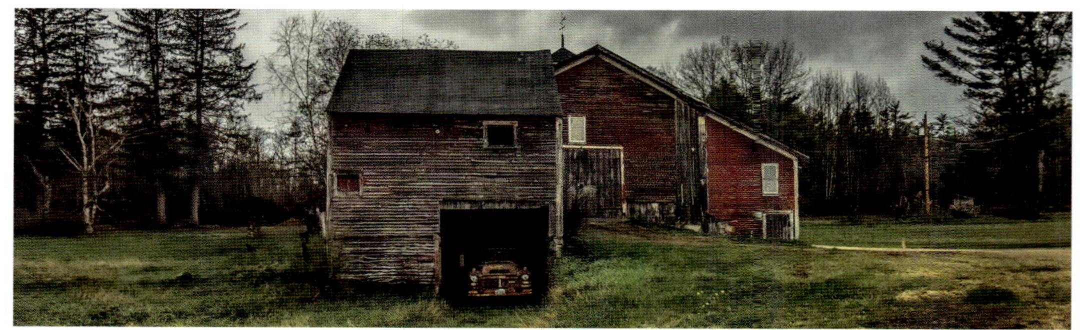

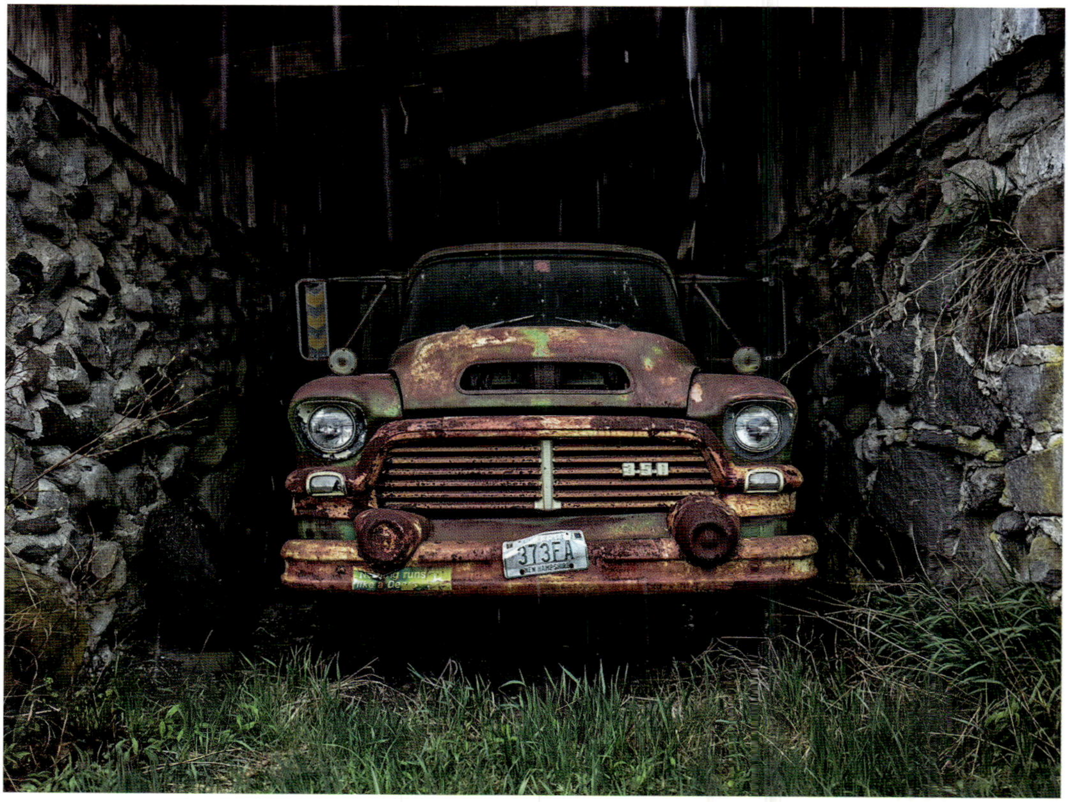

Above: I've seen this 1957 GMC 350 Stake Bed pickup truck parked beneath an old barn in Chichester photographed by others a few times. Understandably so, as she's just begging to be, sitting ever so coyly in plain sight next to the road and winking her eyes!

Top Right: The 1956 International R210 dump truck seems to be lying in wait, and I find the subtle greens and rust colors softened by the reflecting twilight to almost act as camouflage for the hulking beast.

Bottom Right: This 1977 Chevy International Loadstar truck has been in the same spot for many years in a nearby, but now closed orchard in Henniker. The following is from a friend who grew up here. "This old red truck has served the orchard and The Peak (Pat's Peak Ski Mountain) faithfully for years, hauling apples and giving rides to generations of locals and tourists alike as they searched excitedly for 'perfect' apples. The owner has sadly passed away, and with that the orchard and truck will likely follow, gradually fading to cherished memories" *Steve Fisher, Master Furniture Builder*

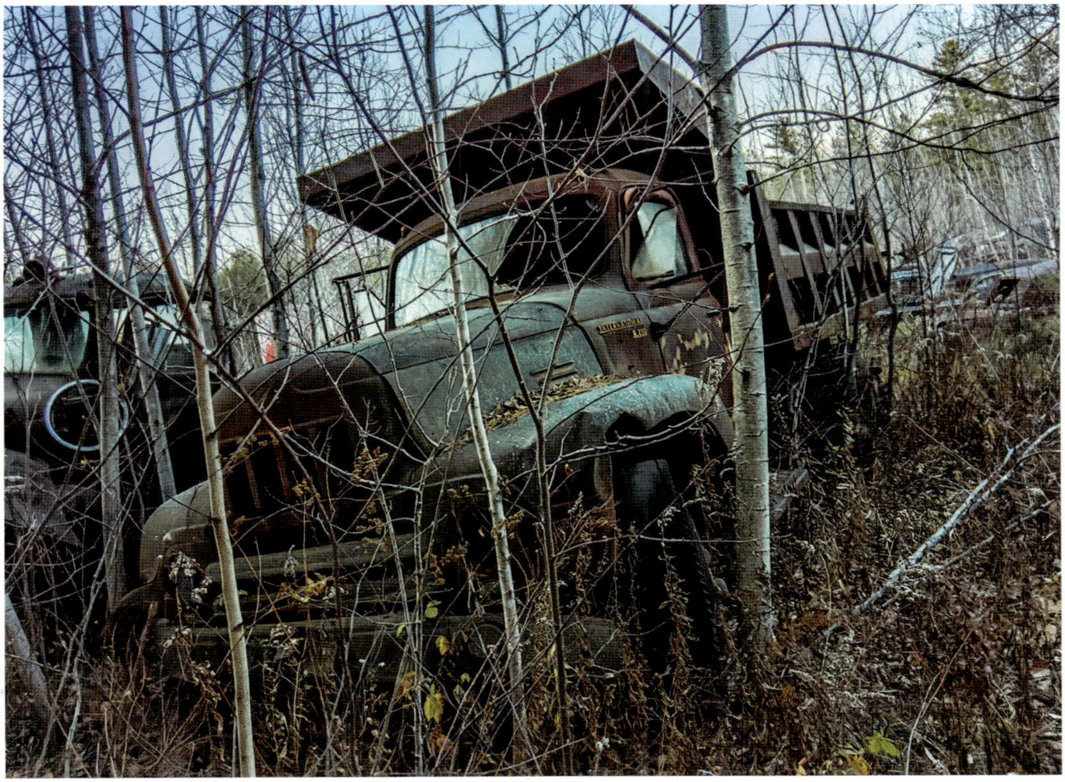

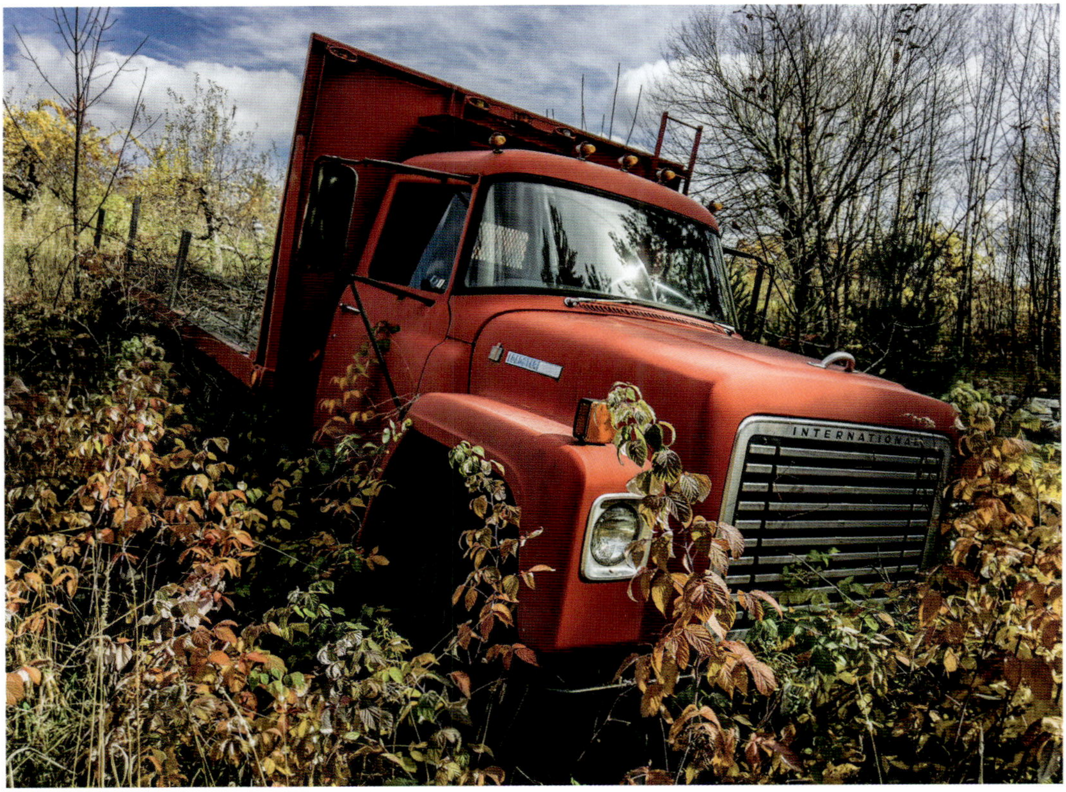

5

MEET THE BEETLES

I don't think any mass-produced automobile ever brought a smile to our face quite like the Volkswagen Beetle, aka the "Bug"—they just seemed to have such an amusing, circus car-like personality. In fact, along with Herbie, Disney's 1968 movie, *The Love Bug*, starring Dean Jones, Buddy Hackett and a 1963 VW with a mind and spirit of his own, helped to establish the Beetle as an icon—despite Volkswagen not being supportive of the film.

This German car was first introduced to America in 1949, but it wasn't until Volkswagen of America was formed in 1955 that sales took off. With well over 15 million vehicles sold by 1972, the company was able to claim it had achieved the world record for the most produced single-make car in automotive history.

Growing up, I have such fond memories of the Volkswagen because of my Aunt Bea, who owned a black Beetle. It was the perfect car for her, as she was a diminutive, yet very lively and effervescent woman. It was always a joy to see her pull up to our house for a visit carting my grandma, who never looked too comfortable stuffed in that little car. In fact, I can still hear her voice in my head as she hollered to my father as he ran down the front walk to the street: "Hectorrrrrr … get me out of here!!"

Right: I had already been to Blanchard's a number of times, but it wasn't until I traveled deeper and peered into a thick grove of pine trees that I discovered this "nest" of Beetles. I know a great artist of fantastic vision, and I was certain he'd have a pretty good take on this photograph. "Almost camouflaged to avoid the predator's eye, this family of forest beetles settle into the dense undergrowth (as they tend to do) and slowly shape-shift toward the forest itself—*its* colors, *its* patterns and tendrils, *its* singular marriage of order and chaos. As it has always been, the living woods eventually reclaim whatever takes residence there. These, like all beetles, will sink and be absorbed, remade into something they were not, could not have imagined." *Ed Binkley, Fantasy Artist, Art Professor*

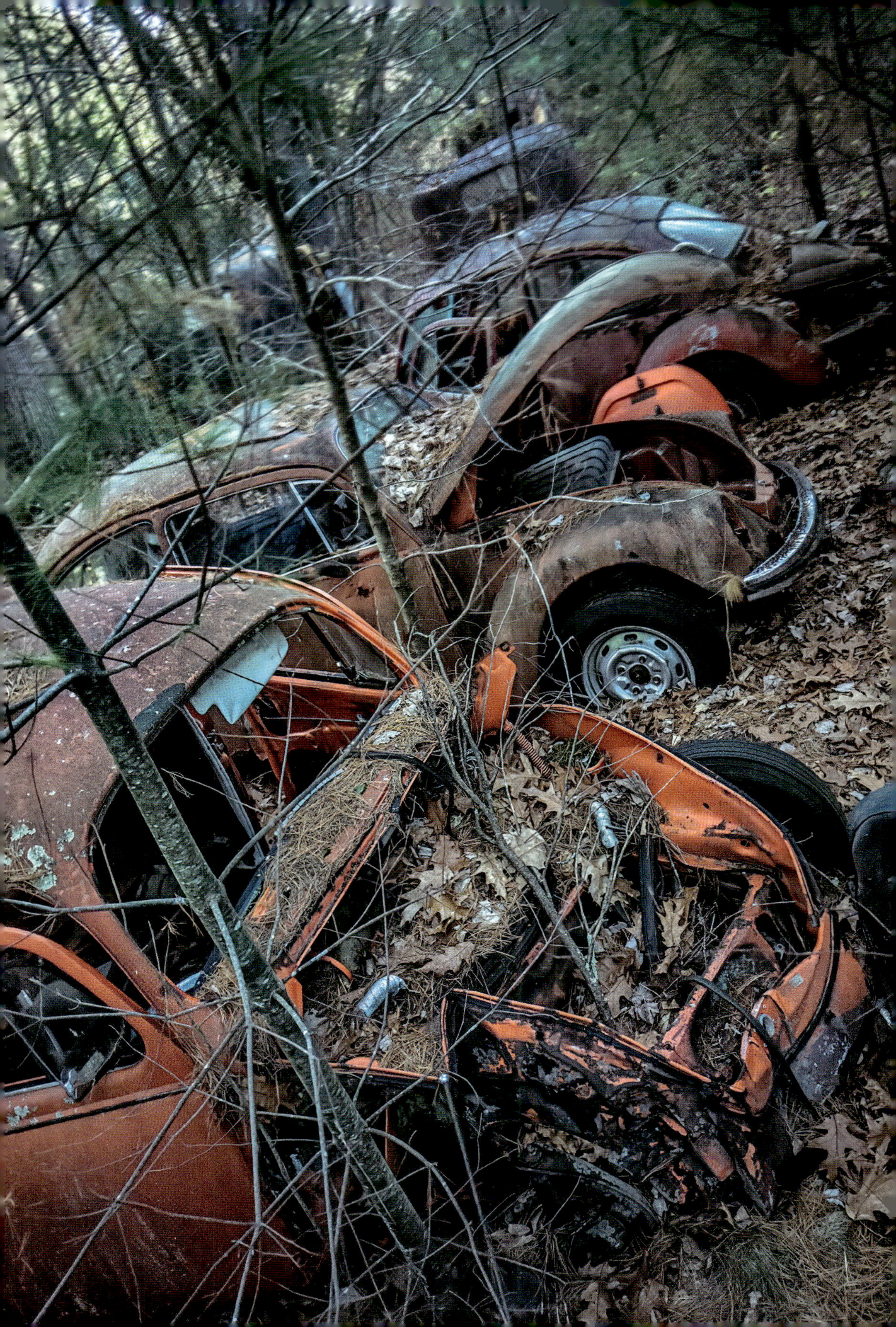

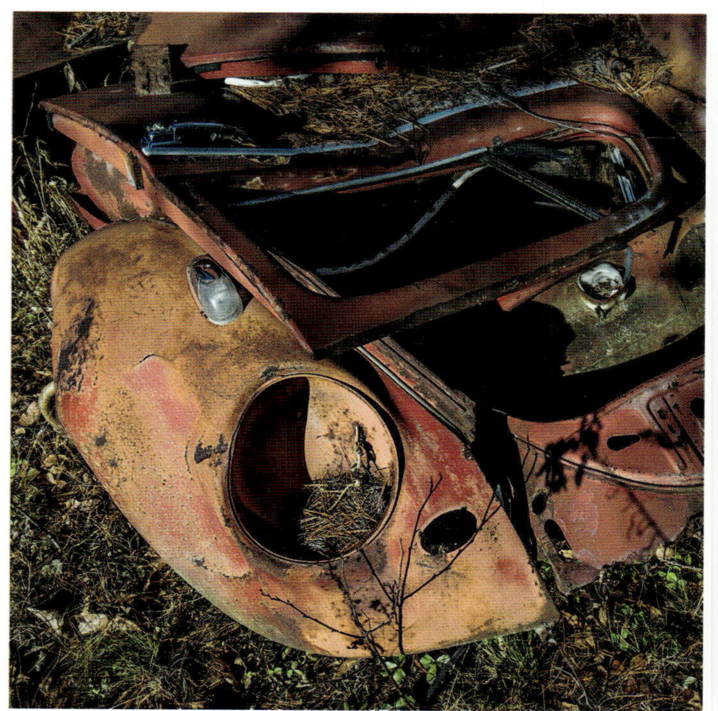

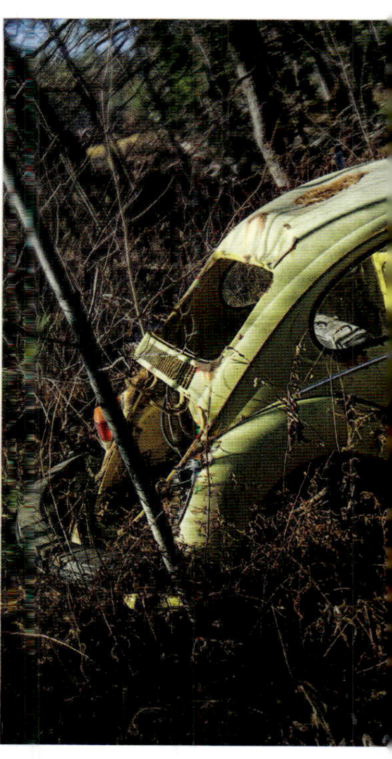

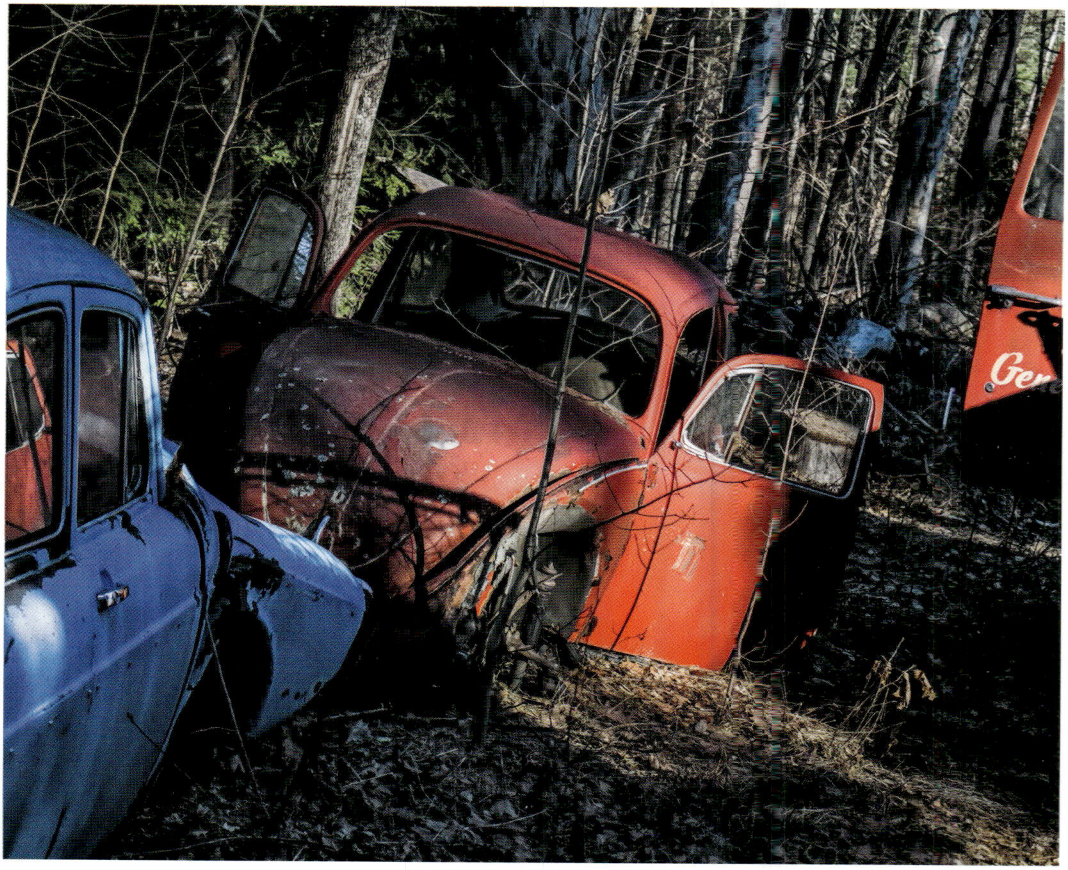

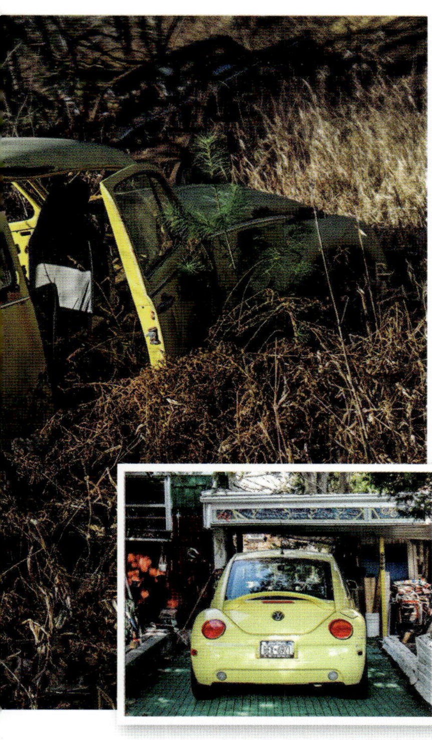

Top Left: Here lies the forlorn exoskeleton of an ancient crustacean, seemingly pried out of its fossil bed slumber.

Top Right: *"Yellow"* Though not the "New" Beetle, this car totally made me think of my dad when I was out shooting that day. Inset Photo: The New Beetle was introduced in 1997, and was produced up until 2011. After owning a Mercedes Benz, my dad also just had to have this screaming yellow bug in 2002 when he was seventy-eight years old (I guess he had a thing for German cars). Pop was a very creative, eccentric and impulsive kind of guy, and when he decided he would like to pull into his back driveway AND be able to drive completely around the house so he wouldn't have to back up, well that's what he did. The problem was, there wasn't enough room even for a small car like this, and he ended up hitting trees, fencing, poles, etc., and severely scratching and denting both sides of the car!

Bottom Left: *"Red"*

Bottom Right: And to complete this page of primary colors that also happen to be song titles, *"Blue."*

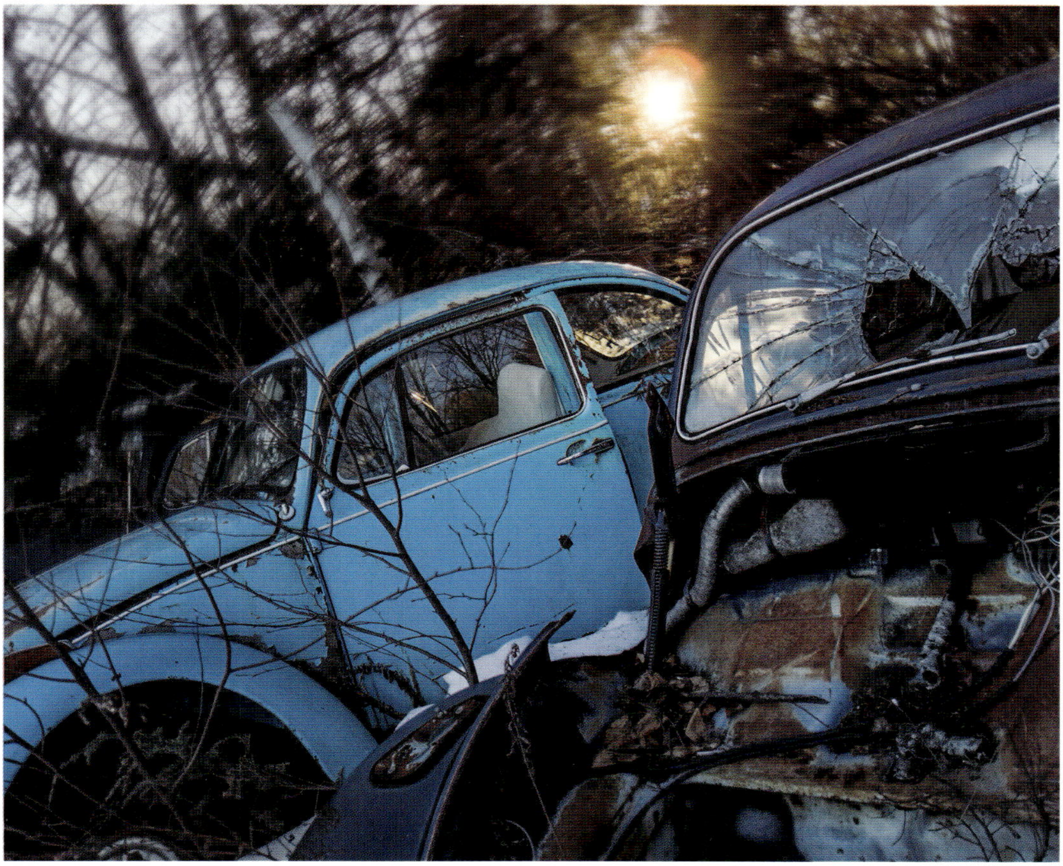

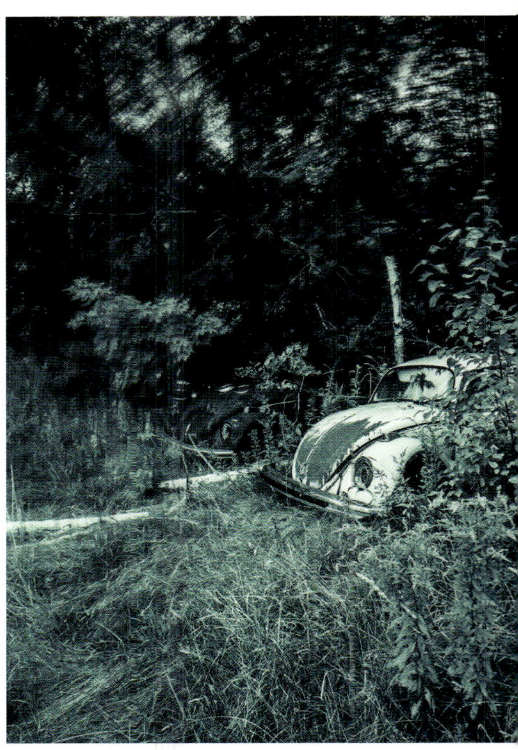

"The Bug Stops Here" It's really groovy to come across so many of these domed-shaped carcasses (I like that there's a "car" in carcass), which makes sense considering the large number manufactured over the years. On my list is to visit is a Beetle graveyard in Pennsylvania, where hundreds are strewn across a wooded property. The perfect title for this page comes courtesy of my old friend and hometown art mentor, who owned a Beetle in the early seventies. *Ned Levine, Illustrator, Designer (Newsday)*

Another creative Farmingdale High School 1977 classmate chimes in: "My Aunt Lillian and Uncle Jesse would only buy a Beetle, and owned a few over the years. I remember when I was at Pratt, the advertising mogul George Lois told us when he did the advertising for Volkswagen, it was a real feat to sell a 'Nazi' car in a Jewish town (NYC)!" *Adam Osterfield, Artist, Animator (Blue's Clues), Art Teacher*

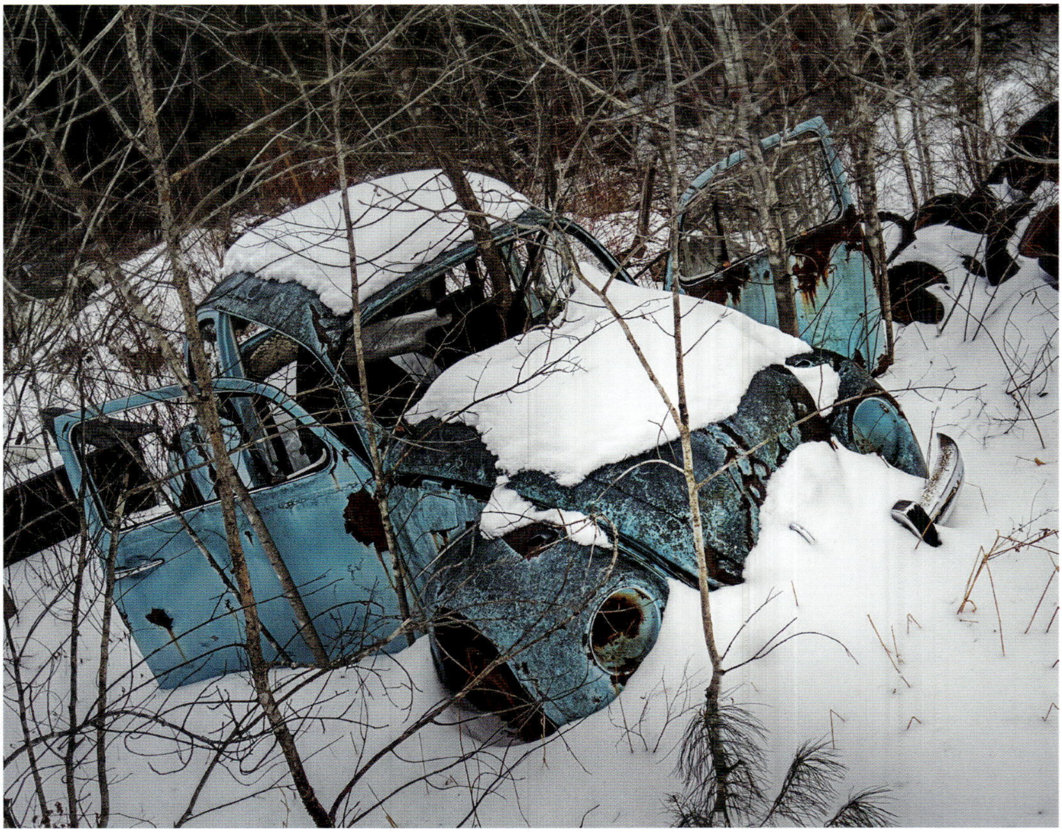

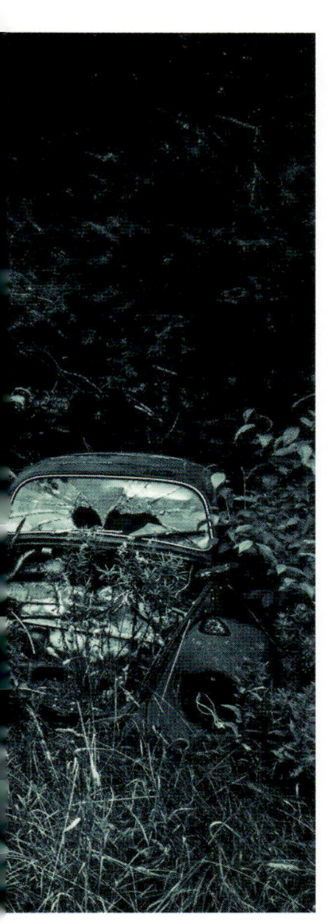

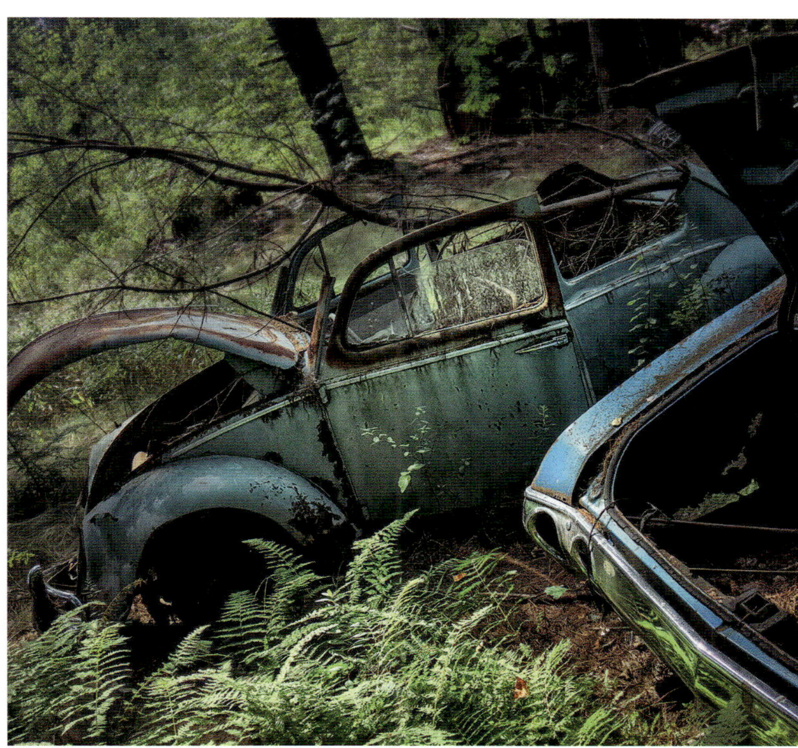

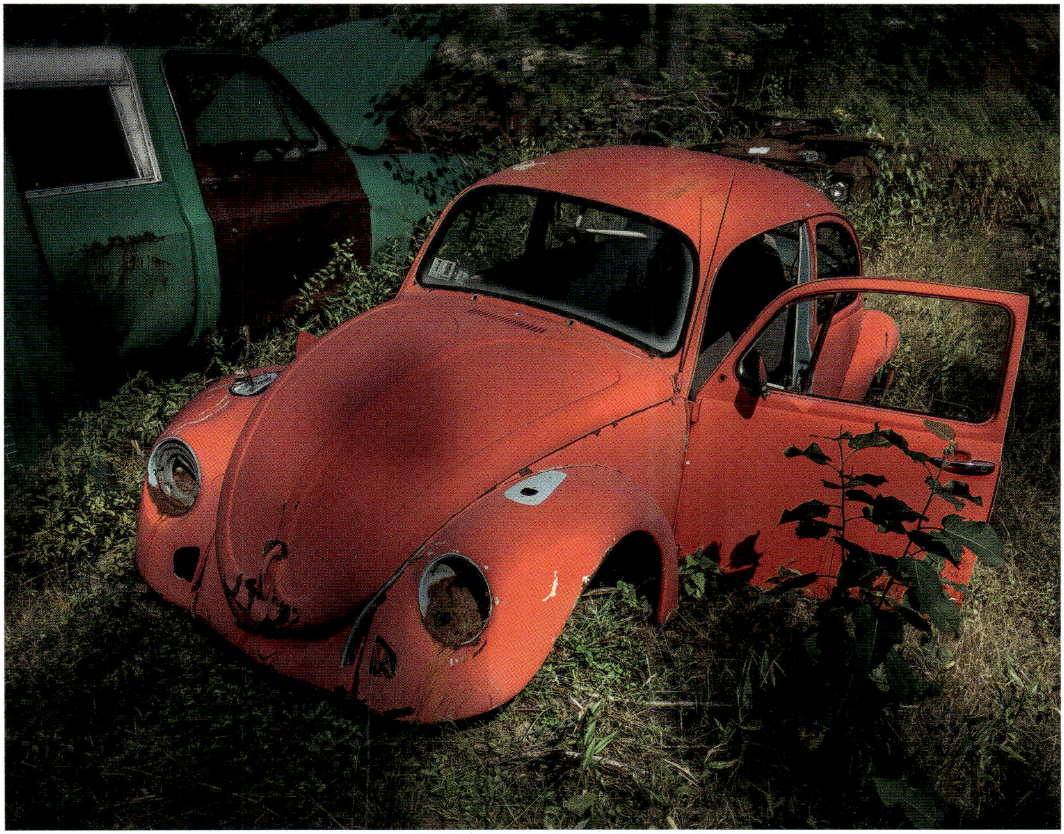

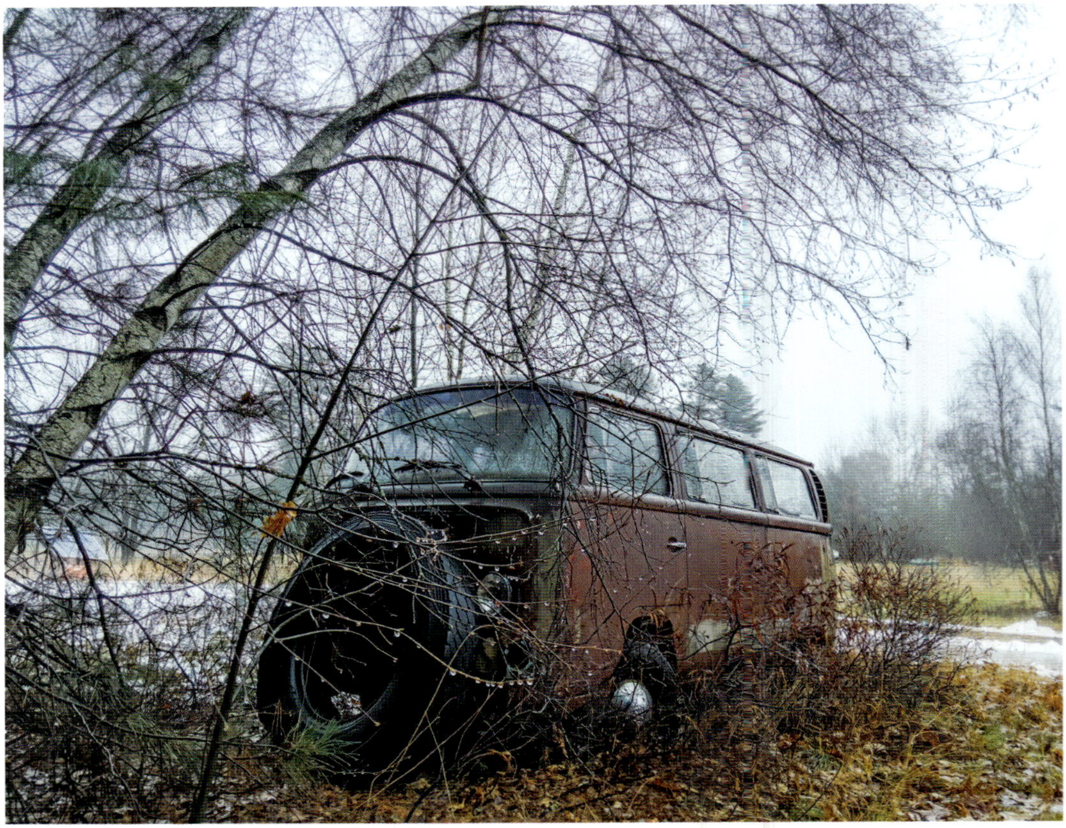

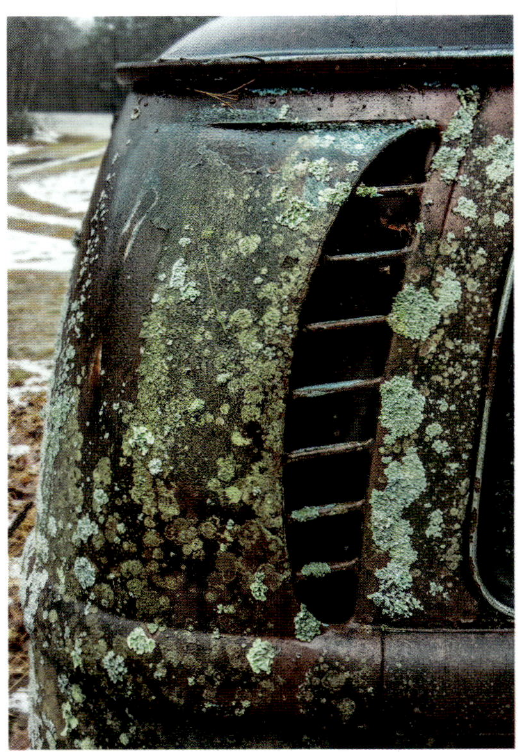

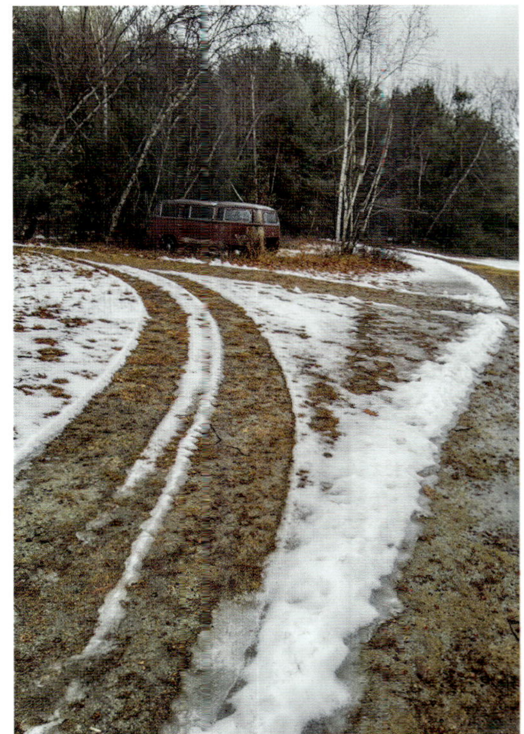

While driving back from the dentist's office one dreary day, I slammed on the brakes when I spotted this old VW van parked at the edge of the woods. My day got brighter after I knocked on the door, said hello, and got permission to shoot. It turns out the owner knew who I was, as friends of mine stayed at his Airbnb when they attended one of the music events I hosted at my home. Rick and his wife, Patti, now attend my concerts, and I asked him to give me a few words about this van he's owned for a very long time, and still dreams of restoring even as the elements grind away at it. "The first sentence from a song by Jon Butcher Axis that was released in '87 is, 'If wishes were horses dreamers would ride.' I believe it originated in the seventeenth century as, 'If wishes were horses beggars would ride.' Okay, enough trivia! I can best describe this as a thirty-year theoretical restoration project. And, to address people's curiosity as to how long the van has been sitting there and why it hasn't been disposed of, the shortest version I can come up with is ... 'Someday'" *Rick MacMillan, VW Van Owner, Proprietor of Breakwind Farm Airbnb, Hopkinton, NH*

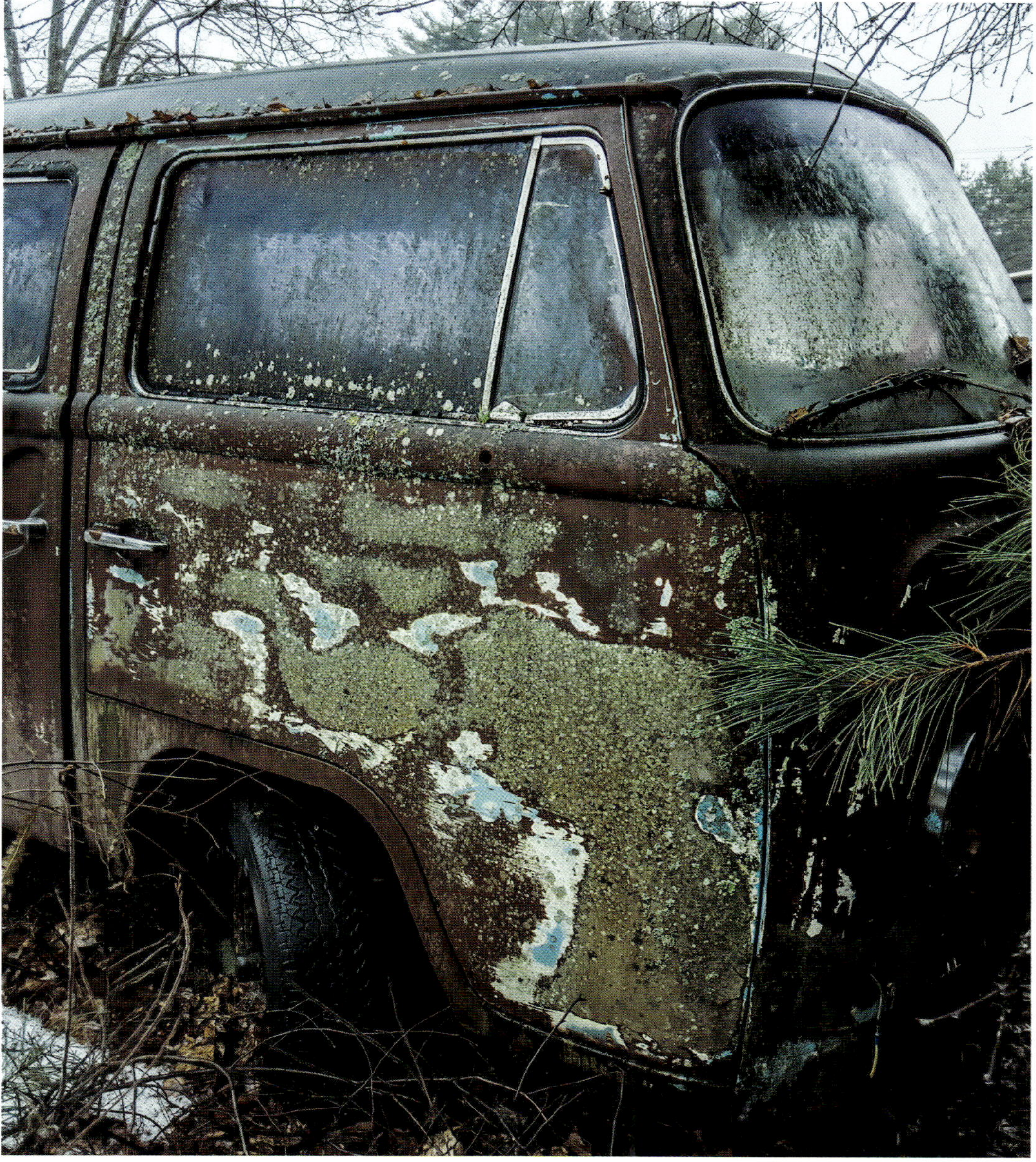

6

SCHOOL'S OUT ... FOREVER!

All the vehicles I encounter are filled with mostly unknown stories and memories, but there's something especially wistful, and even unsettling, about coming upon a school bus out in the wilds. I will on occasion carefully step inside one to explore further, though I'm less concerned about encountering *Children of the Corn* than I am about finding a cornered raccoon that has moved in, or a battalion of angry hornets. More often than not, all the seats have been removed and the interiors are filled with car parts and other assorted items that are stored away, most likely never to be used again. However, I'm always aware that at one time they were filled with laughing, screaming and joyful children, and the contrast in the imagination is as stark as these fading yellow hulks that lie in permanent recess in the woods and fields.

Right: This photo was taken at Lane's, and I can't think of a more appropriate way to start off the chapter than with this touching caption provided to me by an acclaimed children's book illustrator and author. "Long after the last ride home, when the seats are carpeted with moss, and dry leaves gather in the rusted aisle where boys and girls once tramped, none will remember how many friendships were forged here, none will know how many plans for the future were hatched. All journeys have an end, but dreams go on forever." *Daniel Kirk, Children's Book Illustrator, Author*

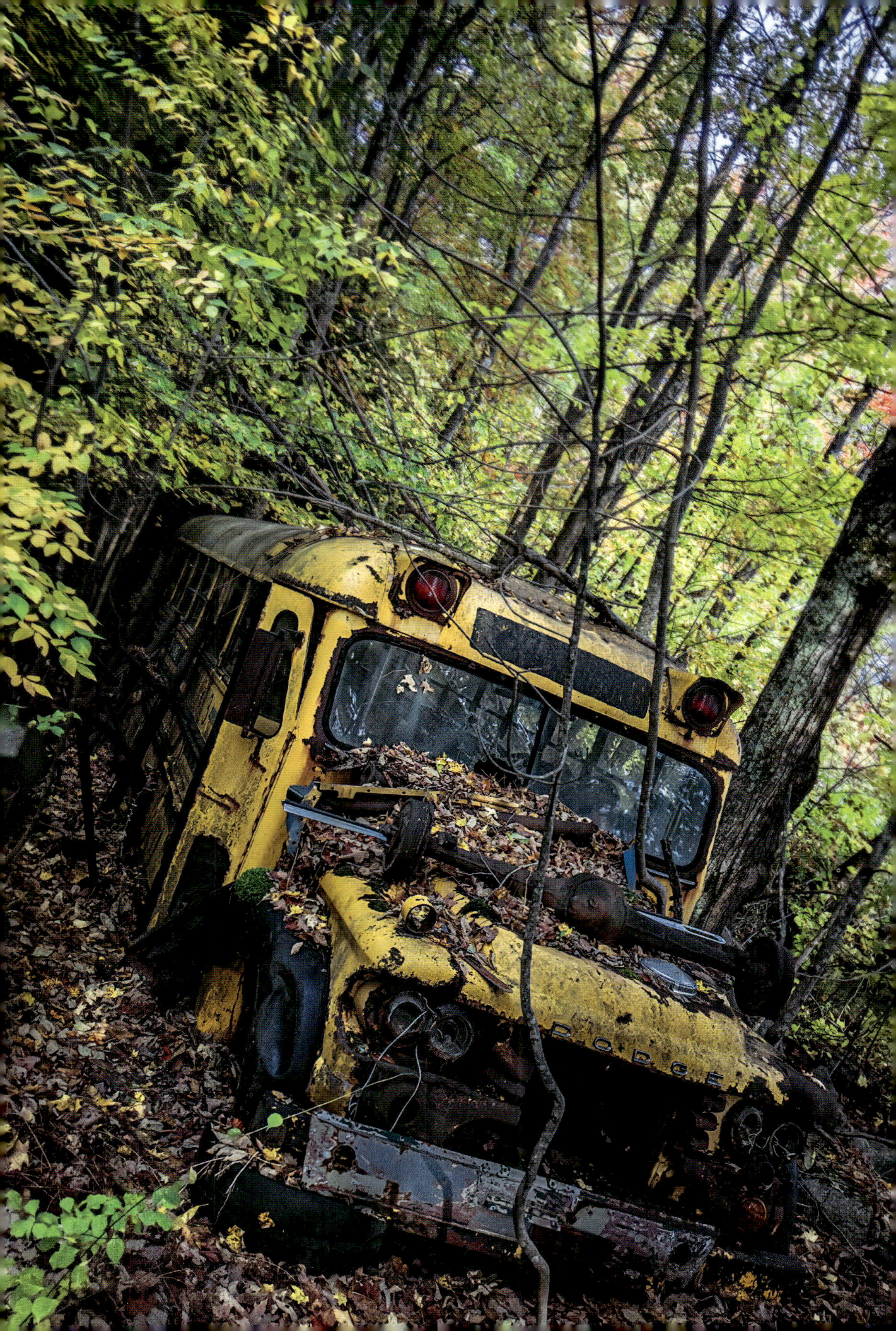
DODGE

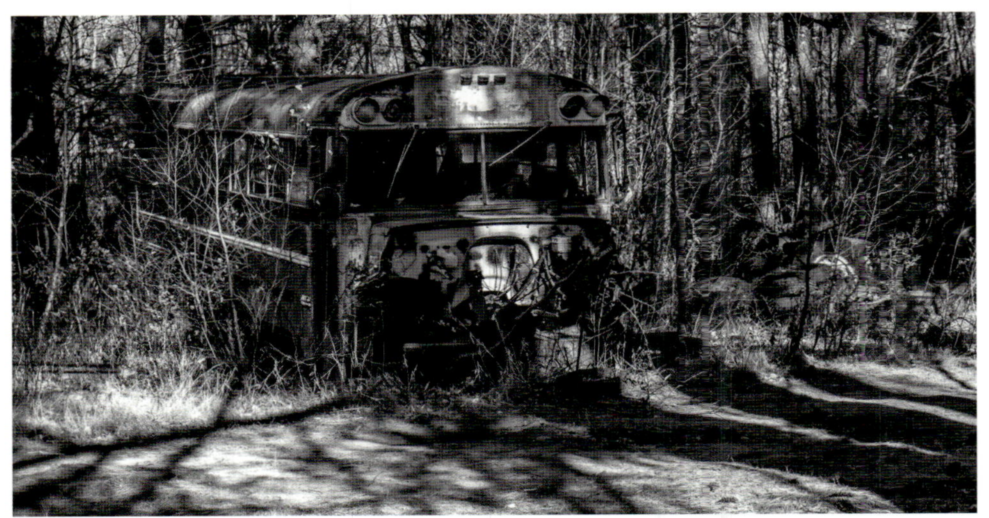

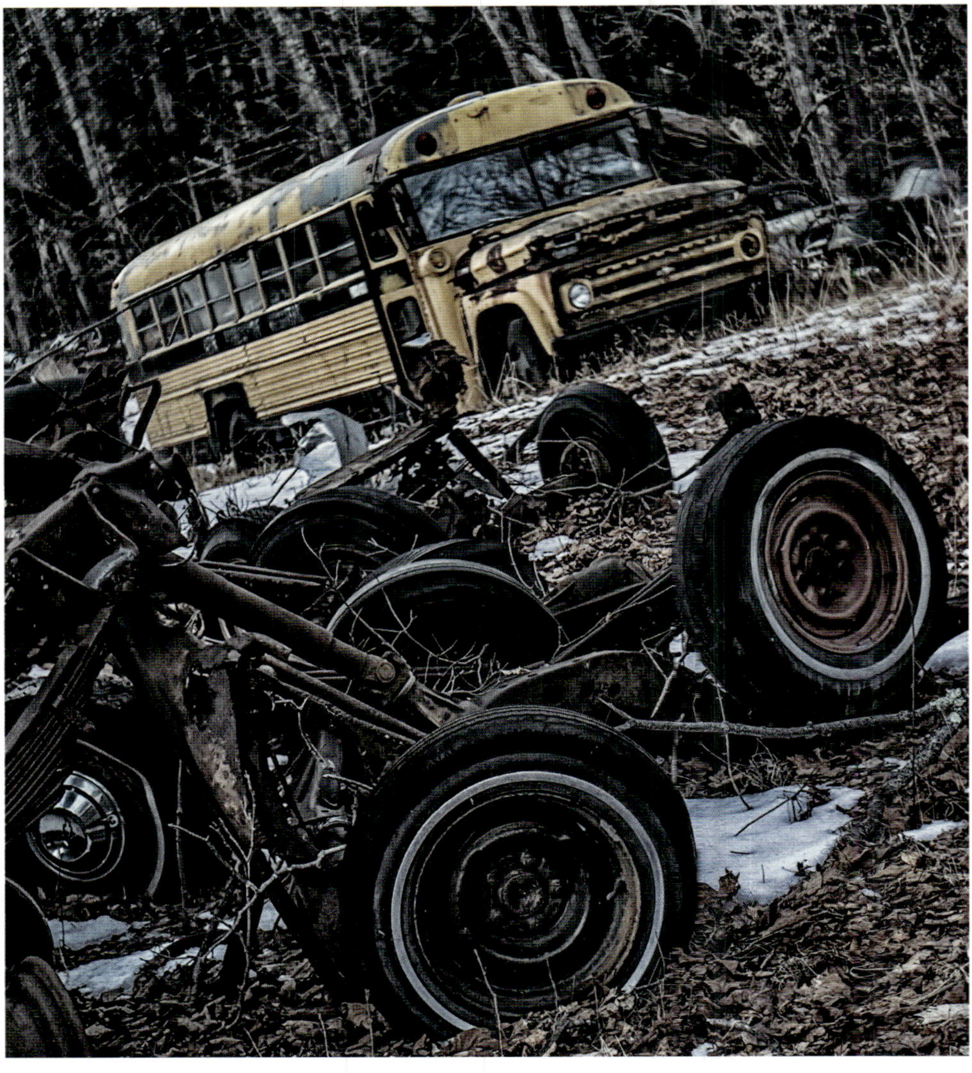

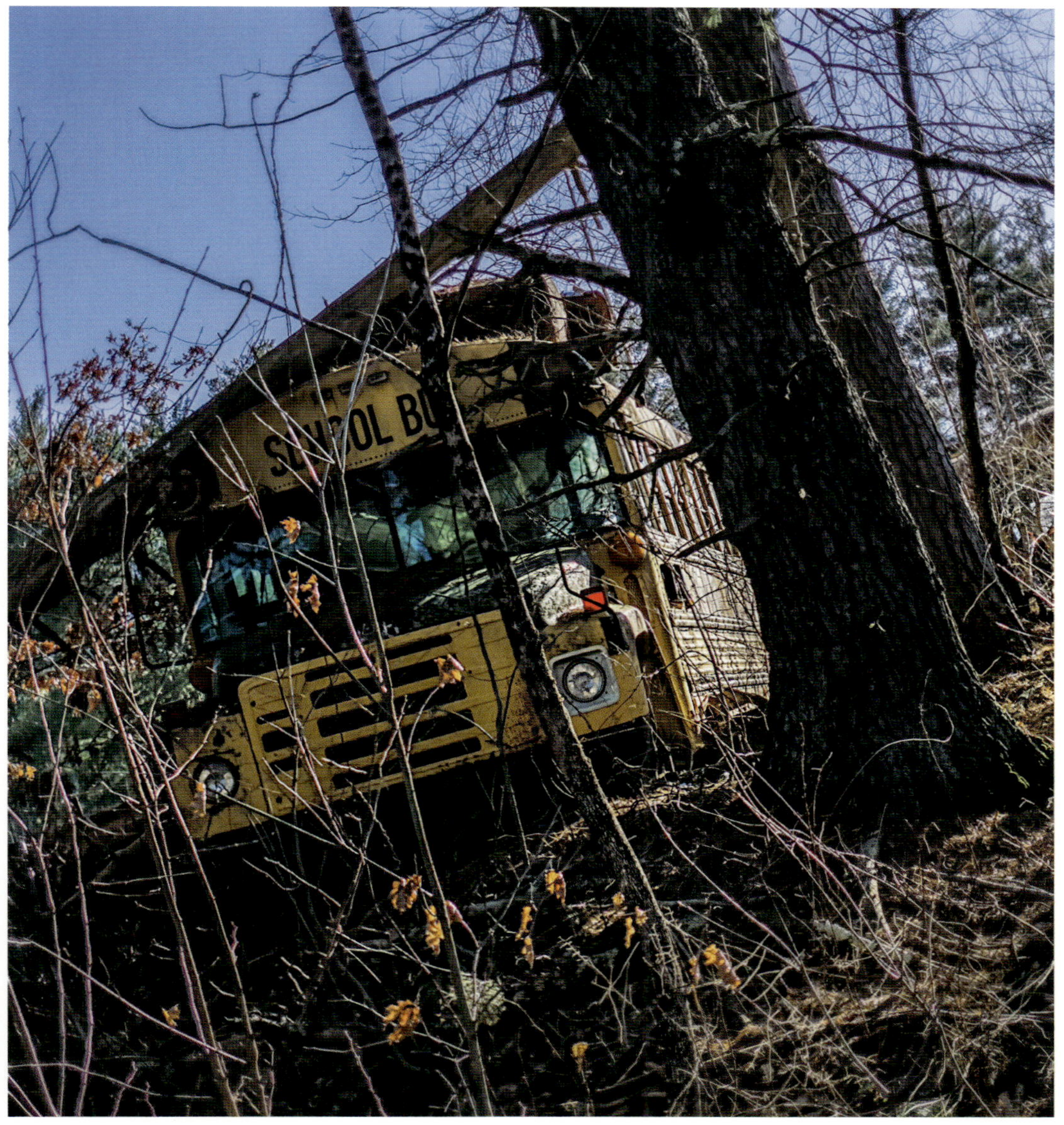

Top Left: *"Permanent Detention"* Missing its front end, this bus inhales the ominous shadows as it peers out of the overgrowth with blackest eyes.

Bottom Left: There's a more cheerful look at this bus at Lane's on the next page, but I quite like the composition and apocalyptic feeling captured in this shot.

Above: One of the things I noticed in salvage yards is that buses often serve as platforms for other automobiles, and parts to be piled on top of. It also appears their size makes them a bigger target for falling trees. I assigned this fellow from England a photo that I thought would be a slam dunk based on the series of paintings he was working on, but was surprised when he responded back instead about his great love and interest of school buses! "I love school buses, but from afar in the UK. I first saw one in *The Monkees* TV show in the 60s (was it in the title sequence?) with each Monkee in a back window. What great color, and particularly with the older ones a funky design too. While traveling in the USA last year, I was forever pointing out to my friends how much I like them every time I saw one! As of all those kids who went to school in this particular bus, I wonder what they are doing now? Do they remember it?" *Mark Harrison, Illustrator, Fine Artist*

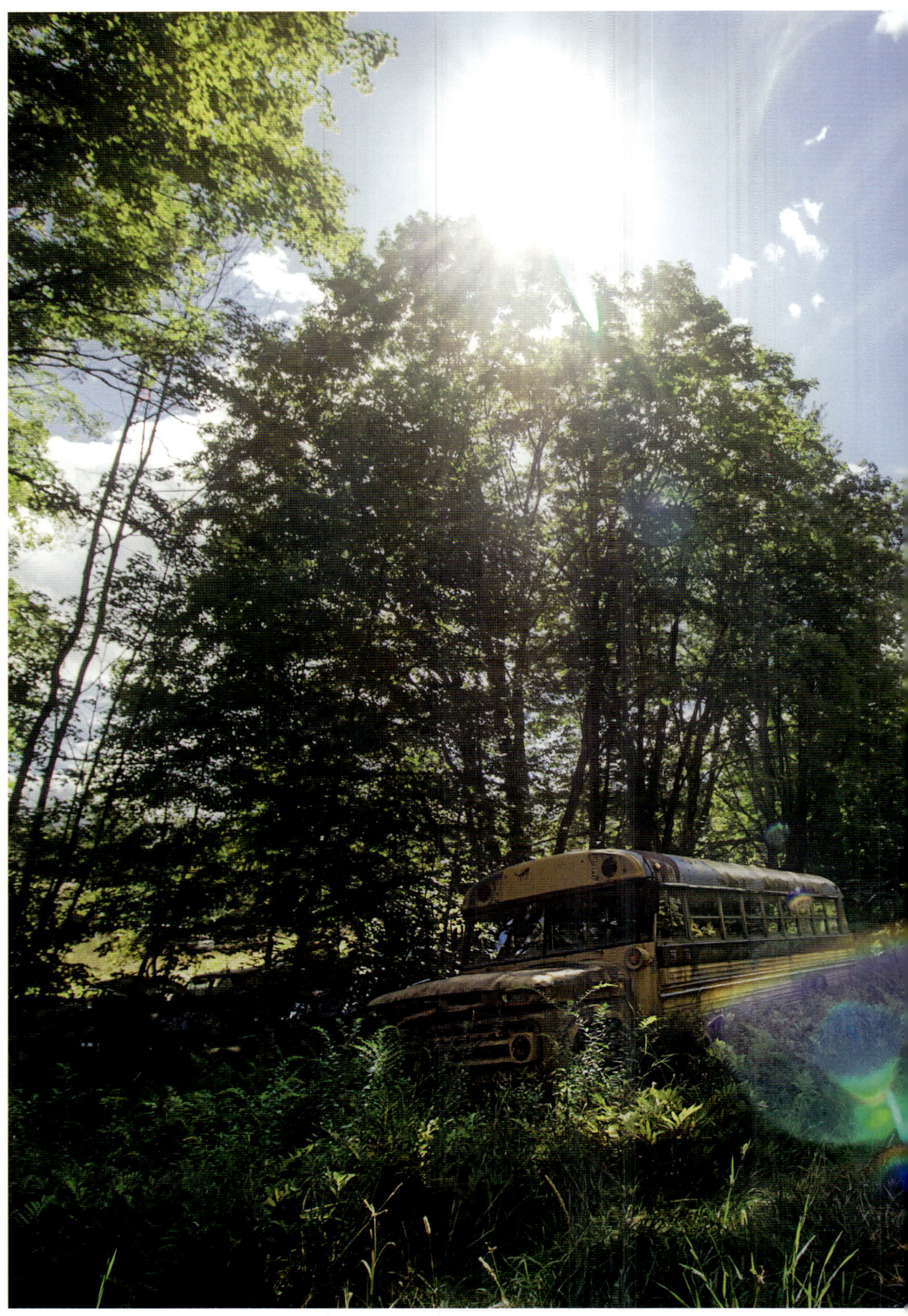

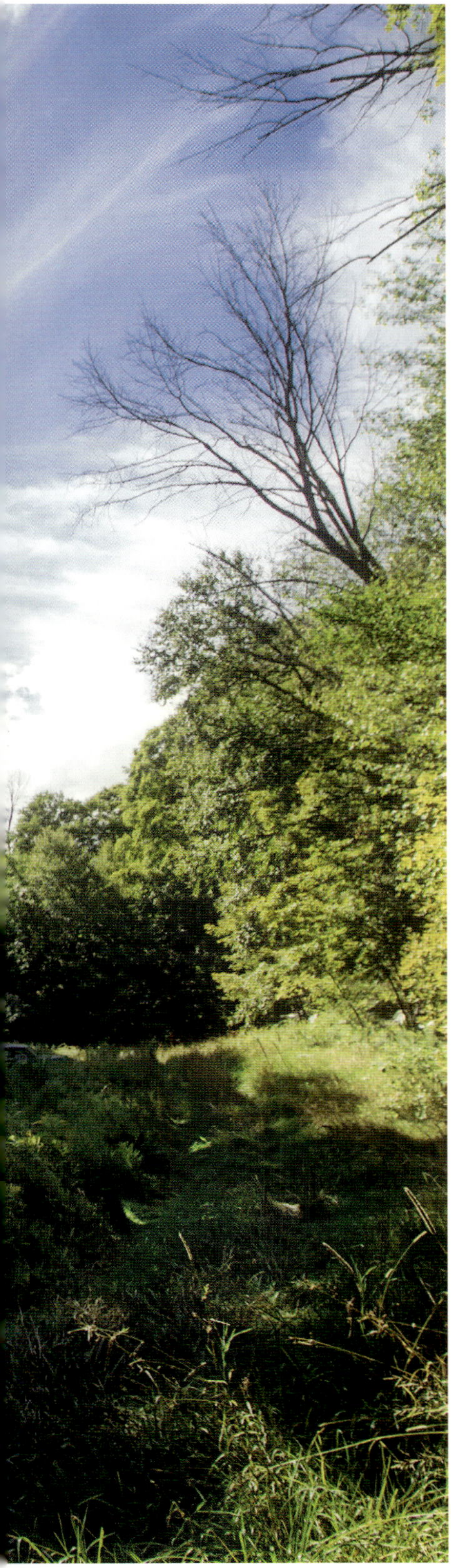

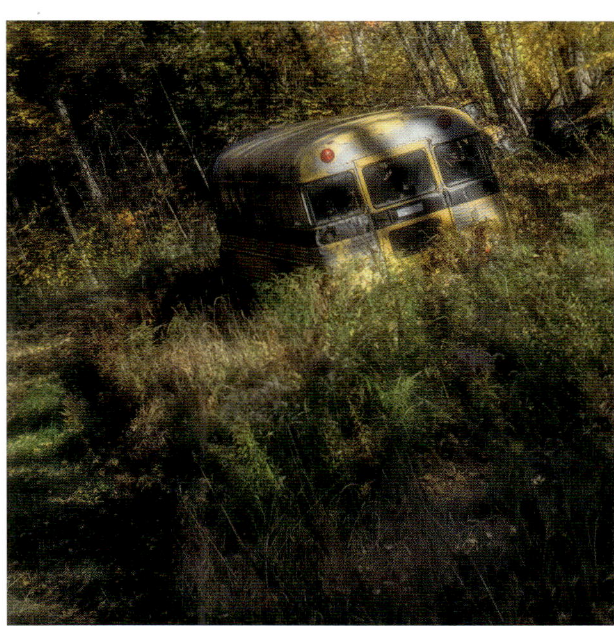

Left: Bright and uplifting, you can almost hear the birds singing in the woods while imagining the happy squealing of kids as they're being dropped off after school. This photo's serene nature had me ask my gifted friend (who also performed twice in my studio) for a memory. "As a youngster on my way to school in the 4th grade, it turns out our bus driver was also a DJ. He knew I loved records, and he gave me many DJ copies of some of my favorite hits. He would also play the Top 40 AM station for us kids. When I was in high school, I'd hear Donavan's *Mellow Yellow* as well as many great tunes from the 60s playing on the ride to school. Then one day, while sitting with my school friends on that yellow bus, my own band's record came on called *Come With Me*, by the New Hudson Exit. What a thrill that was for a little kid like me!" *Phil Keaggy, Musician, Guitarist, Songwriter (Glass Harp)*

Top Right: One of my oldest friends offers a few quips, as well as something deeper reflecting her occupation of many decades. "I love going on class trips! Oh no—I guess I will be late again for class! Just how long are we going to stay here and observe nature? My students immerse themselves in everything we study!" And: "We are part of the change, the story, the lessons of life. We are integral life-long students, observing and staying in the beautiful moments. Stop and see the changes." *Alison Rosen, Elementary School Teacher*

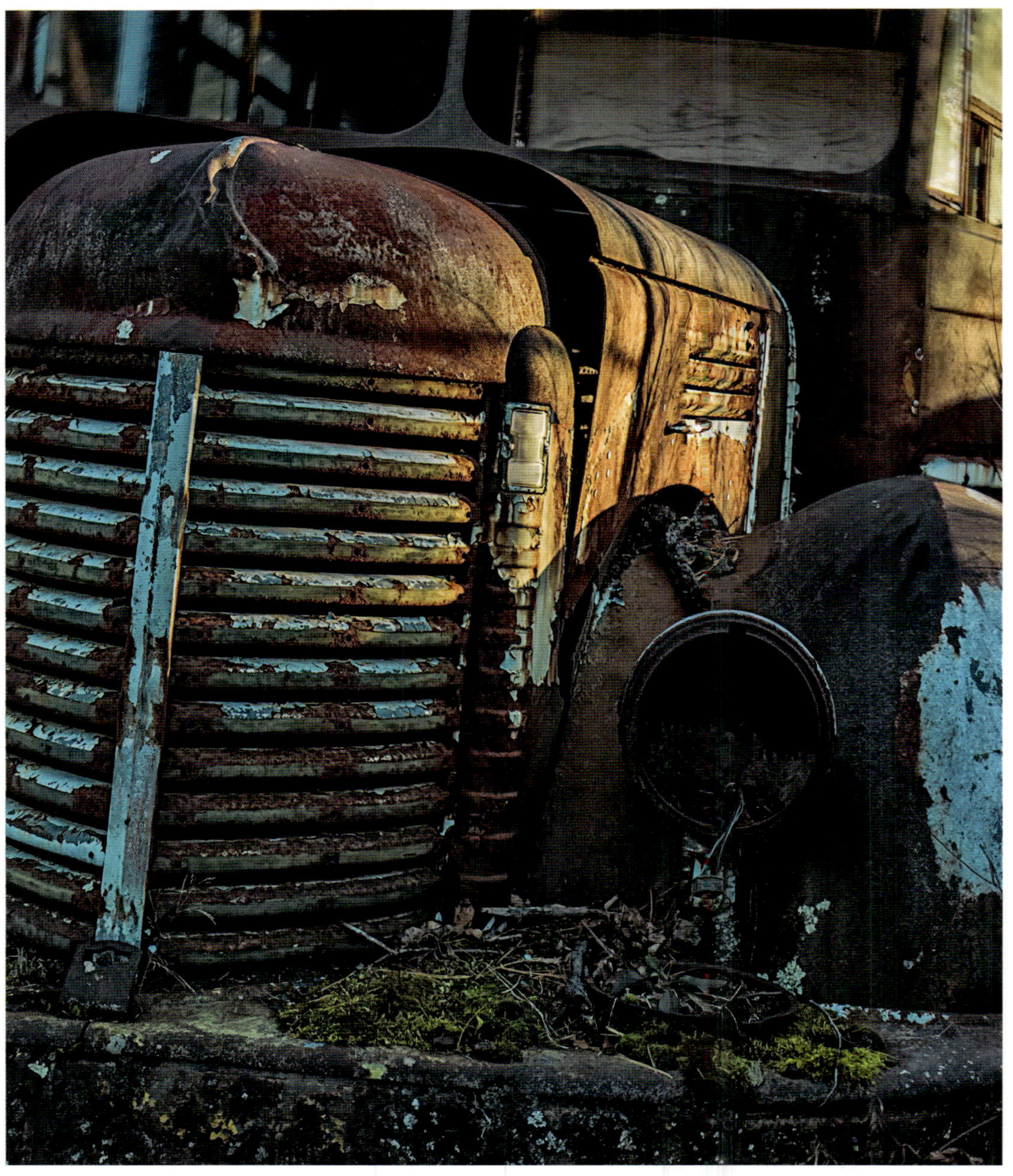

This bus from 1940s displays so much character as it catches the late afternoon light, and its color and gravitas reminded me of the wonderful work of a dear friend, who provides some evocative thoughts. “These photographs really speak to me … they remind me of a scene from a thriller movie—an ominous shot of a long-abandoned school bus, all rusted out and stranded in the woods where it now rests as part of the natural landscape surrounding it. One might ask, ‘What dark secrets from a distant past haunt this bus as it sits in the shadows?’ However, a lesson of hope emerges from the lonely narrative on display, that in the form of the sun’s reflection on the back window of the bus. The bright light reminds us that no matter how dark the season we find ourselves in because of the ravages of time and circumstances, as long as the radiance of hope shines through, we still have a future to look forward to! To me, these photographs are an inspiration, especially in light of the changes that have recently taken over our country and the world brought on by the coronavirus pandemic and racial discord.” *Thomas Blackshear II, Illustrator, Fine Artist*

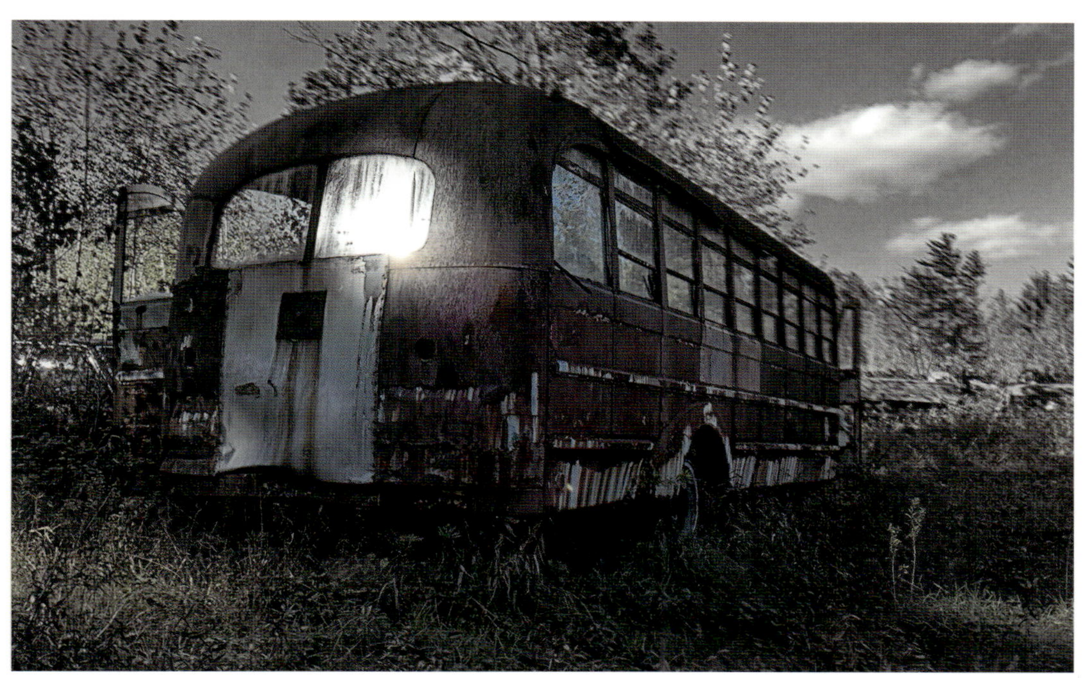

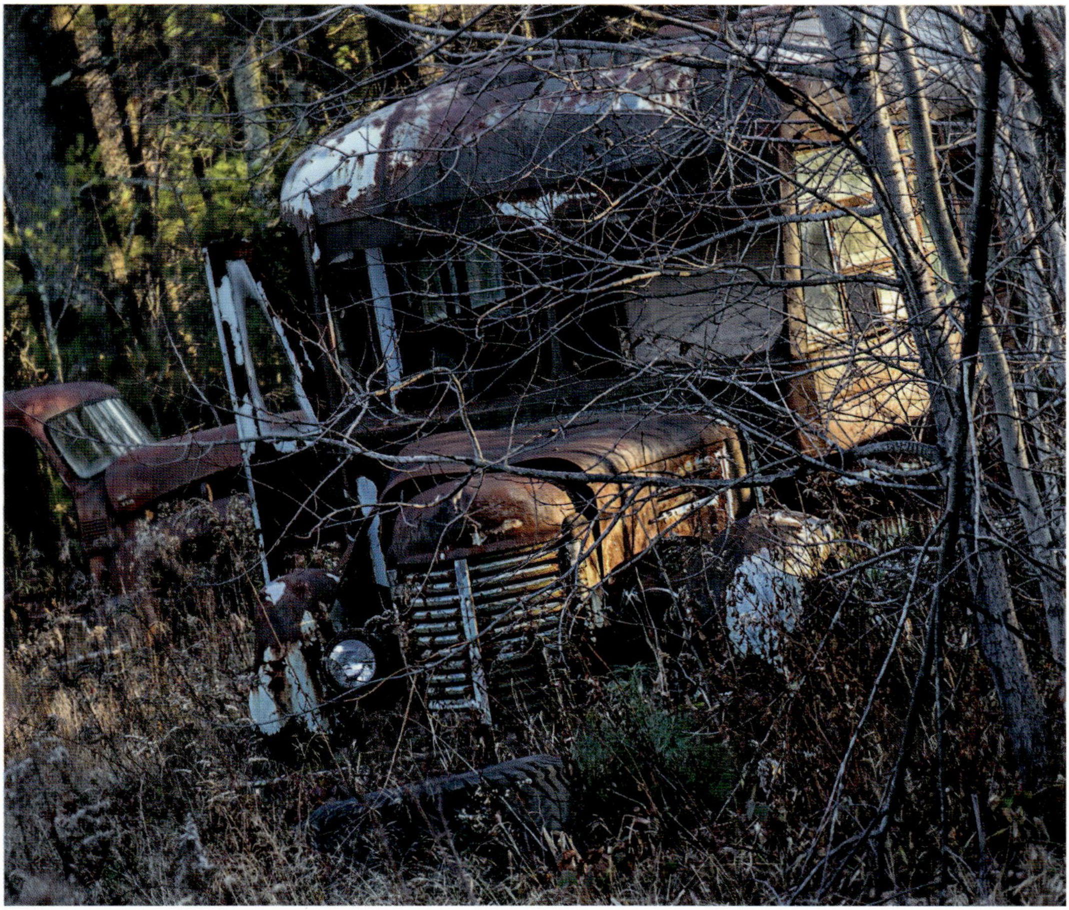

7

LINCOLN SLEPT HERE

It's always a bonus to find cars that seemed to be "posing" all by themselves, giving me the chance to shoot them from a lot of different angles, or frame them nicely in the landscape from a distance. I don't know of any particular backstory for this 1968 Lincoln Continental at Lane's except that it was separated from a whole bunch of other cars that were being moved around or finally crushed, and it was deemed worthy enough to be saved. Owner Ronnie Lane recalls driving around in it when he was a kid, and the car only has around 70,000 miles on it. I particularly enjoy photographing this symbol of luxury where it lies all stretched out in eternal slumber on a gentle hilltop. Perhaps it's just biding its time, waiting for the day it will be reborn and take off to the heavens like a retro-starship!

Right: I've been friends with this fellow since the start of my illustration career, and I was a longtime contributor to his magazine as well as an instructor and leader of his sponsored airbrush workshops. His kind words are meaningful, and resonate for knowing me so well. "Jerry LoFaro has made the fantastic metamorphosis from world-class illustrator to photographer in his new series of images that magnificently resurrects the life of abandoned cars in dramatic fashion. In this photo of a 1968 Lincoln, LoFaro's composition, light, and depth are impeccable; an otherwise mundane subject seen completely differently through the lens of a master." *Cliff Stieglitz, Founder and Publisher of Airbrush Action Magazine*

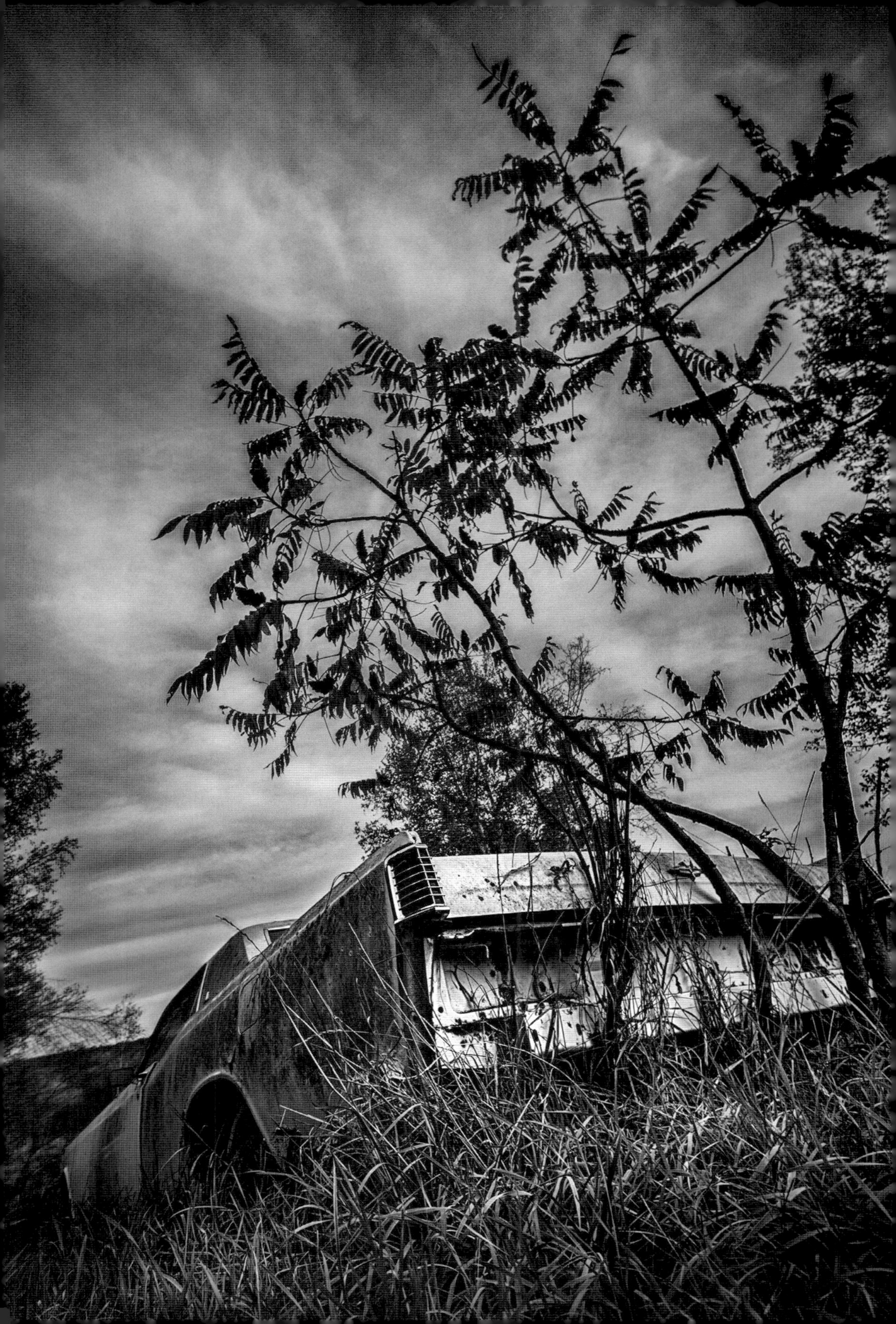

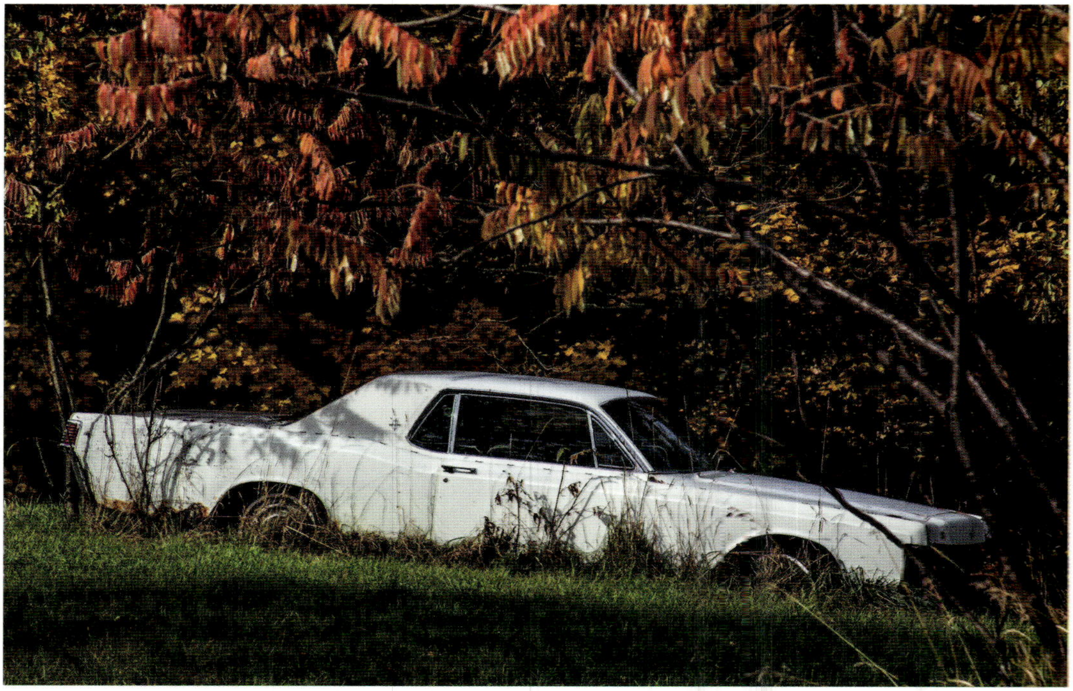

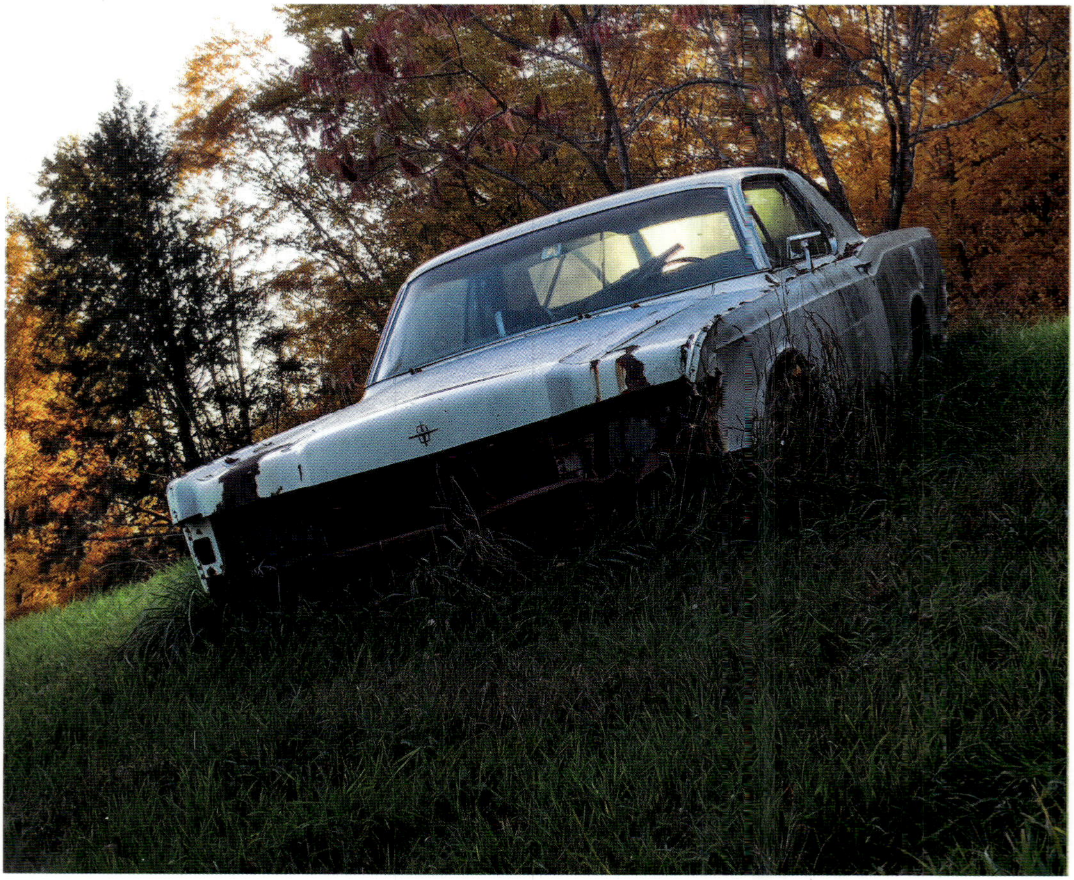

Left Page: I knew my talented artist friend had a connection to New Hampshire, but I was unaware he also had a deep love of cars. "I moved to New Hampshire right after graduating from Connecticut College, first living in Derry, and then just north of Concord. After a bit, I moved south to Virginia and then sometime later moved out to the southwest and put down some roots. Roots are curious thing ... they sort of happen when you're not paying attention, and then you look back over your shoulder and realize you've been hanging out in the same place for decades. As time passes, you also realize the cars you are driving turned into 'classics' a while ago, and have now become 'antiques.' Anyway, my memories of old rusted cars always seem to be from New Hampshire—nothing rusts a car like New Hampshire or Michigan. There was always a marvelous excitement of seeing something peering out of the weeds and imagining that it could be resurrected with a little TLC, and a lot of Bondo!" *Colin Poole, Artist, Painter, Sculptor*

Bottom Right: Like a painting beautifully framed, the Lincoln's reflection lies within, roughly 200 feet away from this 1940s relic hiding in the shadows. It appears to be a portal into a jewel-like micro world, and made me think of my friend Vince's art. He shares the following: "A faded reflection of a life and times long left behind; I see ghosts in the machine." *Vincent Natale, Artist, Illustrator*

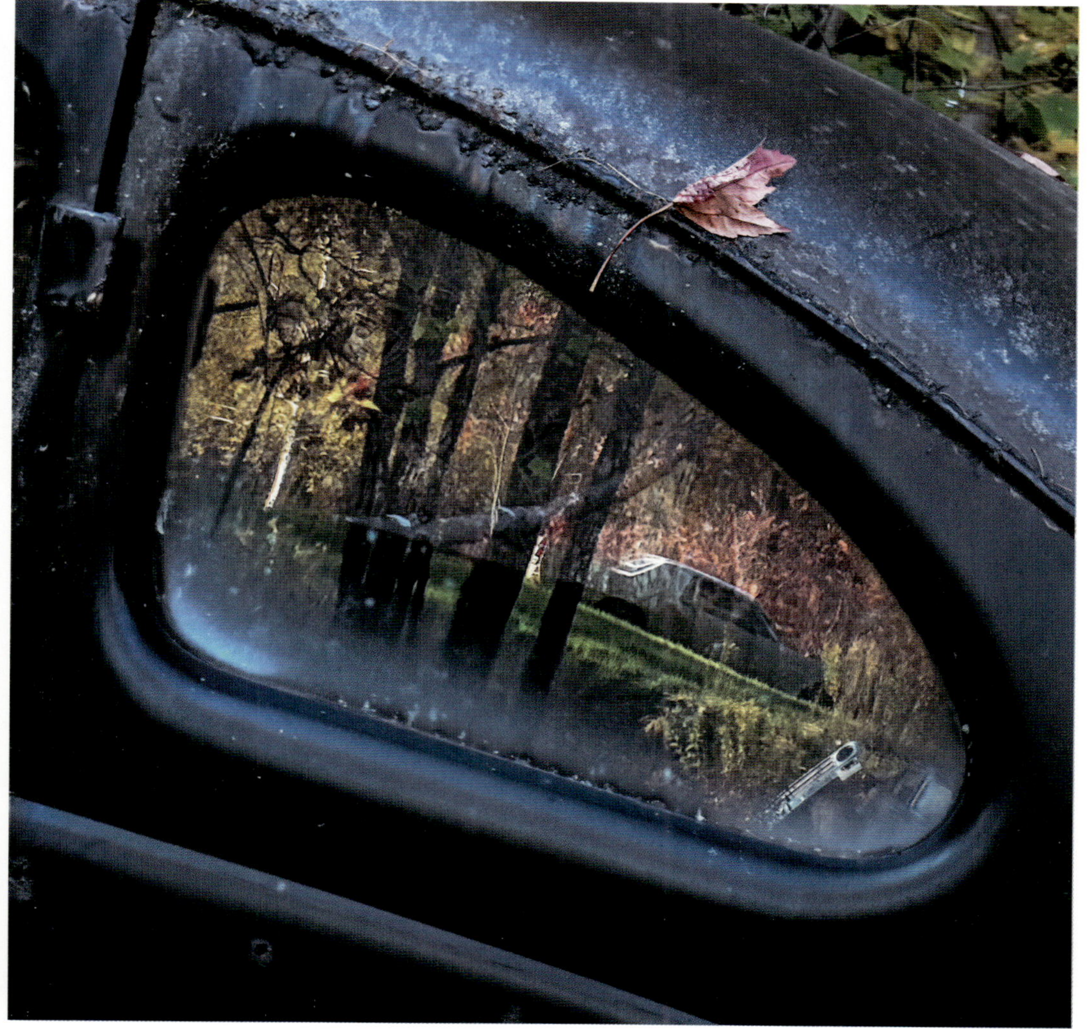

Another reason I enjoyed photographing this car so much is that since it's out in the open, I get to include my other favorite subject—clouds! I wanted to get famed car enthusiast and collector Jay Leno to comment on this page (if memory serves me right, I THINK he is also a comedian AND former host of *The Tonight Show*), but pftttttt ... I never heard back from him. Of course, I thought of him because of his New England roots, as well as the excellent show he hosts called *Jay Leno's Garage*. I was finally prompted to try and contact him after seeing the episode that features a white 1966 Lincoln Continental Convertible. Hey, close enough!

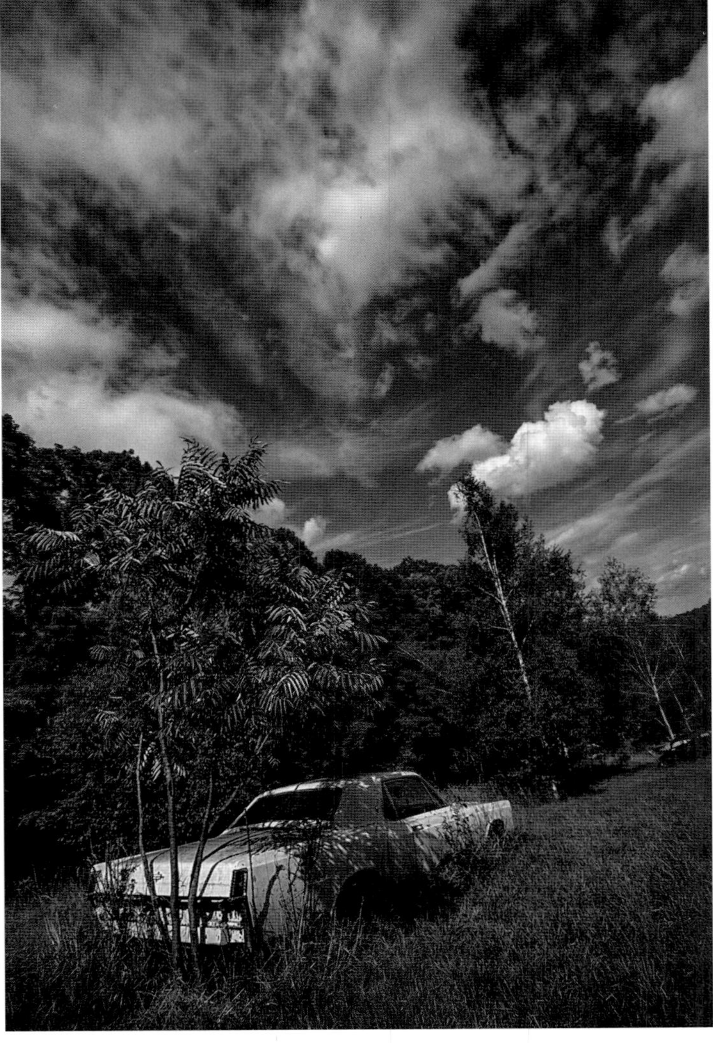

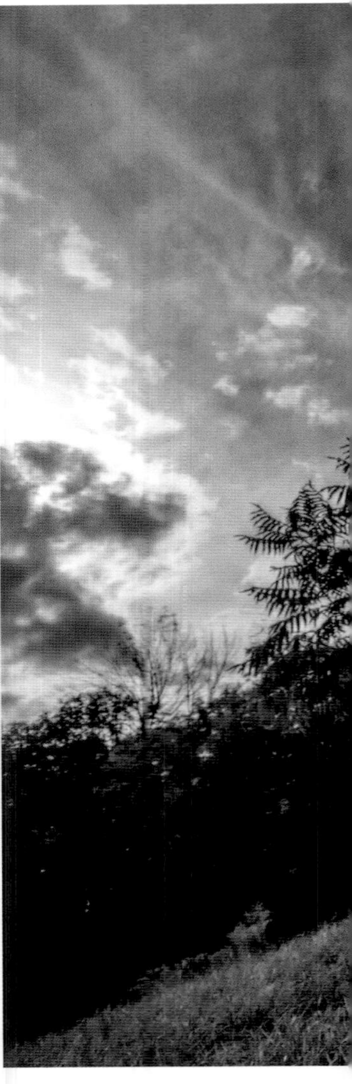

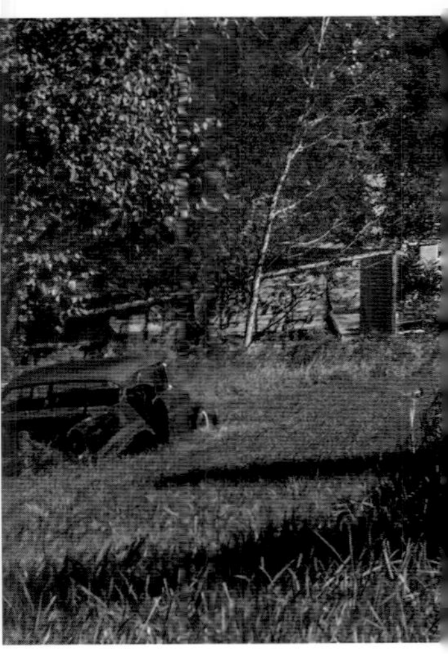

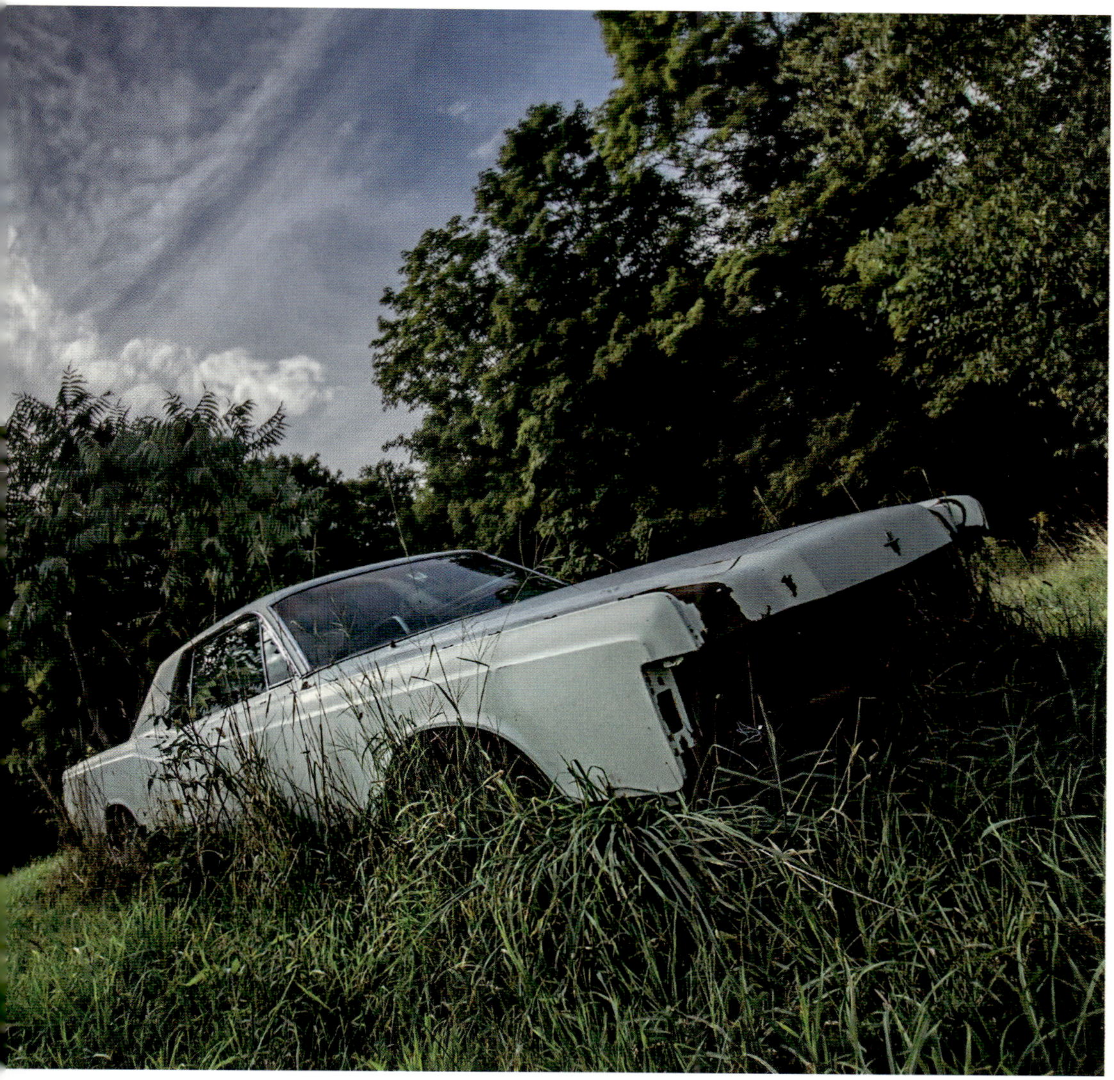

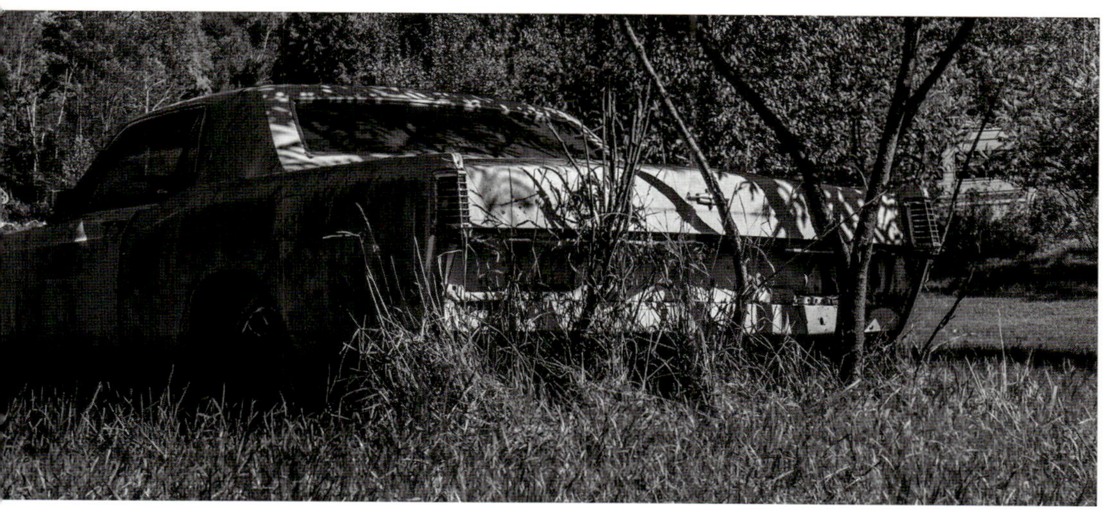

8

COLOR, TEXTURE AND DETAIL

Everything about photographing cars excites me: from planning the expedition, the anticipation of wandering around all by myself unhurried, the actual shooting, and THEN—opening the photos to see what I got. My love of "chiaroscuro" propels my tendency to shoot dark, and often times the RAW files are so murky and indiscernible I'm even fooled at first into thinking I blew the shot. Happily, nearly every time I edit a photo in Camera Raw, I'm able to reveal surprises, stunning details and colors—it's like opening a gift on Christmas morning! For the record, about three quarters of the photos in this book are shot with the Light 16 camera, and the rest with a Canon EOS Rebel T6i. One of the great benefits of shooting with the former is that it does really well with a wide range of lighting conditions, and it captures incredible detail. Sadly, the L16 became obsolete in a very short time, but it's been the perfect camera for me as I run both of mine into the ground. As an oft navel-gazing artist, it's the detail that drew me in closer to the decaying vehicles and made me even more passionate about the subject. I'm happy to have a few more of my artist friends contribute captions in this chapter, knowing they would relate to my fascination.

Right: Here's a closer look into the soul of the Ford truck featured on pages 64 and 65, and I passed this photo on to an exceptional Surrealist painter for a thought. "A light once bright, now dim, still illuminates those memories it fell upon." *Steven Kenny, Fine Artist*

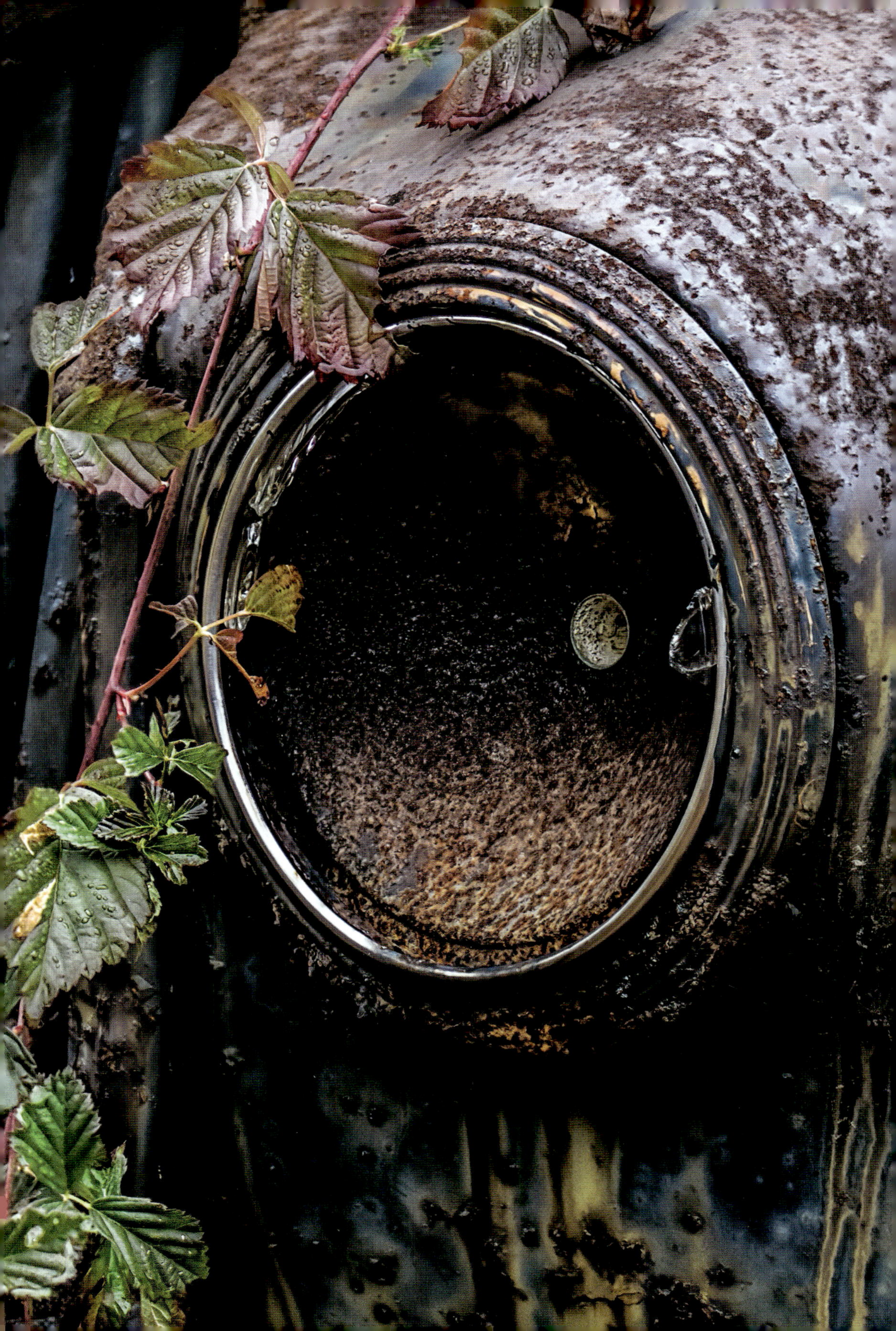

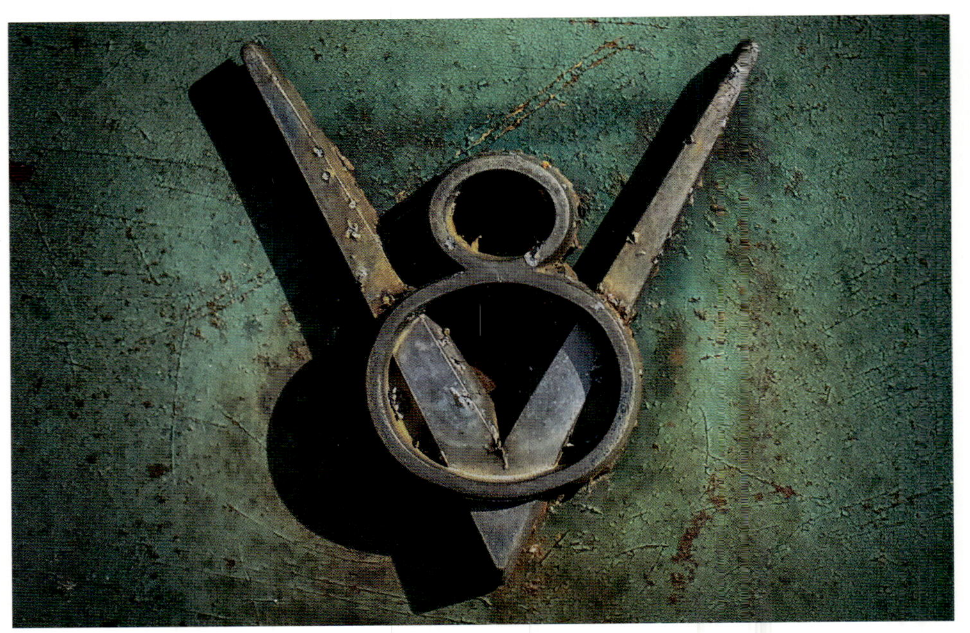

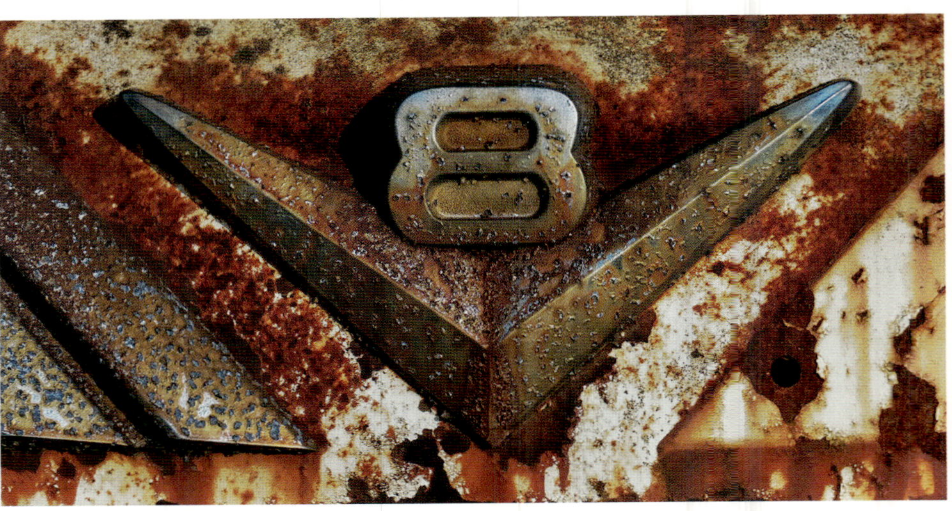

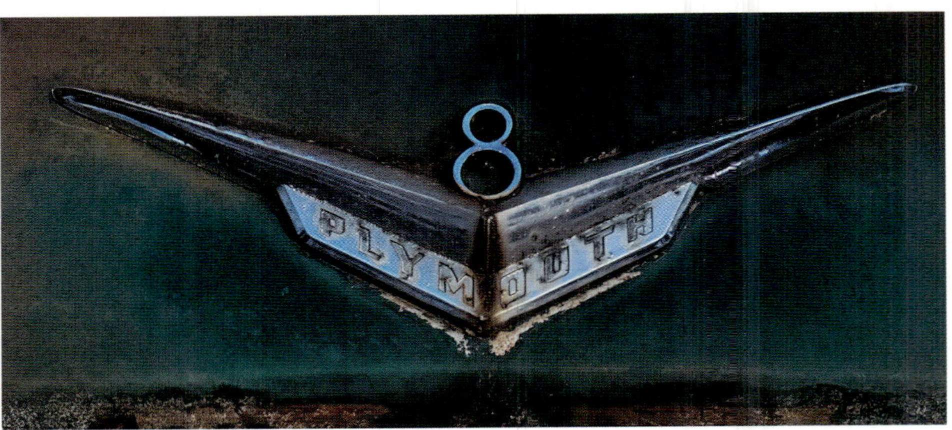
8
PLYMOUTH

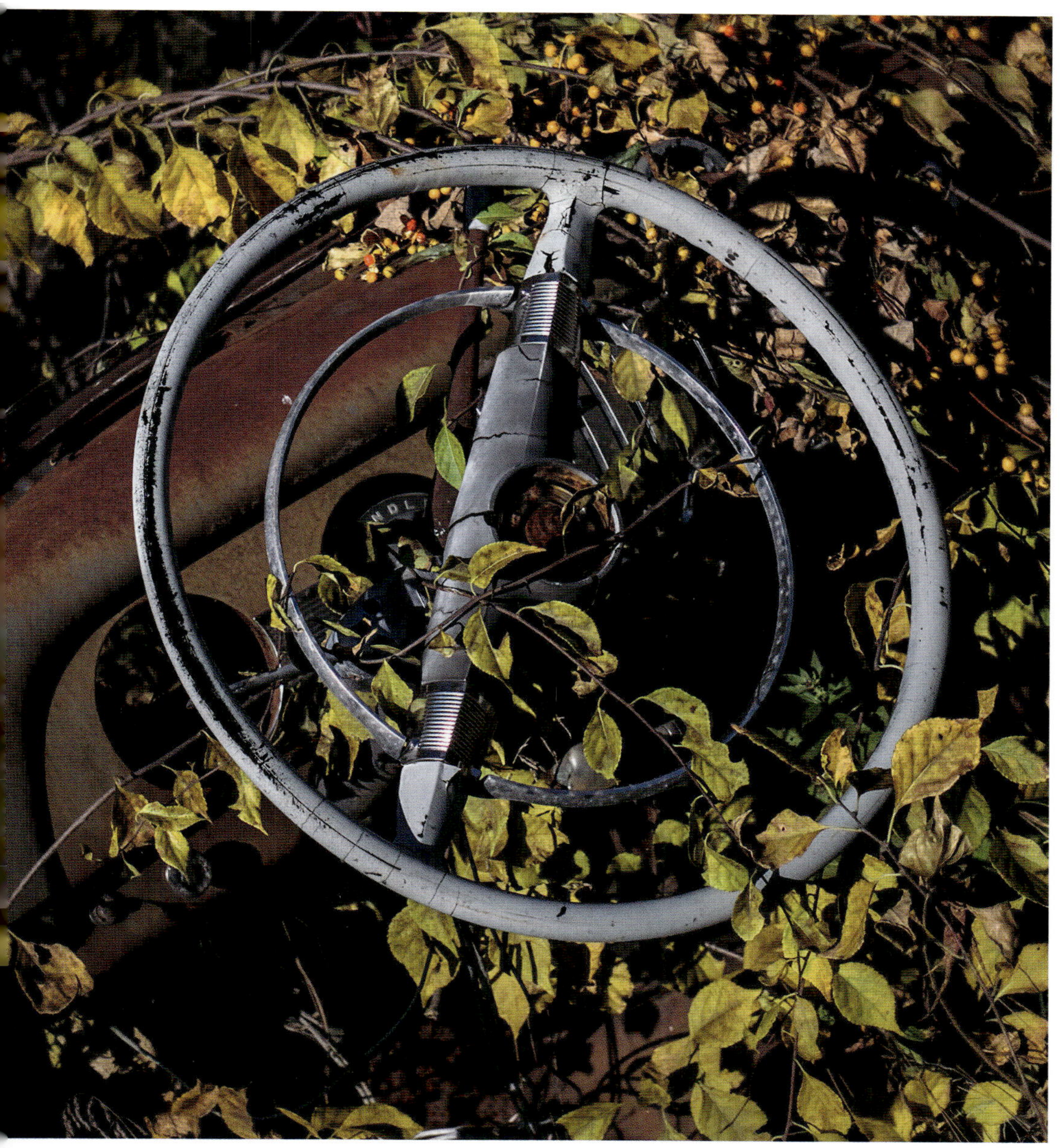

Left: A few words in honor of the classic car by one of the premiere logo specialists of the last fifty years. "The emblem, the identifier, the title, the ornament perfectly beveled, plated, placed and etched in our collective memory of an era wrought with class and character. These are some fine examples of the mastery of lettering and design passed down for future generations. Car emblems have always been a great inspiration and influence on my career." *Tom Nikosey, Designer, Illustrator, Type & Logo Specialist*

Here's a thought from someone who began his career in Robert Fripp's group The League of Crafty Guitarists, which was the ultimate guitar circle. "Circle, upon circle, upon circle, upon circles. What hands gripped these circles? How did these circles arrive here in the leaves and weeds?" *Paul Richards, Musician, Guitarist (California Guitar Trio)*

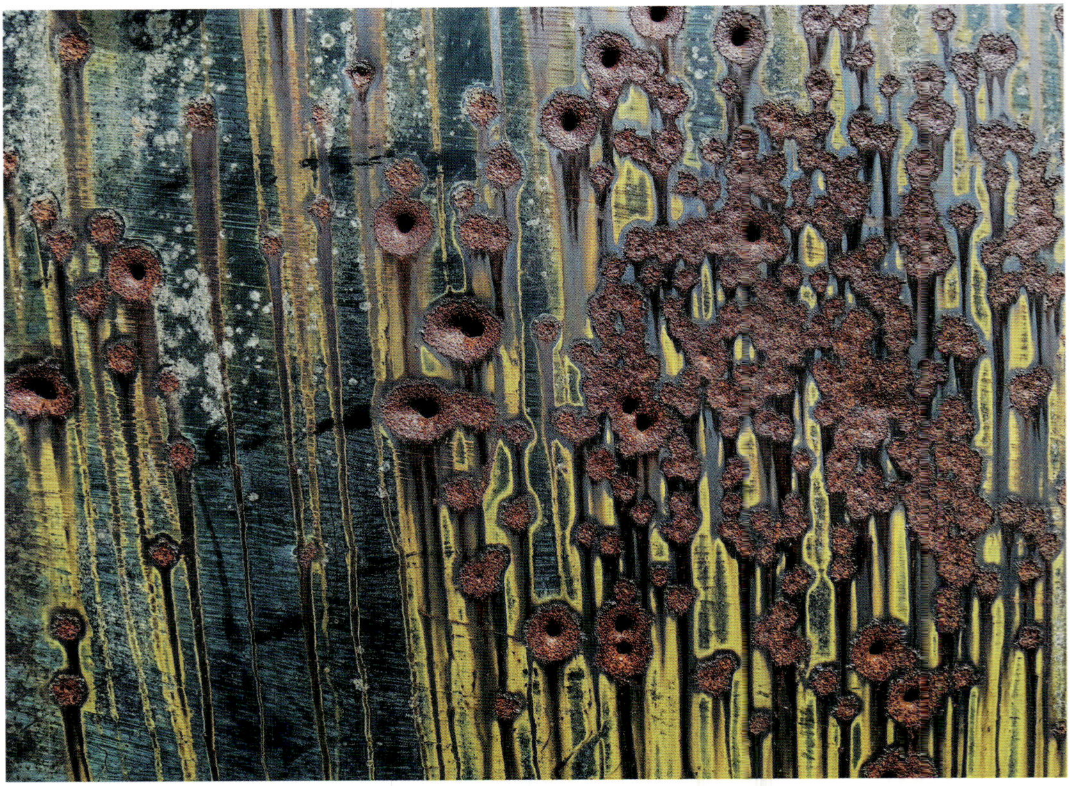

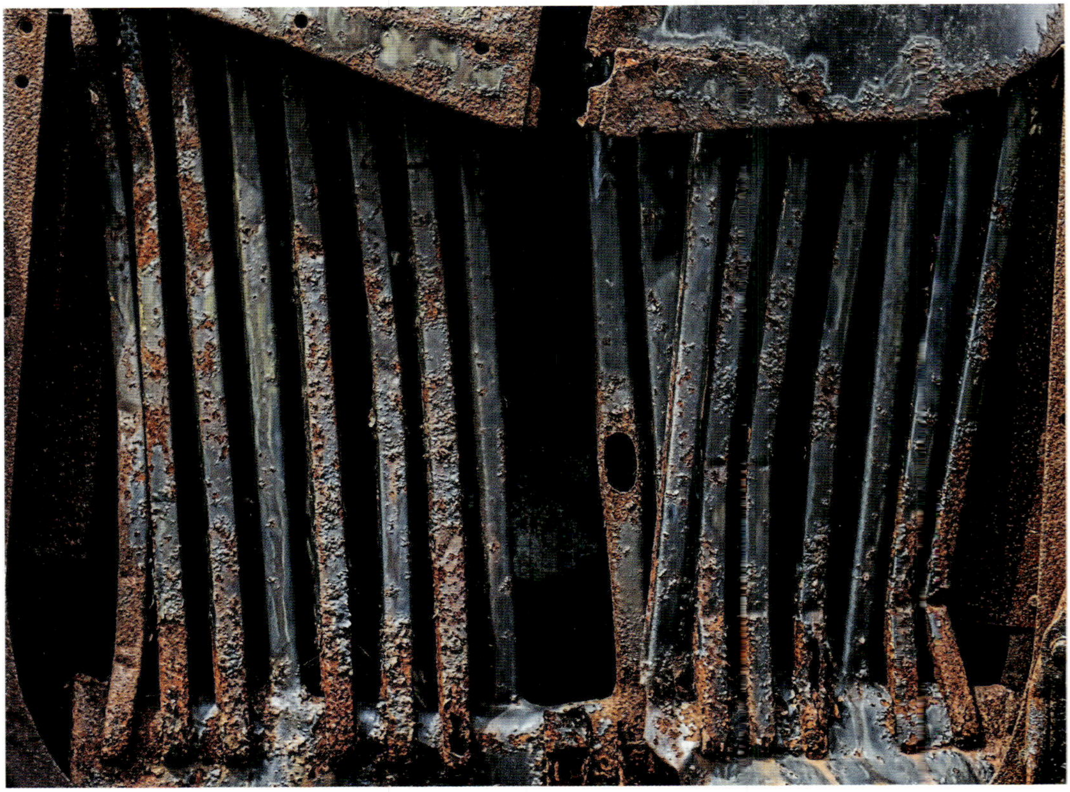

I never stop marveling at the course of metal erosion, and the decaying layers of paint and rust have created amazing pieces of abstract art. Each of the wonderful woman artists I invited to comment have a special kinship with texture and color in their work.

Top Left: "Floral Decay" Another detailed look at the Ford truck on pages 64 and 65, this time displaying the bullet holes on the passenger-side door. Some words from a New Hampshire art stalwart:
"Rust
Well traveled.
Layers of decay that span a lifetime of experiences.
Bruised, defeated, and rebounding with the memories of the past.
Each layer provides a story as it peels away and crumbles,
returning once again to the earth."
Pamela R. Tarbell, Artist, Gallery Owner

Bottom Left: *"The Grate Wall"* Also from the same truck as above, this beautifully eroding grill is one of the very first shots I took with the Light 16 camera. This kind comment is from someone that wants me to gather up all the rusted car parts I've photographed for her to use in her sculptures! "Jerry and I share a deep love for rust, and we both use it in our artwork. He captures the exquisite beauty of rust in such a way that his photographs often resemble gorgeous paintings." *Lucy Krupkenye, Sculptor*

A poem from a texture specialist.
"Crackle, Chip, Erode and Rust
Time crackles.
Time chips.
Time erodes and rusts.
Time adds grit.
Time develops character.
Time ensues wisdom for
the journey back to dust."
Lisa L. Cyr, Illustrator, Fine Artist, Author, Educator

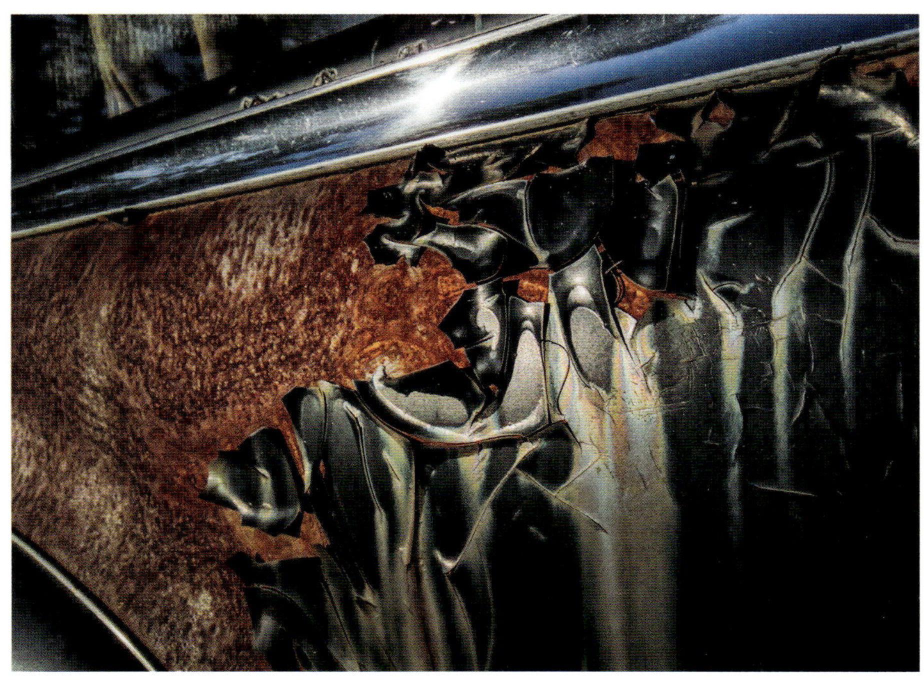

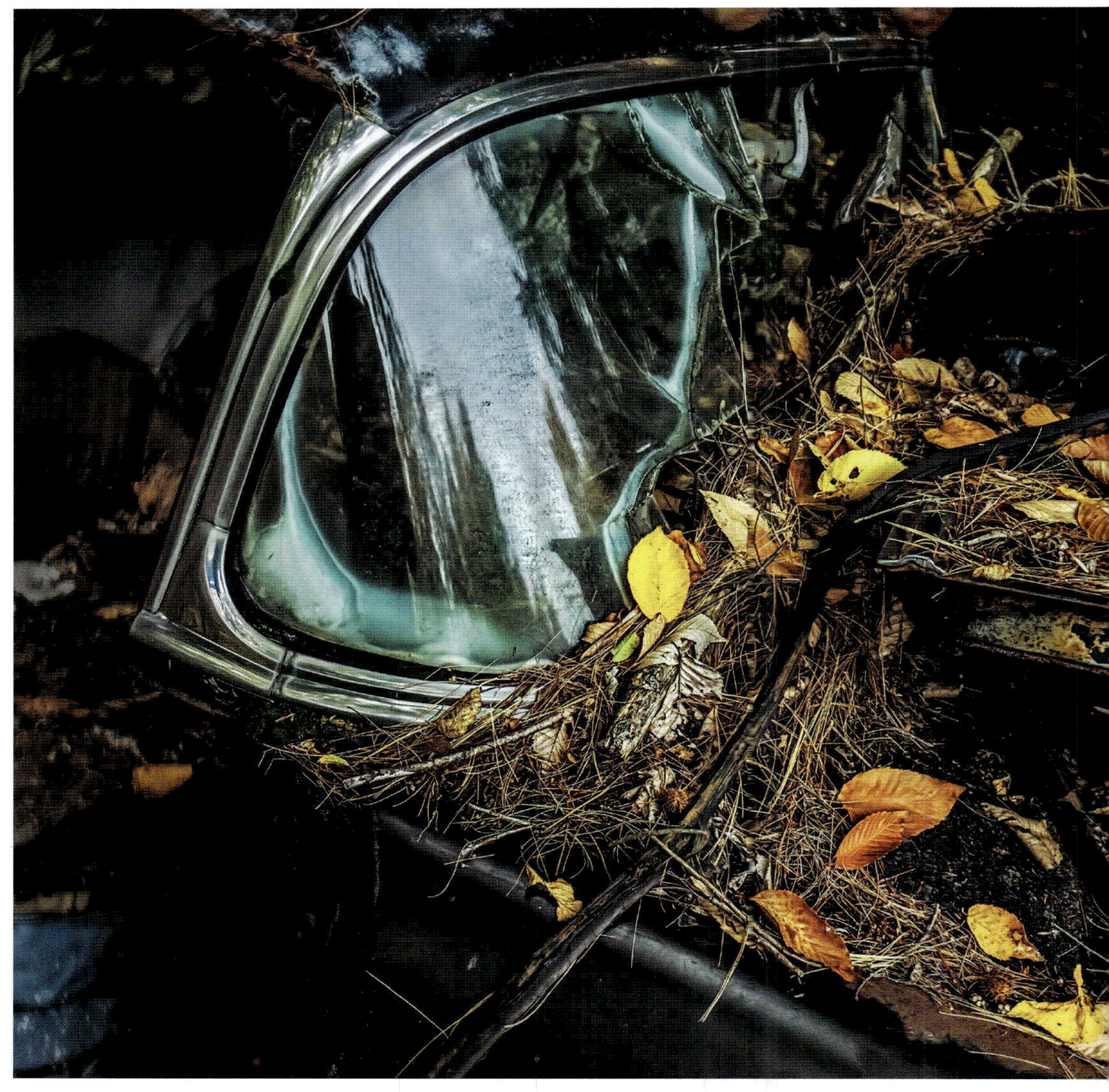

"Window Treatment" Reflecting the sky above while buried beneath the trees and overgrowth, windows are often framed by seemingly decay-proof chrome among the rusting and eroding bodies that still hold them in place. Time and weather have a wondrous and surprising effect on the heavy glass, and the bubbles, patterns, and ghosted discolorations form beautiful and surreal secret worlds within. My friend, Bonnie, has a very significant place in my artistic journey, and I'm pleased to have her kind and lovely thoughts about these photos. "As an artist who has known Jerry for years, I can only call these works LUSH! Each masterpiece reveals the intensity of the photographer and artist who created them, and imbue to us not only thought-provoking works, but also pure beauty!" *Bonnie Zimmerman, Artist, Founder of The Pioneer Computer Arts School, Weare, NH*

Middle Right: With an AMC Pacer as a backdrop, a rumination from a dear friend, NH Institute of Art teaching peer and a gardener extraordinaire: "Ahh … I see with the bloom of asters, fall is near and all will soon be the color of rust." *Jill Weber, Artist, Children's Book Illustrator, Teacher*

Bottom Right: I knew what I was doing when I asked a rising art star to comment on this lava lamp of a photo. "I existed in a liquid universe, infinitely suspended in an intricate ebb and flow of melting contemplation, yet oblivious to the stoic walls of rigid coagulated ore that surrounded me." *Novel Teethe, Artist, Illustrator, Former NHIA Student*

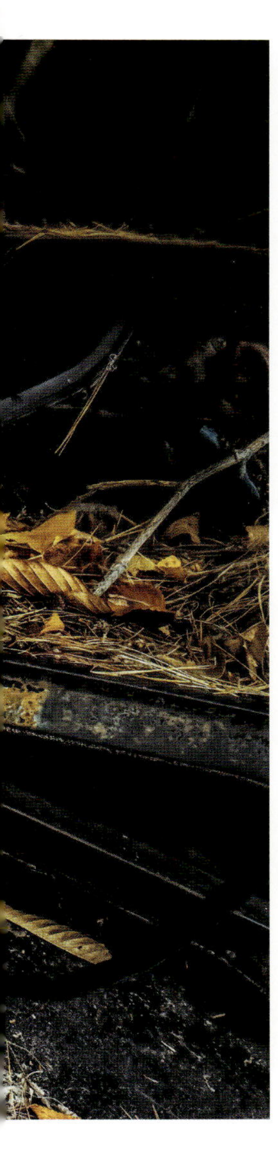
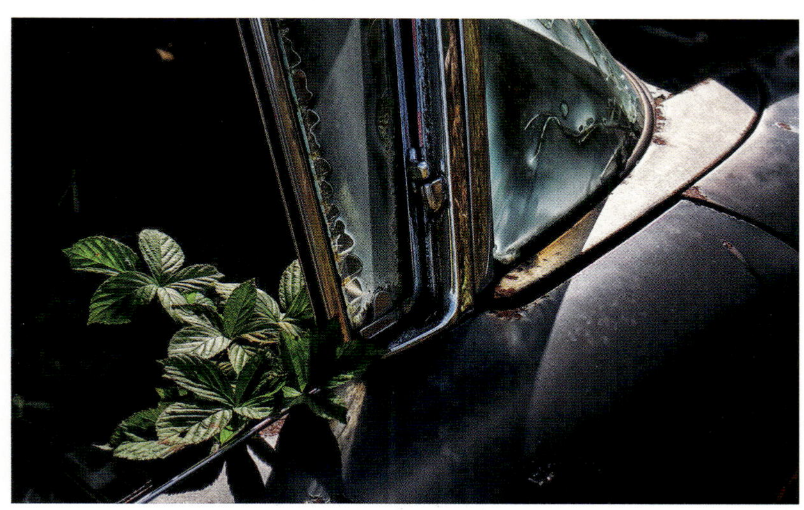
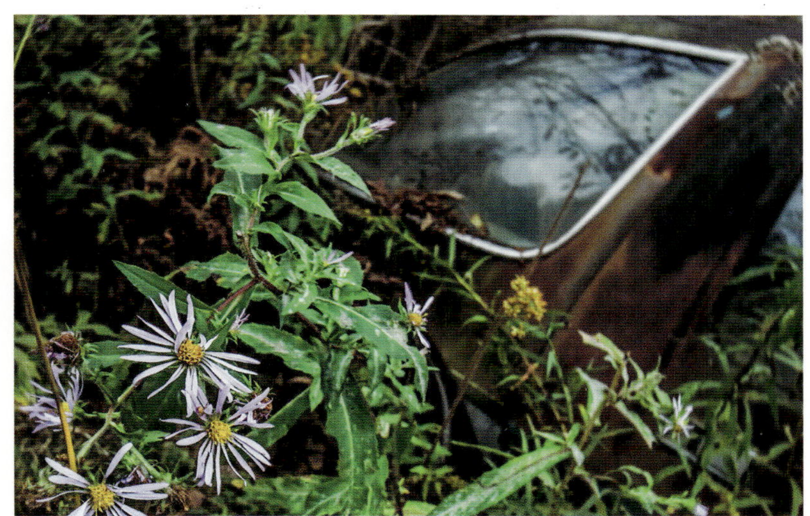
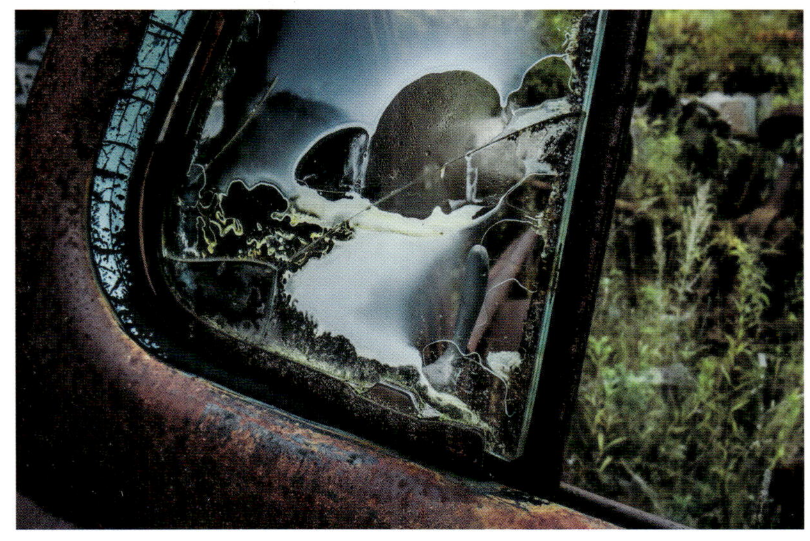

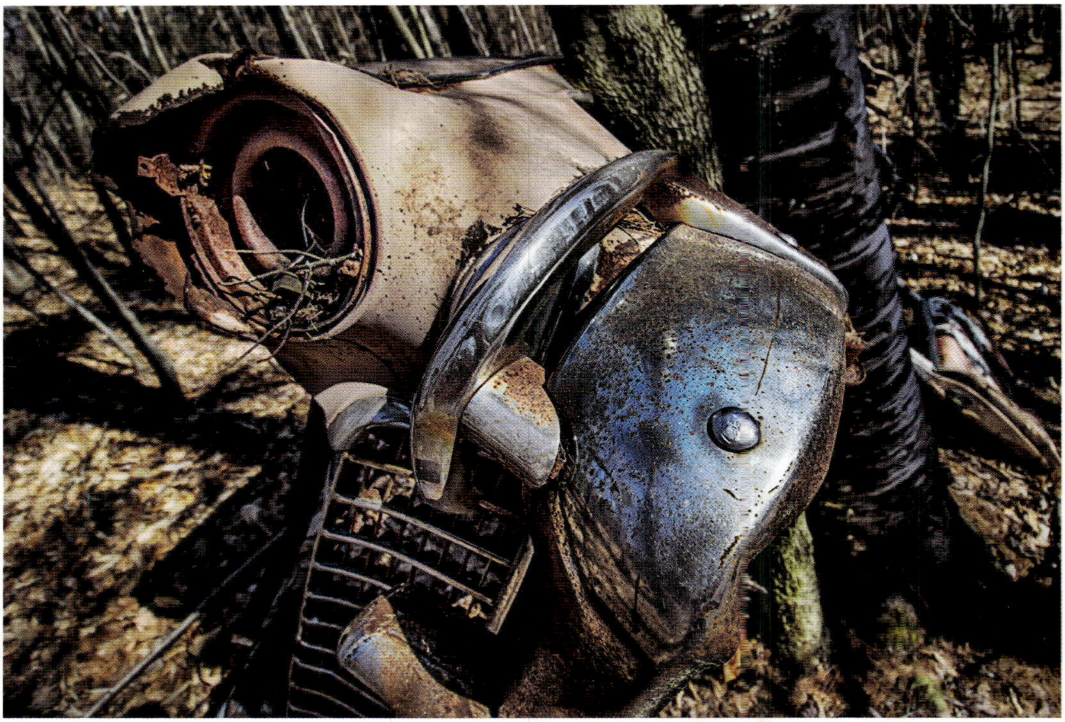

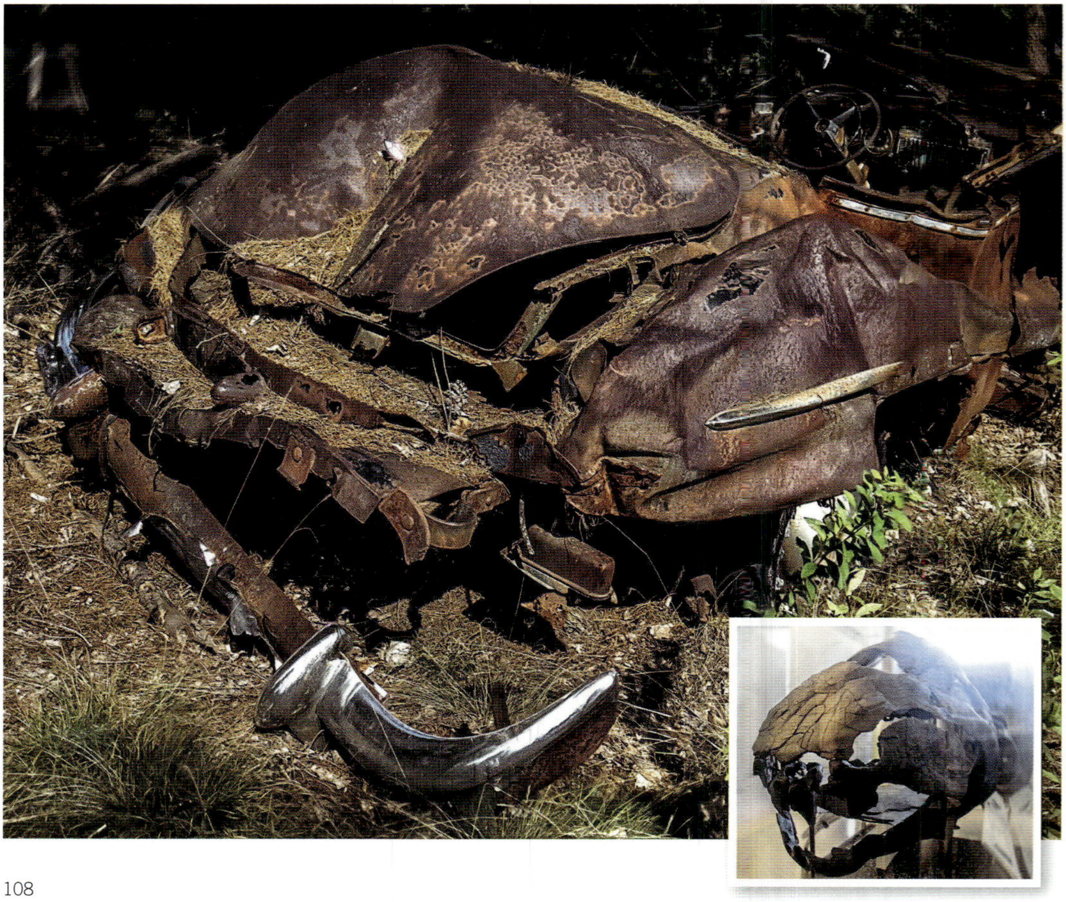

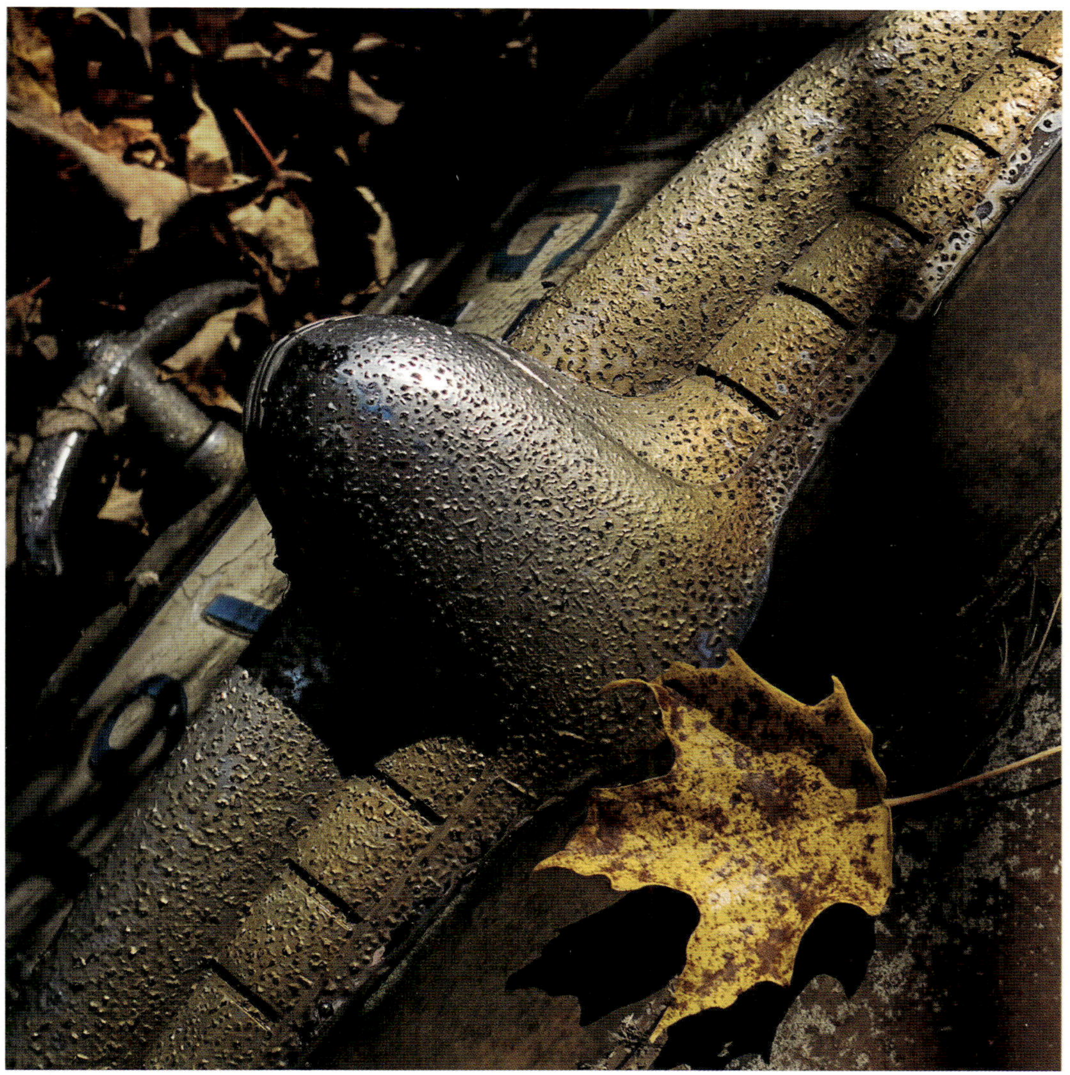

Top Left: Here's another view of the 1955 Belair that appears on page 16, enhanced with an imagined eavesdropping on the arrest. "Handcuffed in the woods, I should have been devastated. But sweaty, bruised, I had never felt better ... 'Damn, that was fun!' The cop couldn't help but return my boyish grin." *Emily Marsh, Artist, Former NHIA Student*

Bottom Left: *"Dunkleosteus"* I've retained my childhood fascination for all things prehistoric, and my first reaction to seeing this wreck emerging from the shadows was "OMG —a dunkleosteus!" I took the inset photo at the Museum of Natural History many years ago, and I think this car has an uncanny resemblance to the gigantic and terrifying ancient fish from the late Devonian period.

Right: The trunk ornament from a 1950 Plymouth (Cranbrook or Cambridge) has such an incredible texture and blend of color, and I was drawn in by the juxtaposition of the equally textured leaf. I particularly like the specks of blue among the warmth and earthiness. Here's a great memory from a fellow artist in Utah, my favorite state to visit. "The family farm of my youth contained many pieces of retired machinery and vehicles that were 'out to pasture.' Their state of decay and the randomness of placement were fertile grounds for children at play. From stagecoach holdups to science fiction battles, the rusted carcasses of these relics helped fuel my imagination. A majestic pitted patina like this still brings a tingle to my soul." *Greg Newbold, Artist, Children's Book Illustrator*

Bottom Left: *"Fallen Angel"* What a soaring symbol of beauty and freedom this hood ornament from a 1954 Mercury Monterey is! Other glorious chrome emblems peer out from the decay and shadows, holding on to their brilliant finish while all erodes around them. These retro-futuristic icons are a perfect match for my old friend, and legendary airbrush artist.

"Once these were loved automobiles on an open freeway, whose mascots proudly cut into the oncoming wind, cranked by the boastful horsepower beneath their hoods. Now they remain forgotten in abandoned places, after having escaped the scrapyards where they would have been crushed into blocks, melted and transformed into new objects. These machines were destined to remain with us, be a reminder of the past, to quietly rust into dust in their final parking places."

Stanislaw Fernandes, Artist, Illustrator, Graphic Designer

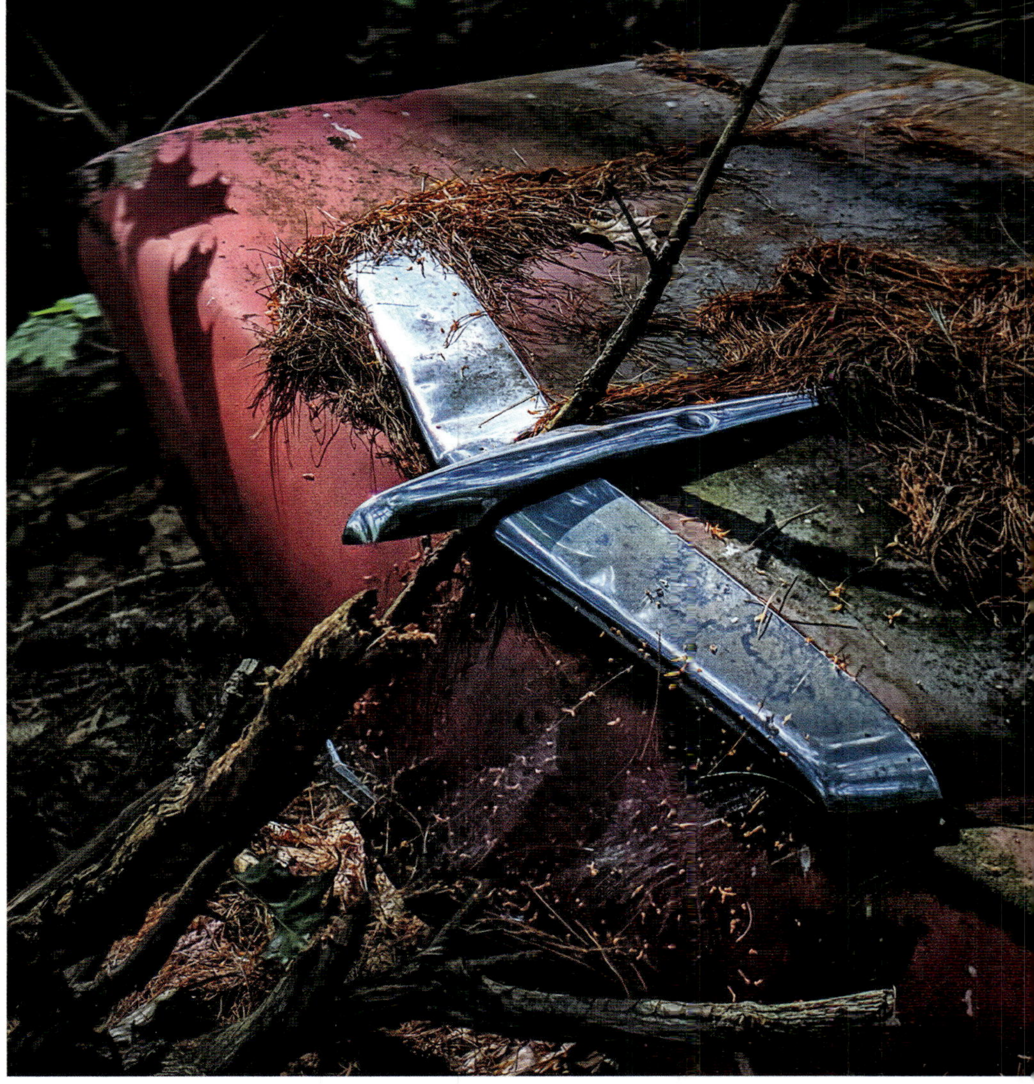

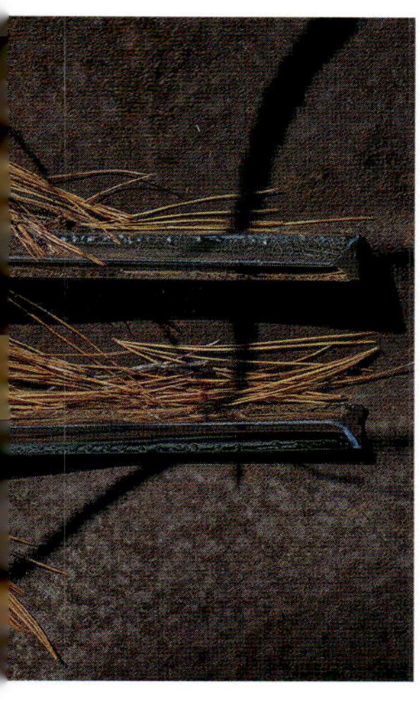
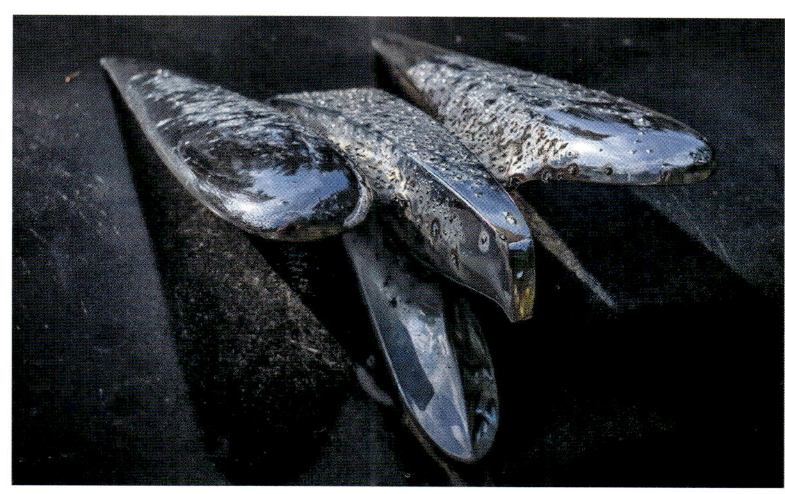
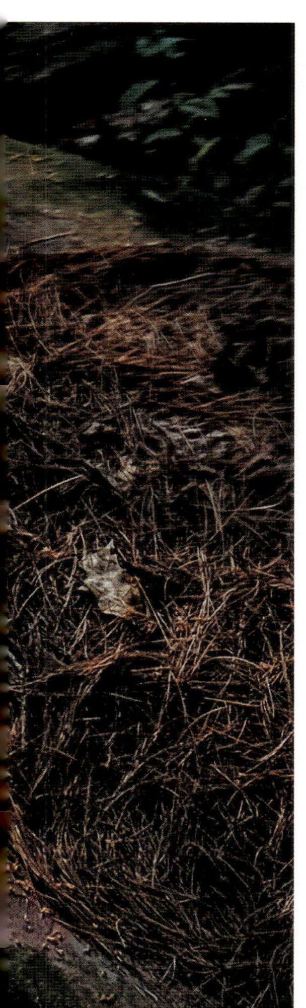
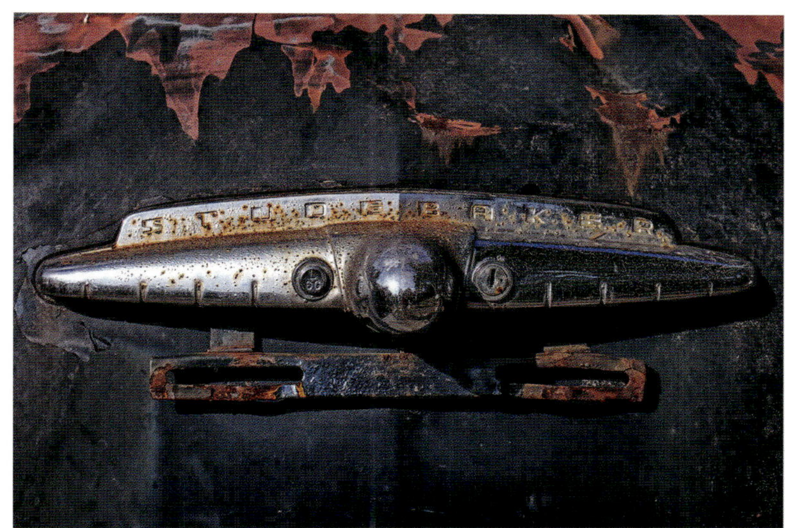
STUDEBAKER
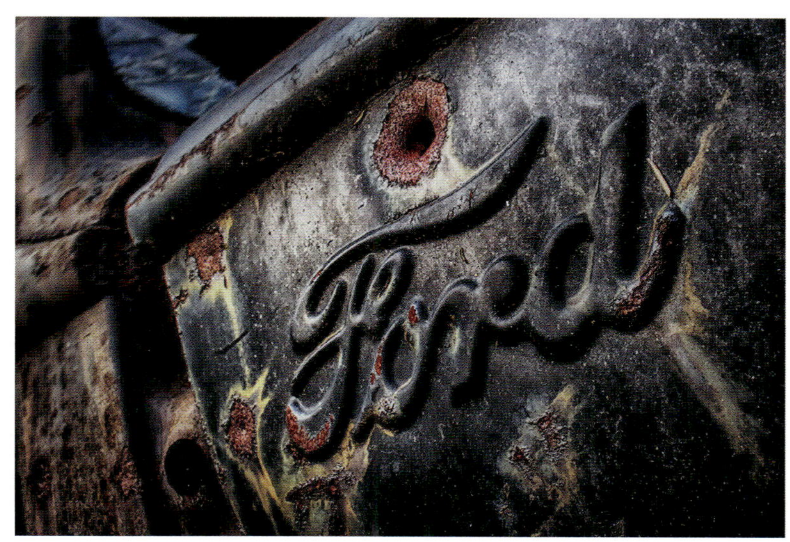
Ford

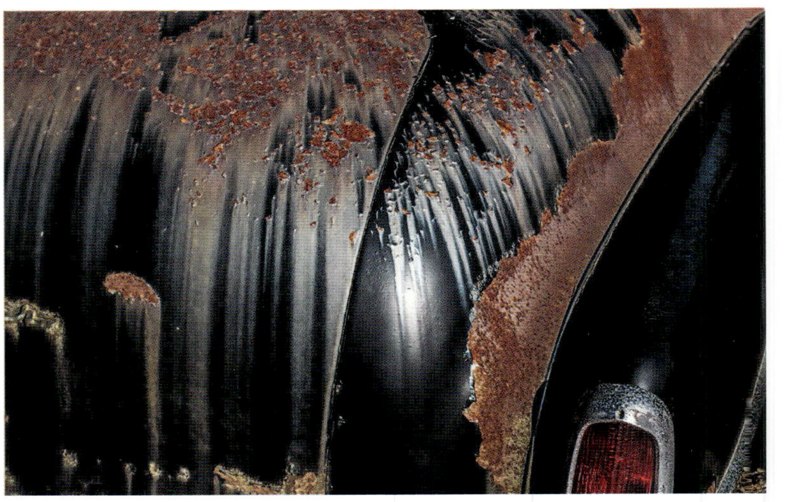
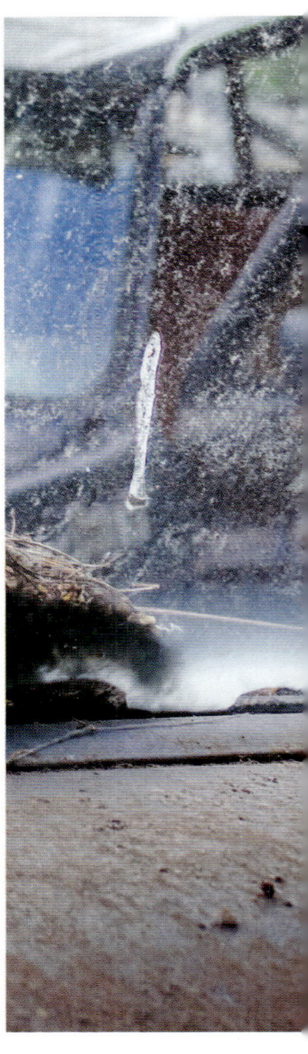
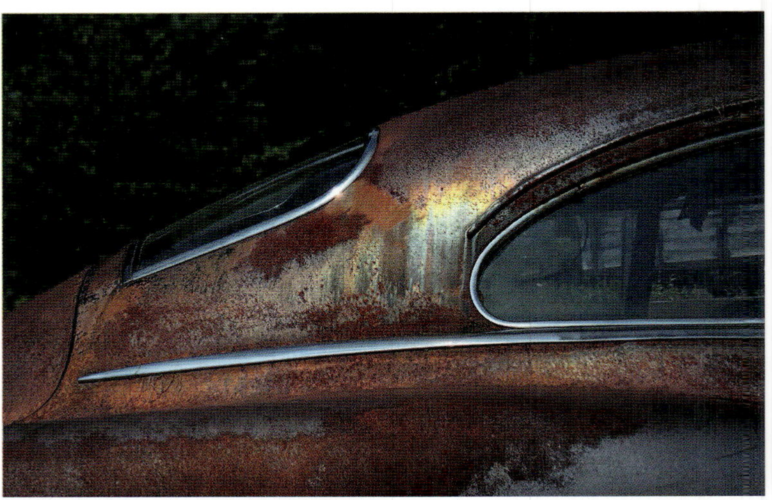
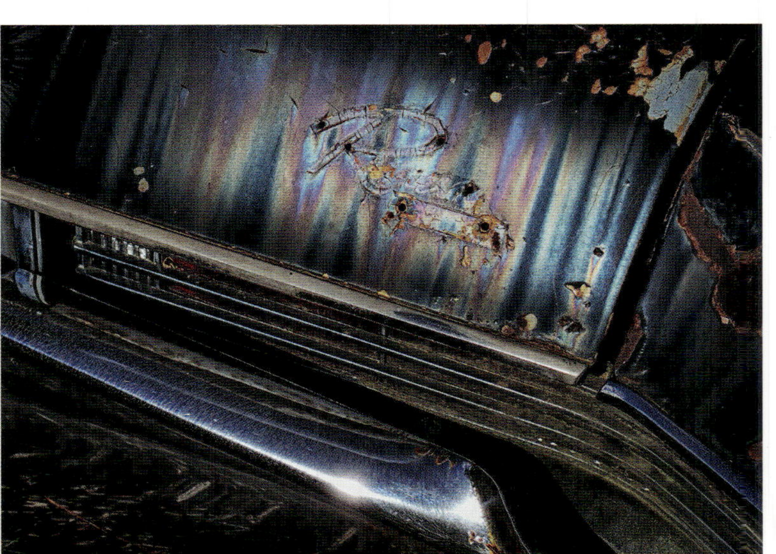
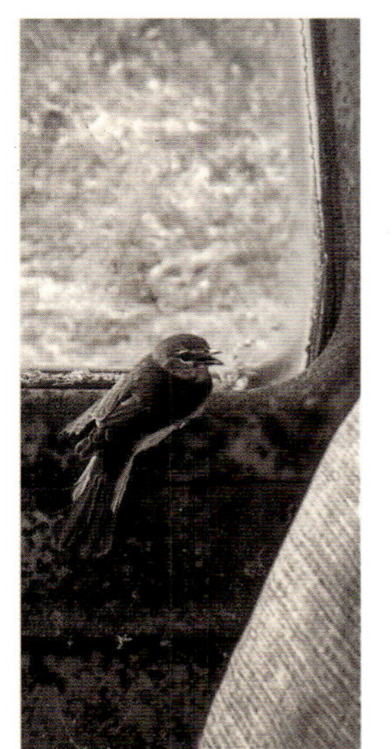

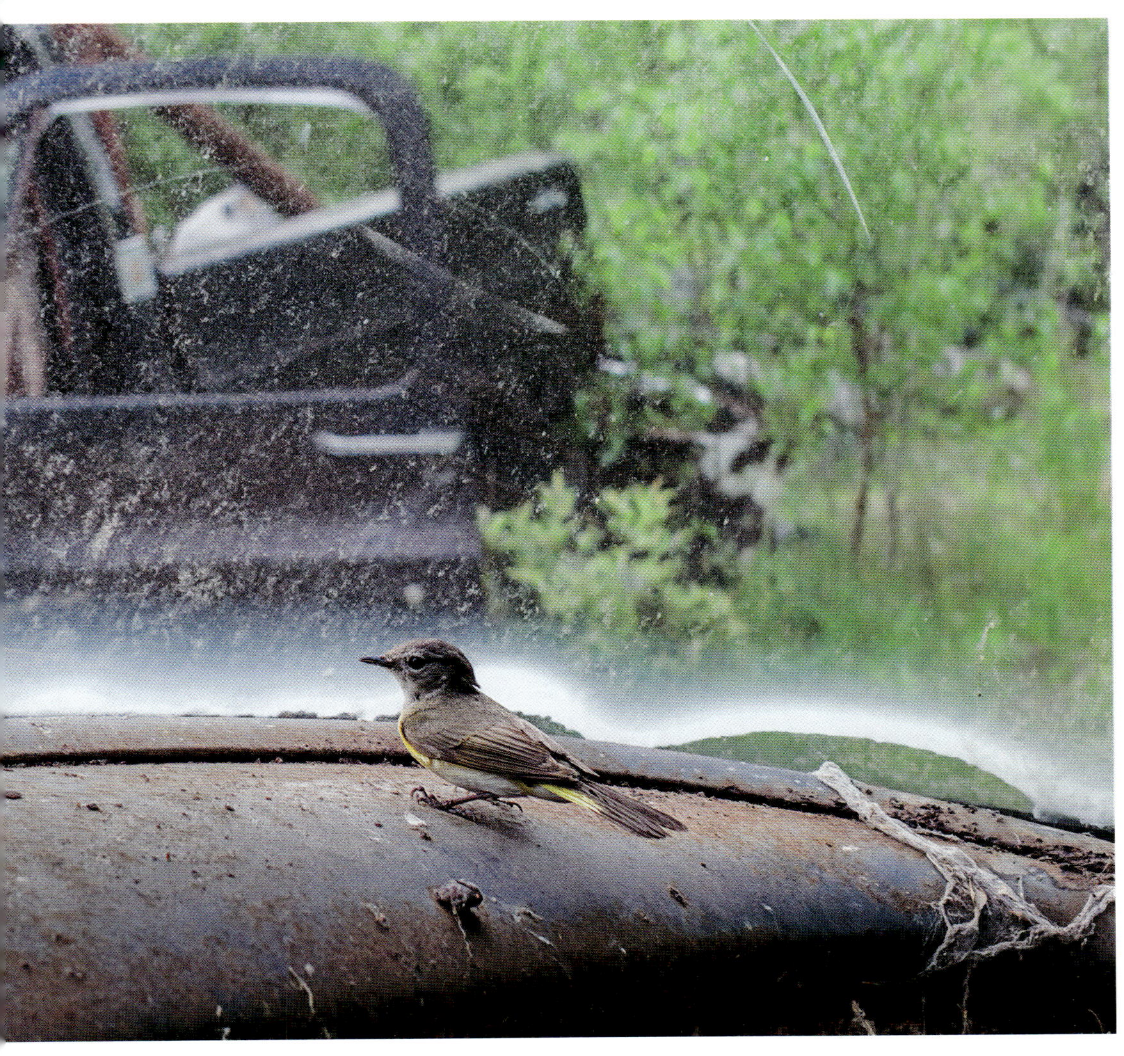

Left Group: *"Sun Basking on The Riviera"* What the elements do to a car's finish is just remarkable. I asked my very first Photoshop instructor to share a thought. "Time is in constant movement and represented through change. A photograph is a captured second in the life of a story. Those vehicles that once roamed the land and echoed the sounds of life, now can only project an impression of loveliness gone by. Paint and colors will fade, and metals will rust, but never after that captured second. These are lovely, colorful photos brilliantly shot, but also great lessons in life." *Alhan Irwin, Illustrator, Artist, Teacher*

Top Right & Bottom Middle: *"The Cinema Show"* What a sweet little guy! No, actually it's a girl ... a female American Redstart, which is a member of the warbler family. As I was walking by an old pickup at Lane's, I saw her fluttering away inside. However, she was only momentarily trapped, and didn't seem to mind me taking a few quick shots before she exited without the help I was about to offer. Here's an interesting thought from an actual Guy, another old friend and legendary illustrator. "An ancient fatal accident revisited." *Guy Billout, Illustrator*

9

THE HUDSON

I spent many years illustrating book covers, many of which were conceived after I read and conceptualized visual ideas from raw manuscripts provided by the publishers, and I even illustrated an entire, science-based children's book called *How Life Began*. However, this is a brand-new animal—the first book I've ever authored, and it has been quite the learning process. I'll admit that when I first started, I was in a bit of a panic about what to do. The photography was easy, as I already had plenty of shots to choose from, even as I continued shooting to create a fuller and richer story. My dilemma is that I actually know very little about cars—what the hell was I gonna write about? I'm happy to say the evolving process solved that issue, but I was surprised and even happier that a book about rusty stuff would become so personal and meaningful.

With that, I purposely saved this chapter till last to showcase the Hudson, a car that my grandson coincidently shares his name with. Of course, that meant I had to find a Hudson to photograph. I was so overwhelmed with excitement on my initial trip to Lane's that my quest actually slipped my mind. I slowly wandered around the property that hot August day until I got to the edge of a beautiful field, empty of vehicles except for an unidentifiable one out in the middle. It was picturesquely posed, and I shot away as I got closer and closer. Surely, and magically enough, when I saw the name on the trunk I realized that I found my Hudson—a 1951 Commodore! For car and movie buffs, it was a 1949 Hudson Commodore featured in the movie *Driving Miss Daisy* (starring Morgan Freeman, Jessica Tandy and Dan Aykroyd), and Rachel McAdams drives a 1946 Hudson Commodore Eight Club Coupe in *The Notebook*. However, the car I discovered in the field that day also has a fun and cinematic story of its own to share on the following pages.

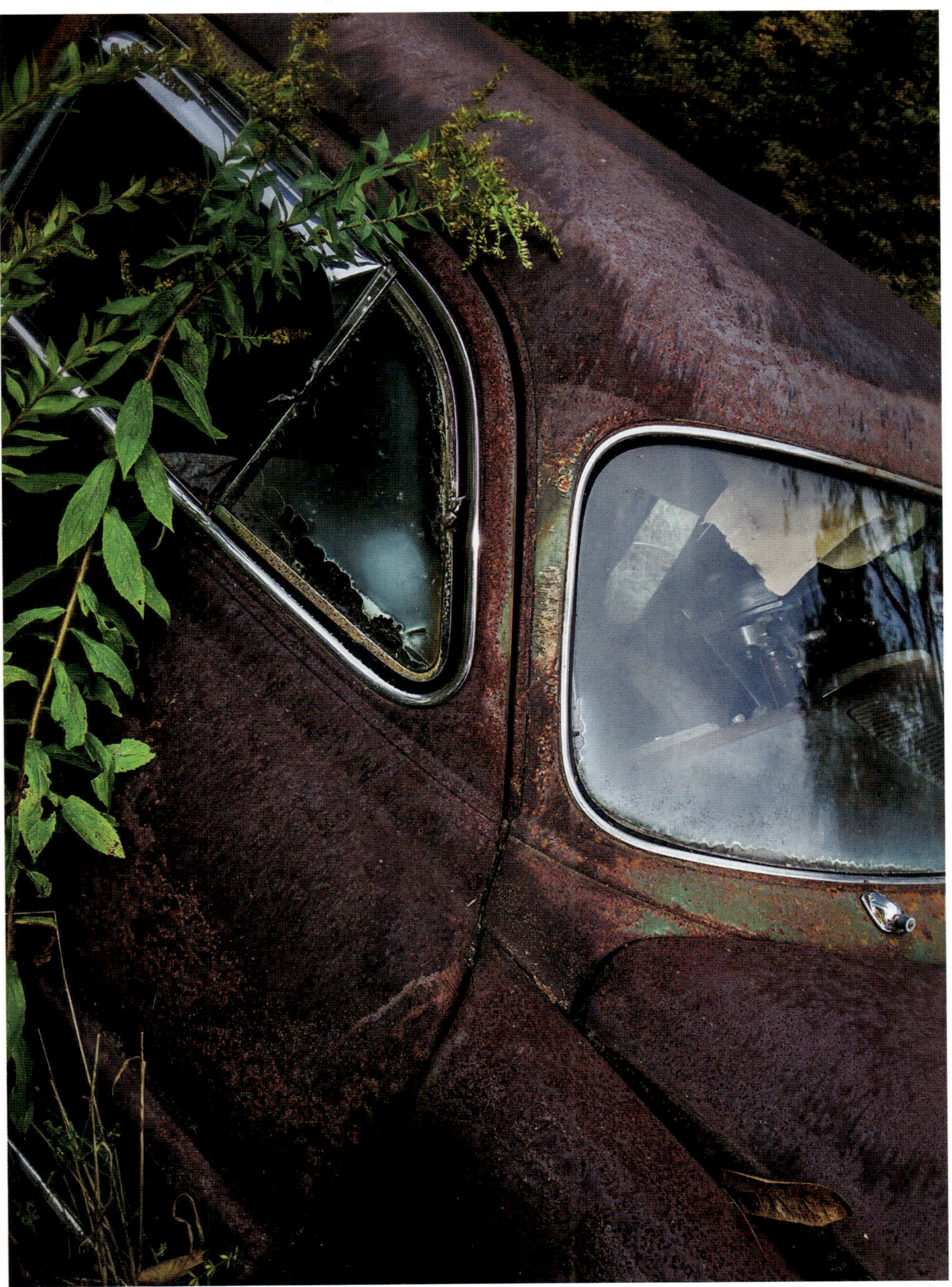

With this photo's clean, elegant, mystery-book-cover quality, I immediately thought of my friend and illustration peer to share a thought. "Like an aging Hollywood starlet who was once an absolute stunner … she's had a hard, long and rich life after a brief but glorious career in the spotlight, but now lives in peace with deep wrinkles and deeper memories. She still has a little sparkle in her chrome; she was a beauty." *Rick Lovell, Illustrator, Associate Chair of Illustration at Savannah College of Art & Design, Airbrush Workshop Teaching Partner*

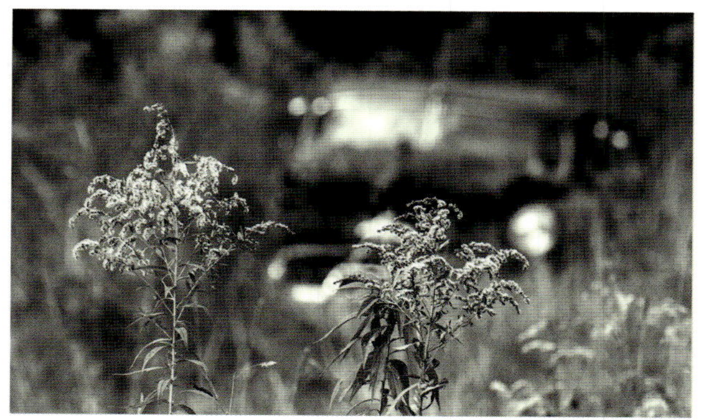

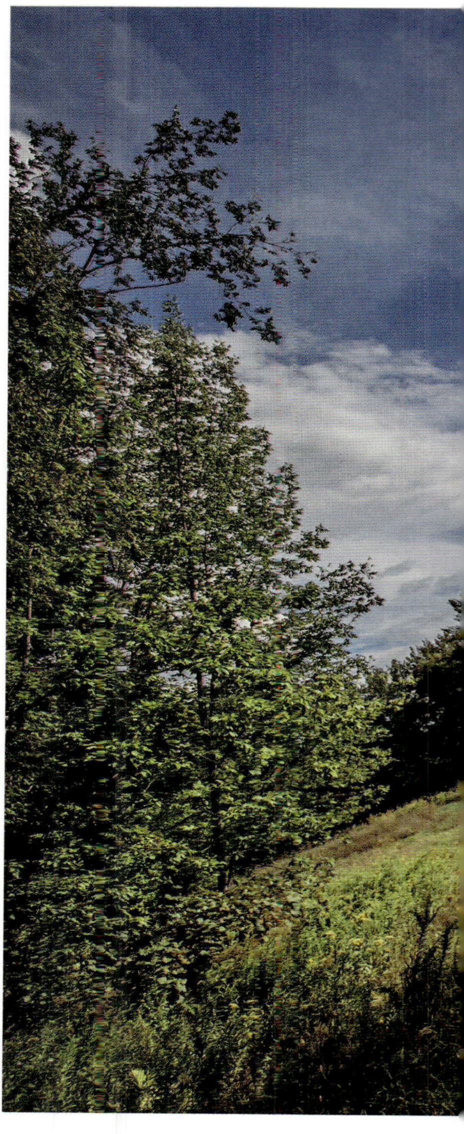

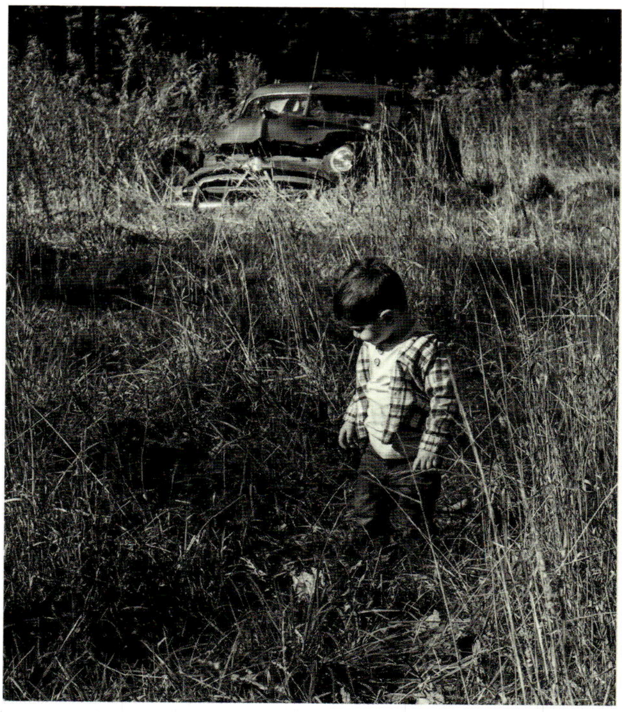

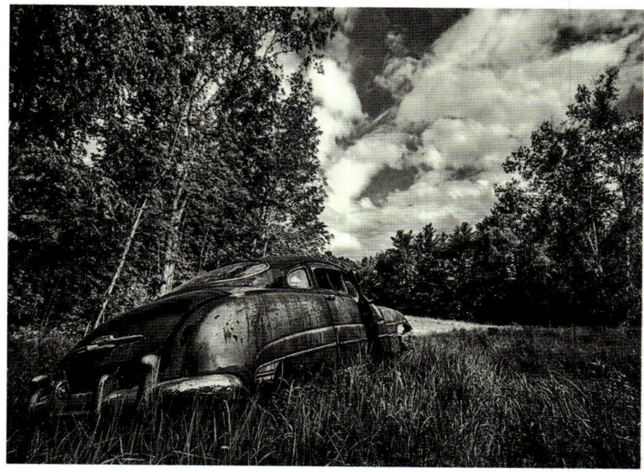

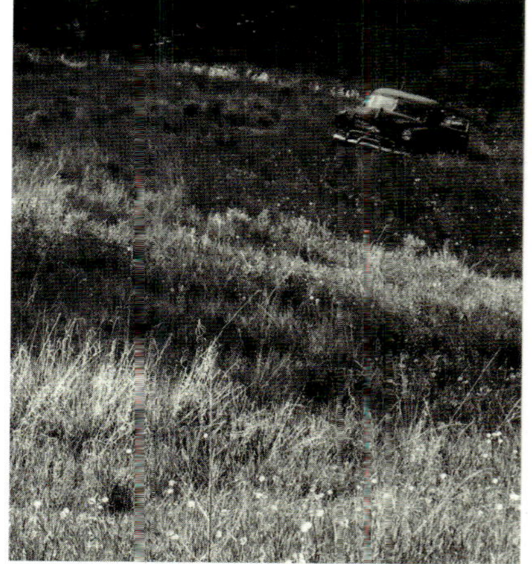

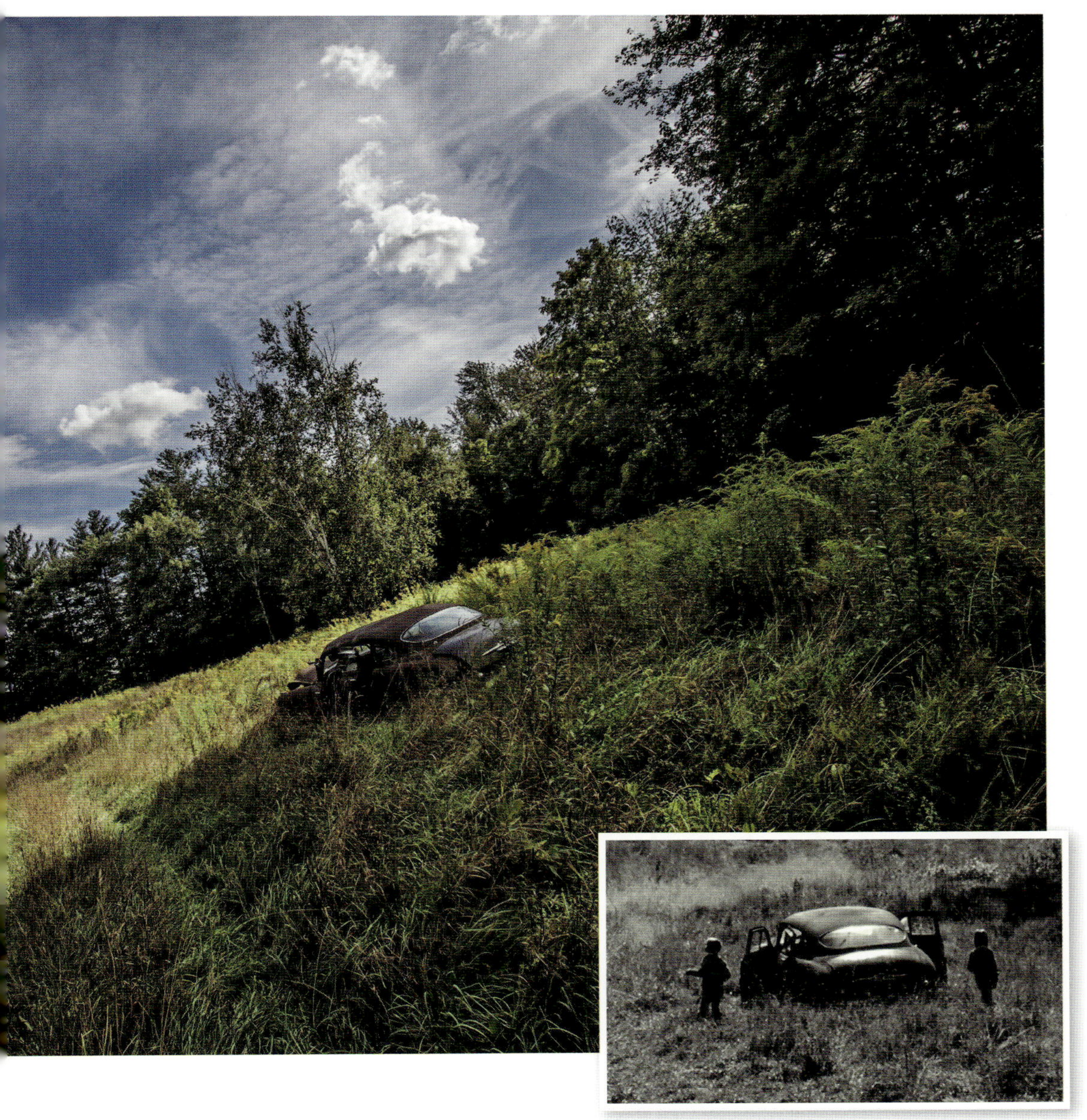

Top Right: My first view of the Hudson was dramatic, beautifully lit and perfectly framed like a still from a movie. It struck me as unusual, so I stopped back in the garage afterwards and asked owner, Ronnie Lane, why the car was out there by itself. As it turns out, he placed it in 2016 for a film company that was making a short horror film called *Bloody Henry*, and they needed a car in a field for the opening scene. It's a very cool and well-done film, but I only let my scream-prone wife watch the first few minutes, as it gets very dark and creepy (think David Lynch). Inset Photo: A still from the movie, with the two young characters encountering the Hudson while out playing.

Left Page: It wasn't until after I brought my grandson to Lane's that I watched *Bloody Henry* online. Not knowing anything about what would transpire in the movie, it gave me a start to see those little kids around this car! I'm glad to have the movie's creator share a thought about these photos. "There is visual poetry in the contours and rust of an old car photographed in black and white. The Hudson is a beautiful relic of America's once thriving automobile industry and provided the perfect visual for the bygone era where my film *Bloody Henry* was set." *Jean-Paul DiSciscio, Filmmaker (Overdue Films), Professor*

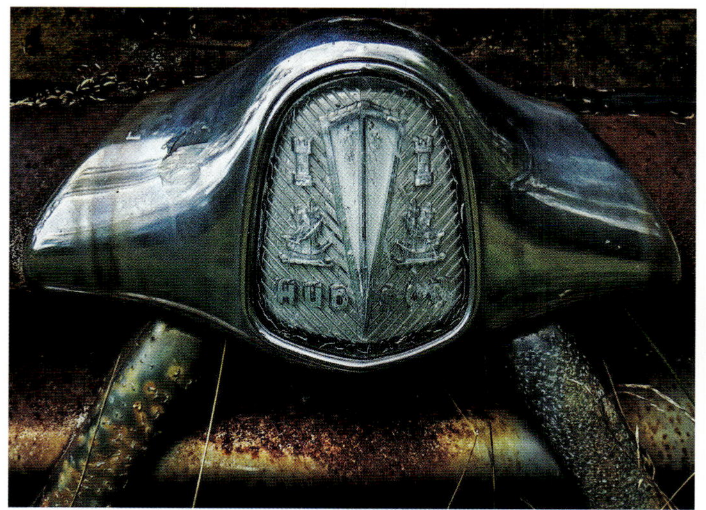

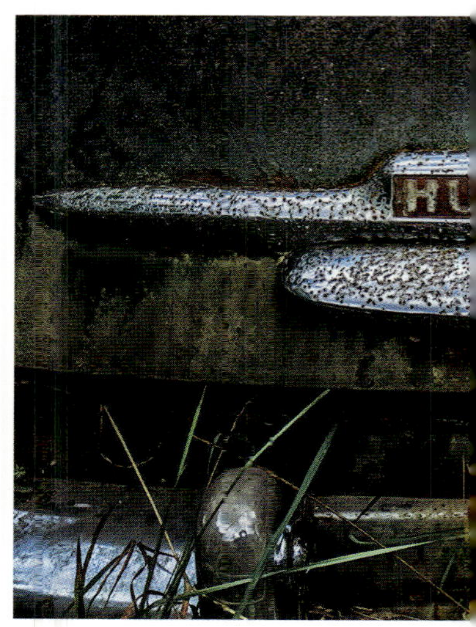

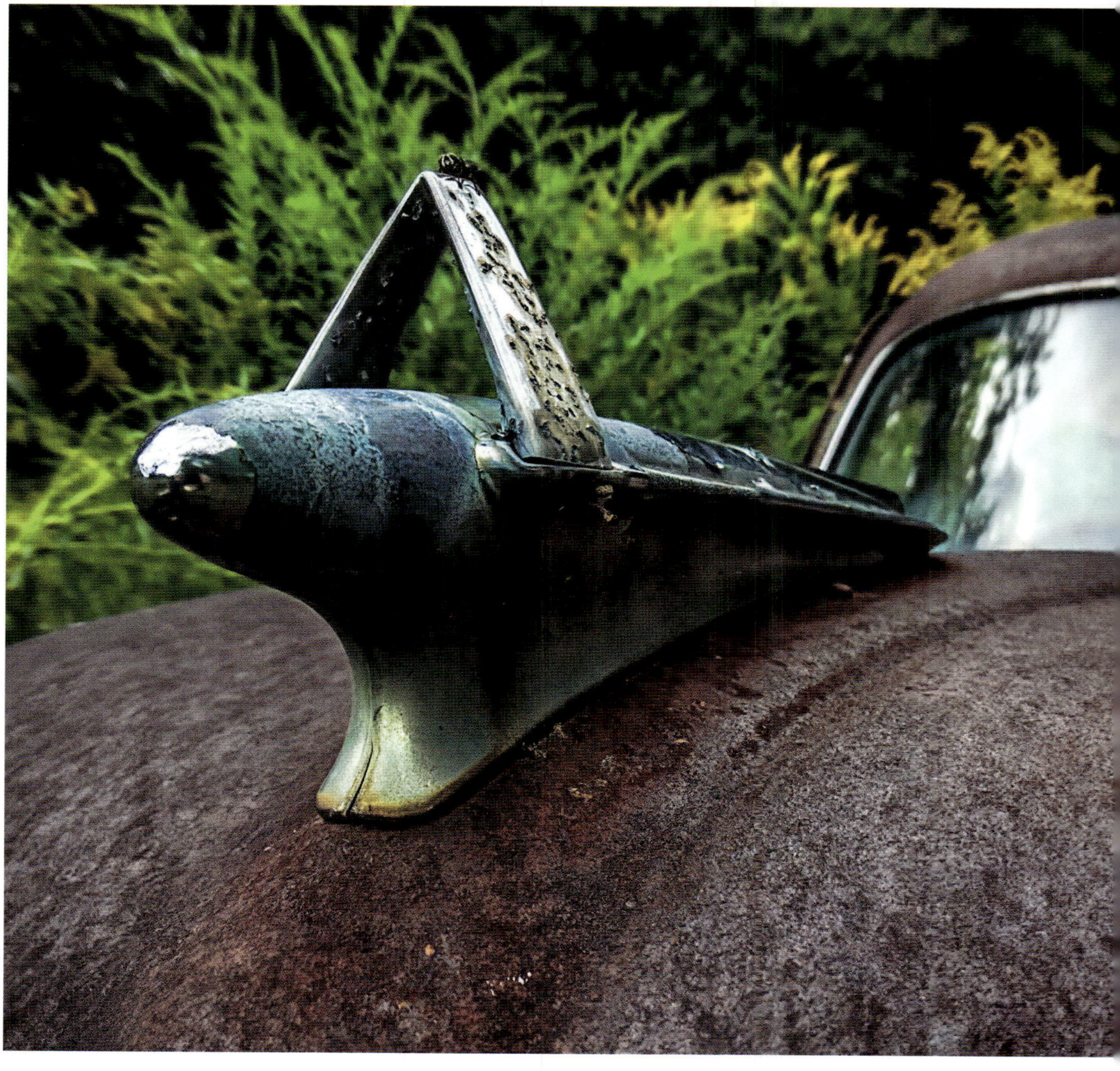

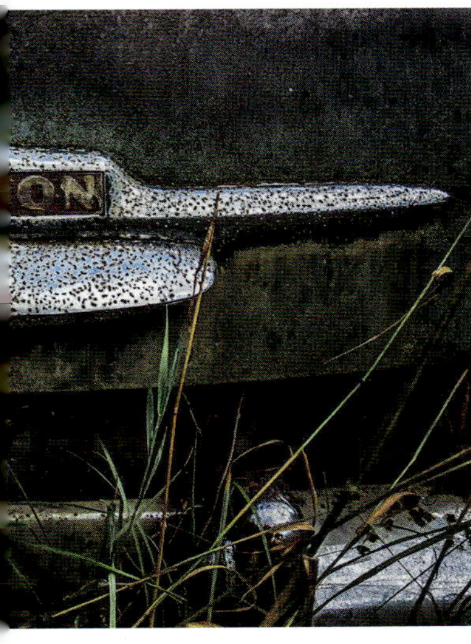

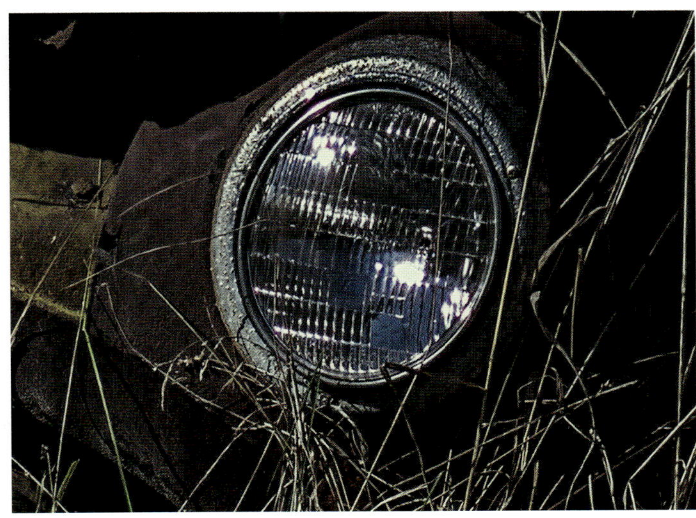

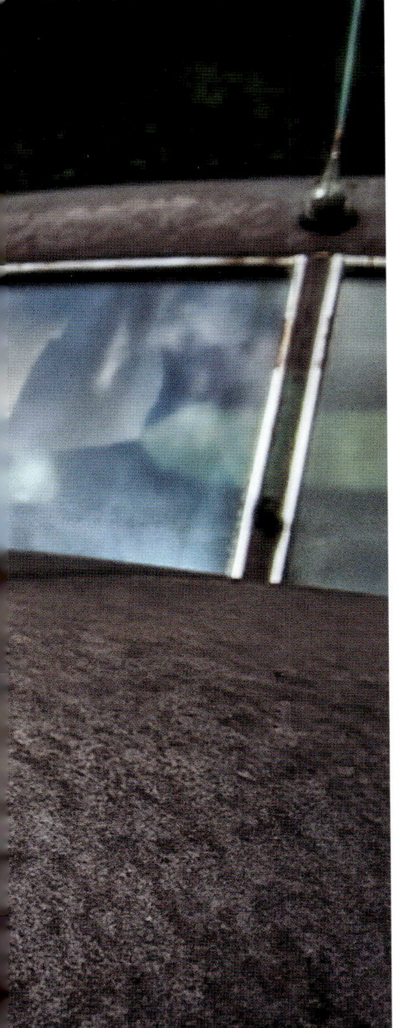

I love all the chrome details, and especially the wide trunk ornament displaying the Hudson name. The emblem located at the top of the front grill is also fascinating, with the plastic work encased within depicting the explorer's wooden ship and a castle tower. Finally, the hood ornament with its beautiful, aging patina seems to have another admirer beside myself. Look close—I managed to capture a fly perched on top as if getting ready for glory like Slim Pickens in *Dr. Strangelove* ... yee-haw, I'm the Dennis Miller of rust!

Below: There was a Hudson dealership (Rowe's Garage) in Henniker on Western Ave., not two minutes from my home. This old post card is from the 1930s, and not only does the building still stand, but my friend Larry Dunn has been lovingly renovating it. In fact, the main showroom space is now the ultimate "man cave."

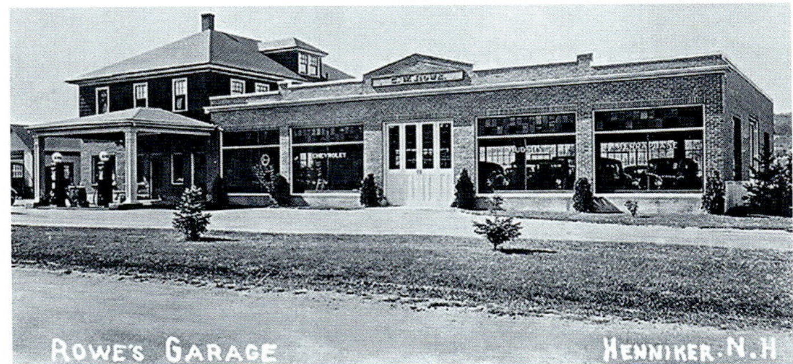

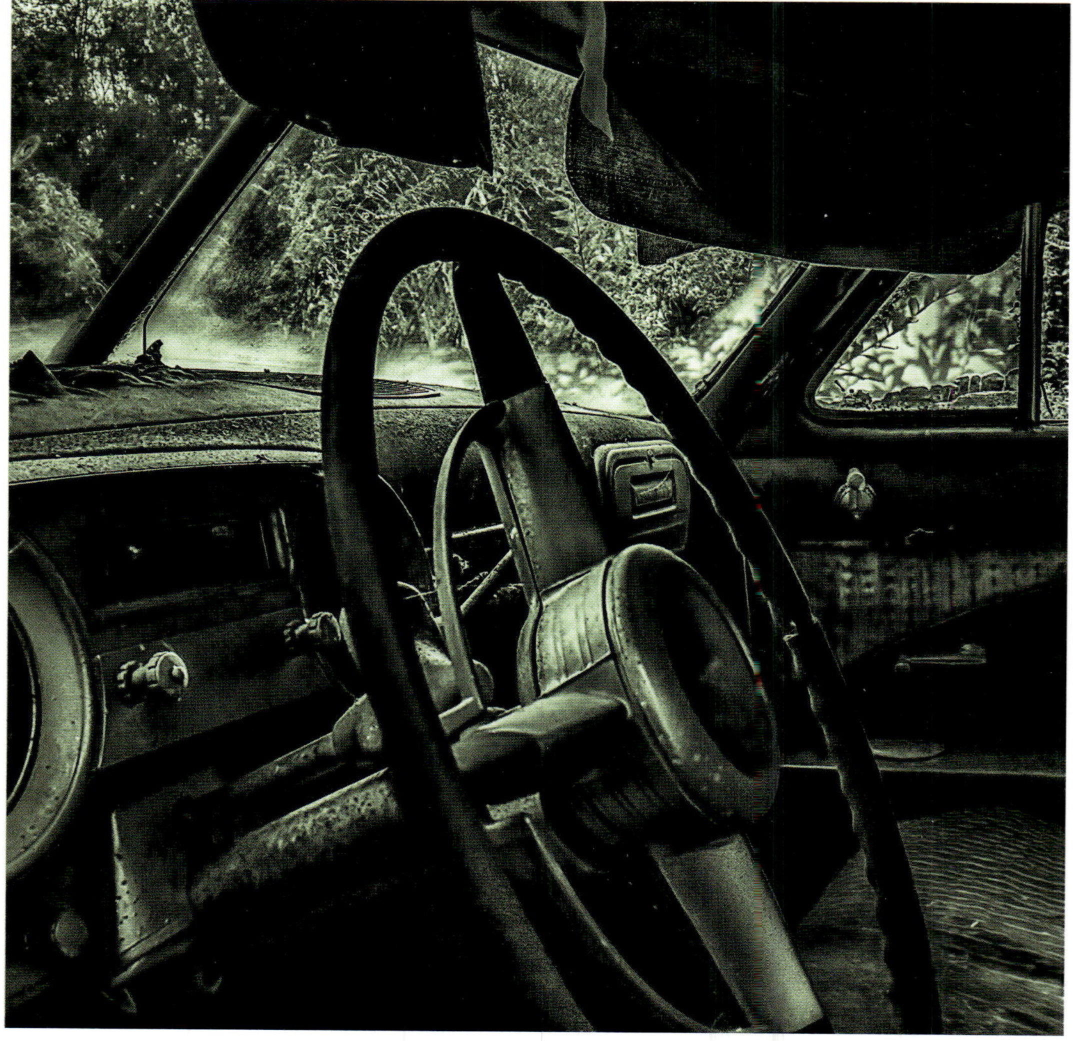

Top Left: I wanted at least one interior shot for this chapter, but it was overcast that day, and the color shot was pretty drab. Converting it to black and white and tinting it slightly green made it much more interesting.

Top Right: This car seems to attract a lot of life to it, and it was enjoyable to quietly observe nature do its thing. Here's a poem from an esteemed friend who I knew would connect with this image.
"Butterfly
Delicate, spotted wings flap gently,
Antennae search restlessly, in contradiction to all that is surrounds it,
Resisting losing its dignity or beauty, in search of freedom."
Dr. Foad Afshar, Psychologist, Professor, Life Consultant, NHIA Teaching Peer

Bottom Right: I love seeing living creatures exist among the decaying, once vital man-made machines. Sitting patiently in the grass was rewarding, and well worth risking the attention of unpleasant creatures—ticks (amazingly, none found me that day)! I'm proud to have this young lady, and a rising art star that I taught, put forth such a beautiful and thoughtful concept. "I can't help but think of whale falls, the extraordinary process of ocean life caring for and inhabiting a whale upon it's death, and continuing once it reaches the ocean's floor. Even the mechanical, non-organic creations of man can participate as hosts for entire ecosystems, finding a way to make use of the skeletons of our fallen artifacts." *Taylor Rose, Artist, Illustrator, Former NHIA Student*

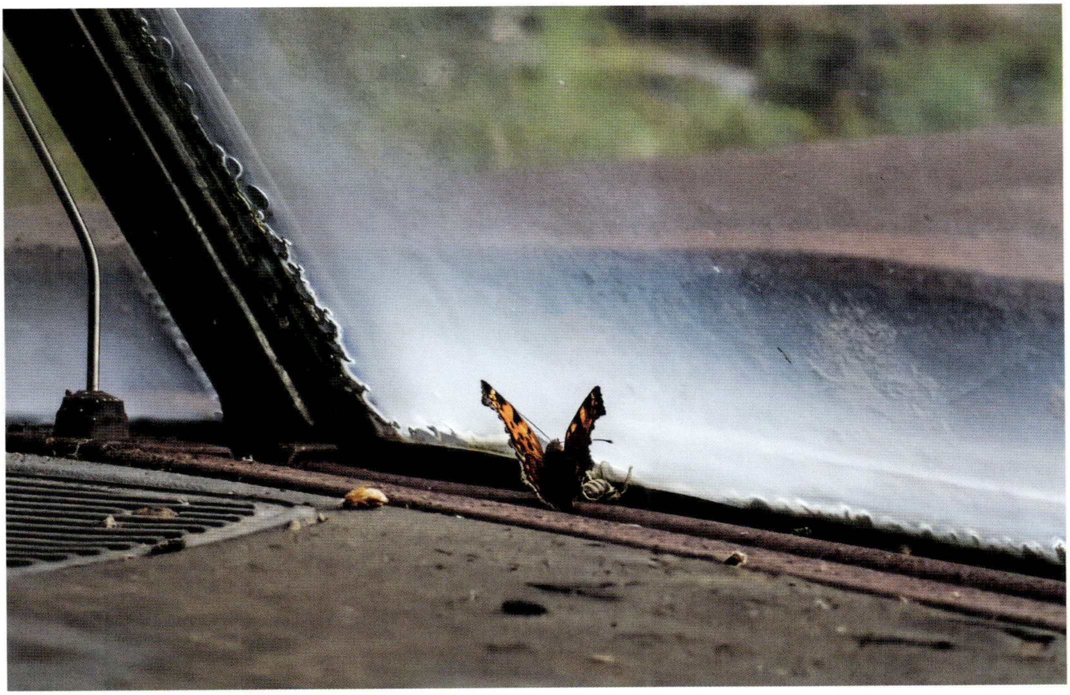

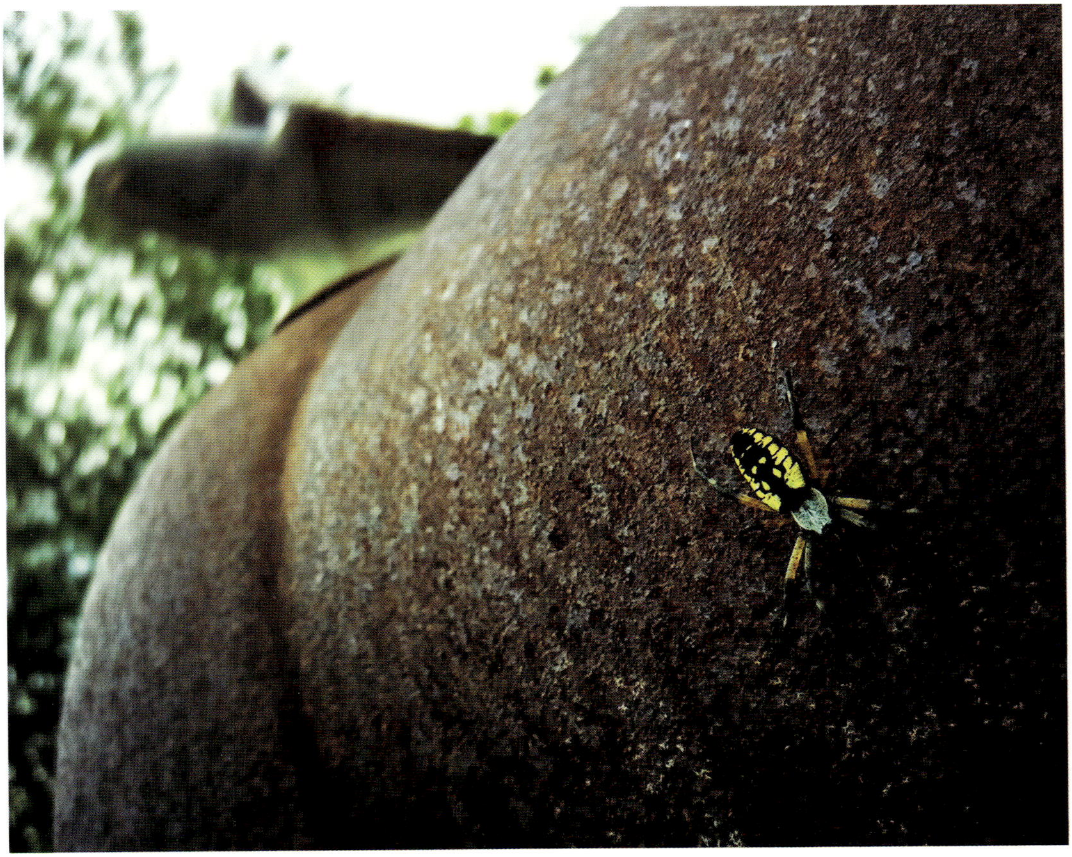

Bottom Left: Something extra special happens when photographing relics bathed in the extra intensity colors and atmosphere of autumn. A masterful painter shares the guiding principle of his career, and one he continues to incessantly preach to his students. "Wait for the light to come and it will change the world ... " *Peter Fiore, Landscape Artist, Teacher*

Top Right: The beautiful late afternoon light hits this car, and my friend, Jeff, perfectly encapsulates what my experience of hanging out with the Hudson is like. "A quiet time to be still and listen." *Jeff Haynie, Illustrator, Whimsical Symbolist*

Bottom Right: I asked quite a few people to share their thoughts about photos in this book, and I was gonna make darn sure that at least one of them was an actual car expert (with a popular TV show to boot)! I'm pleased that one of the top custom car builders in the USA gave me his two cents. "Ran great when we parked it—that's what every car guy says about the junk he's selling!" *Ian Roussel, Custom Car Builder, Actor & TV Personality, Star of Full Custom Garage*

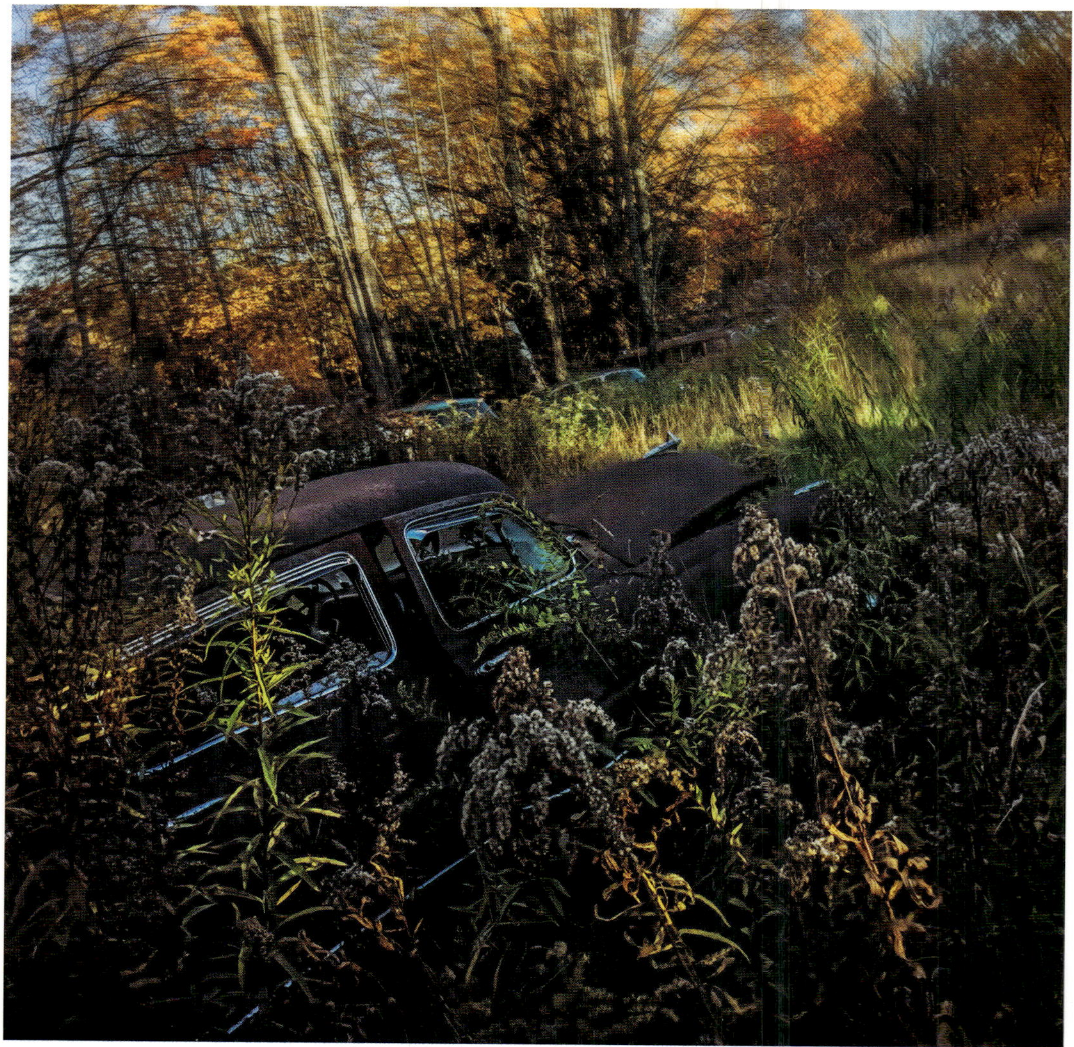

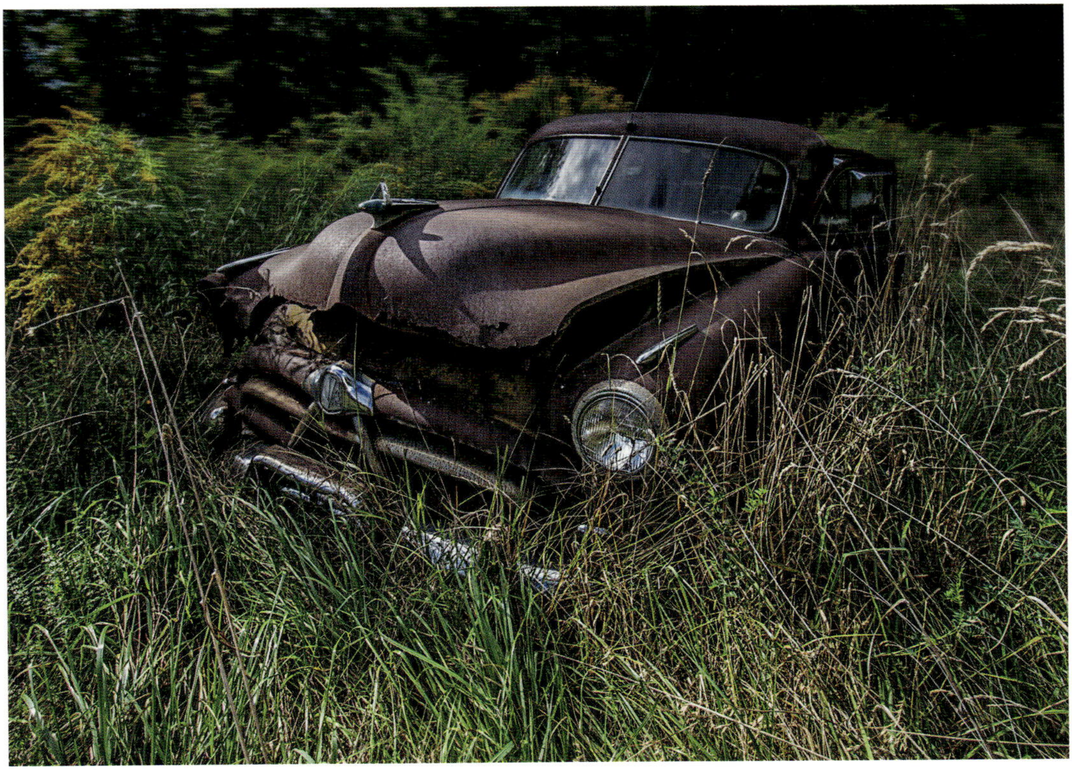

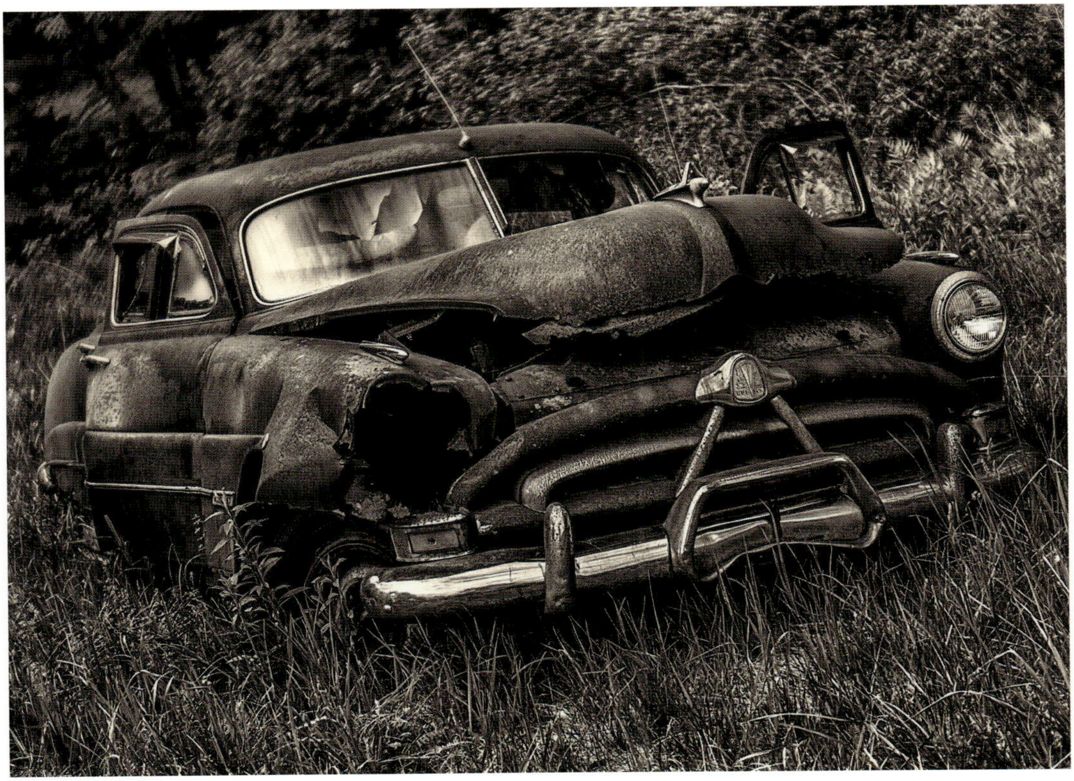

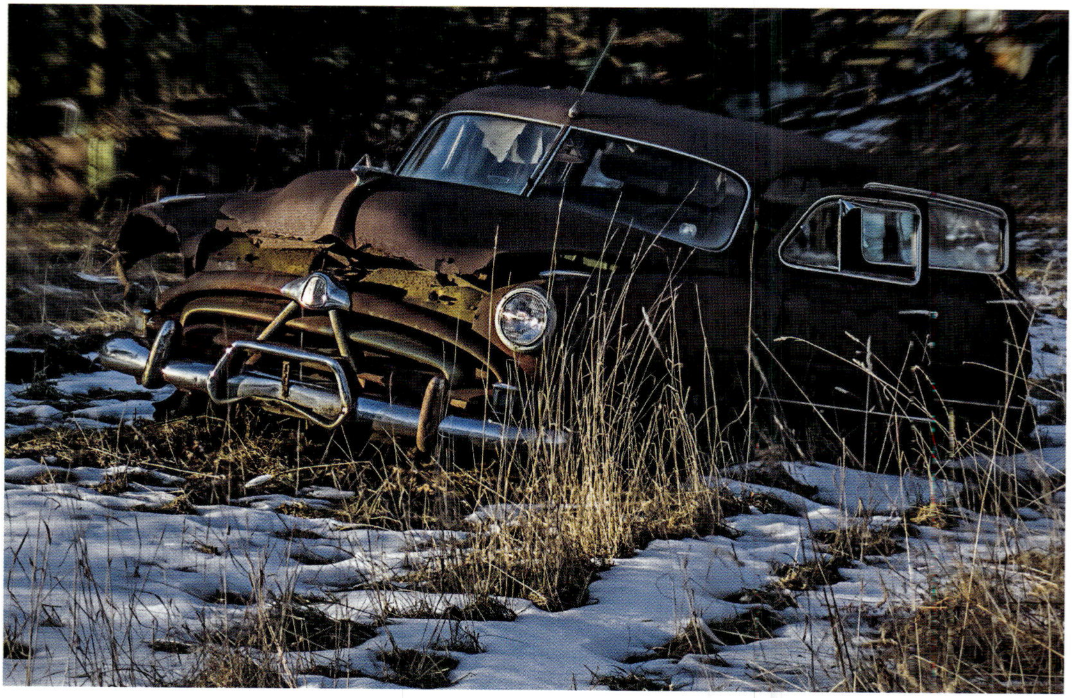

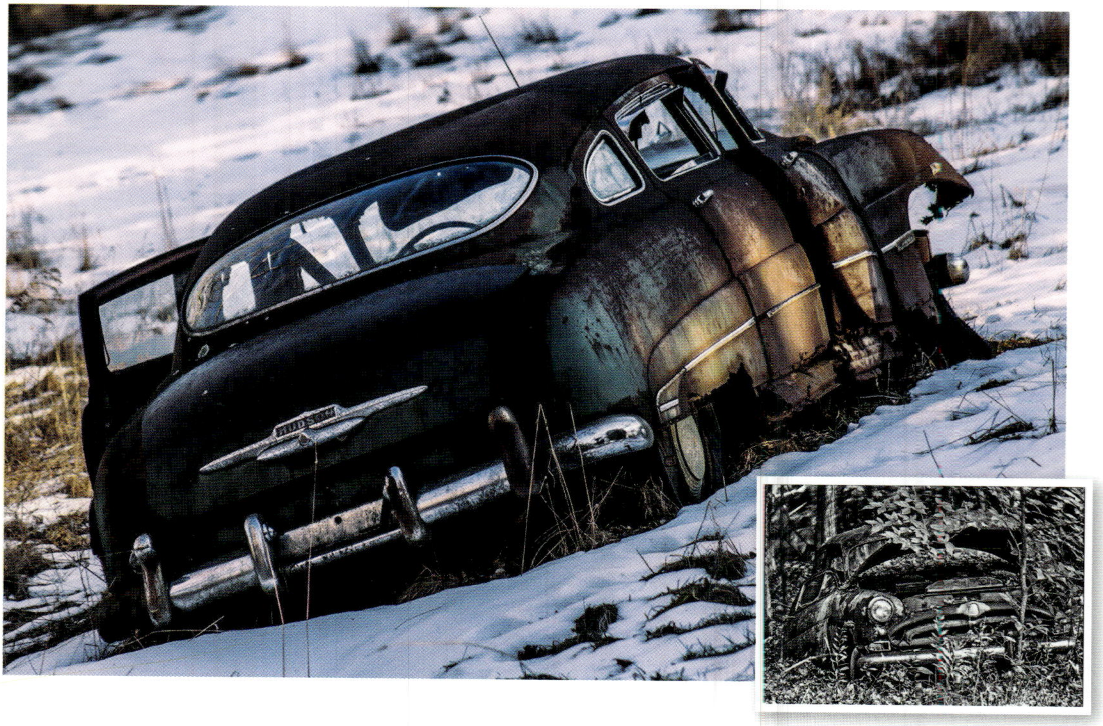

Above: My winter visit to Lane's had just the right amount of snow cover to frame the car's interesting blend of colors and rust. Inset Photo: I was so captivated with the Hudson in the middle of the field, it wasn't until I made a return trip to Lane's that I noticed another Commodore over my left shoulder playing peek-a-boo from the edge of the field.

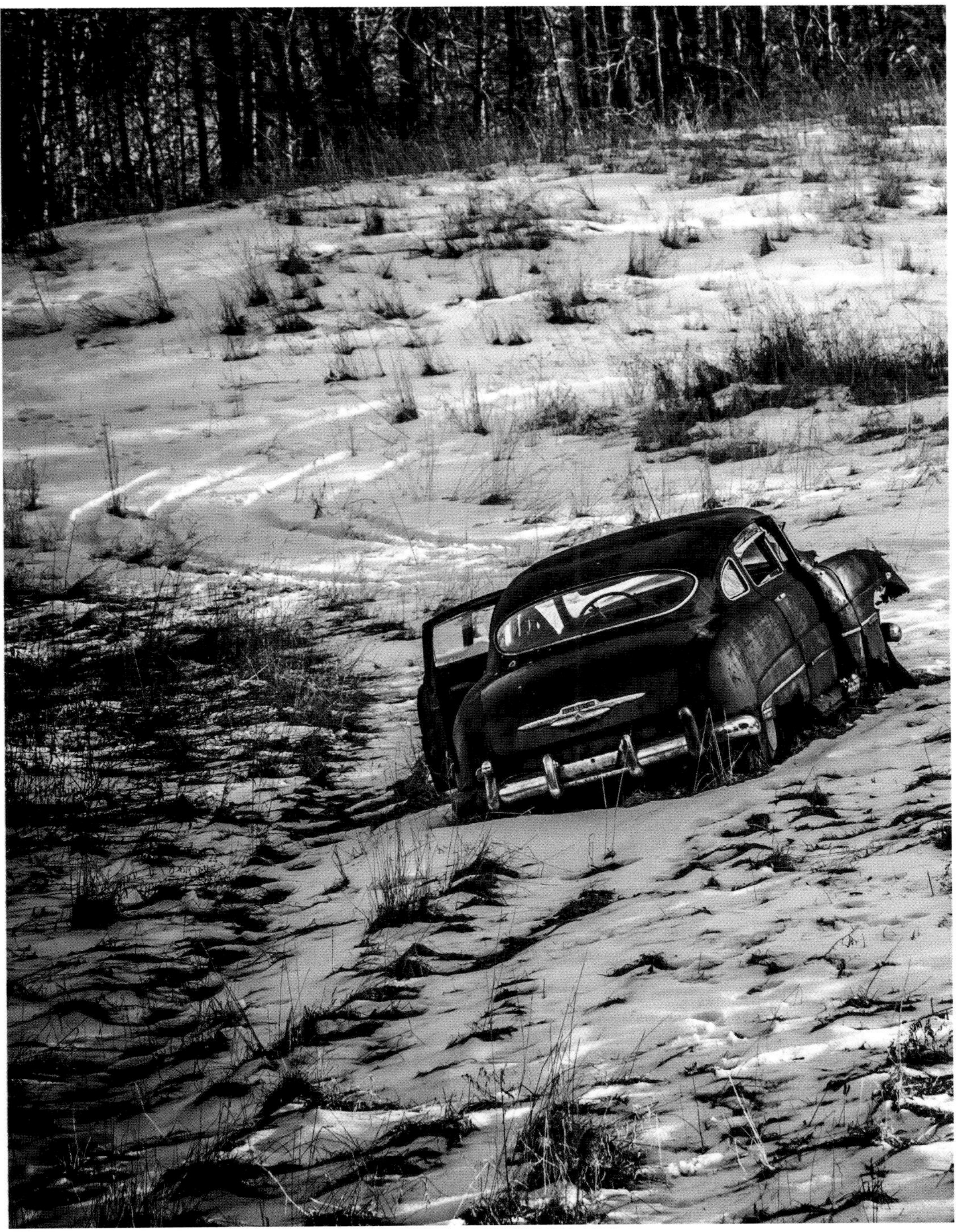

Above: From a very talented photographer, and fellow Light 16 camera enthusiast: "Shakes and fries in the front seat, young love in the back. Road trip along the Lincoln Highway, with bugs hitting the windshield as waves of radio static herald the next town. Sinatra croons, Beethoven rolls over. *American Anthem.*" *Anne-Marie Littenberg, Photographer*

Overleaf: *"All Dolled Up, But Nowhere to Go"* To echo Rick Lovell's comments on the first photo in this chapter, this car was indeed a beauty. Nearly seventy years later, she still is as she lays on a bed of soft, flowing grass, with a gleam in her eye and the sun on her skin … for however long, no one knows.

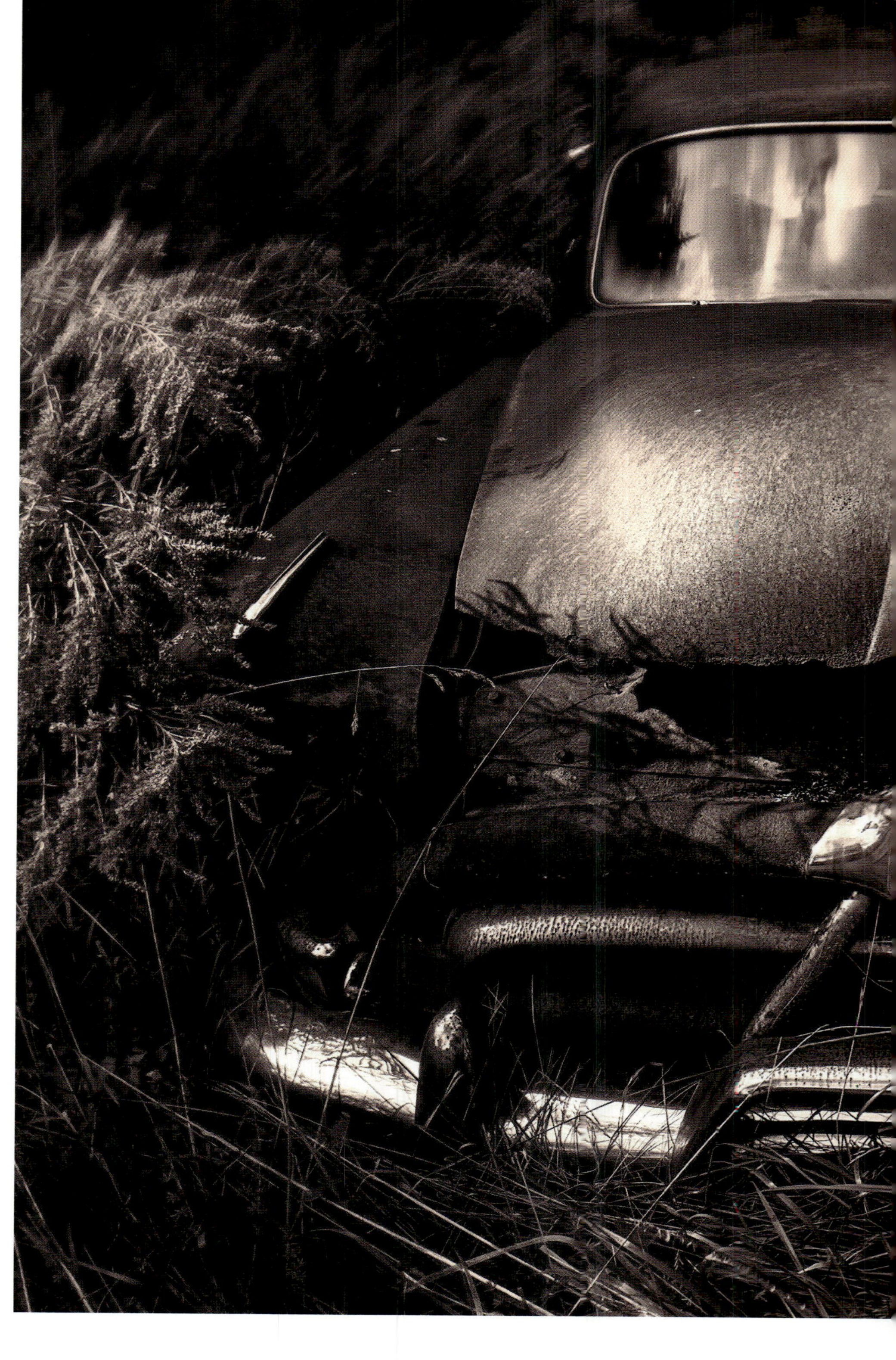

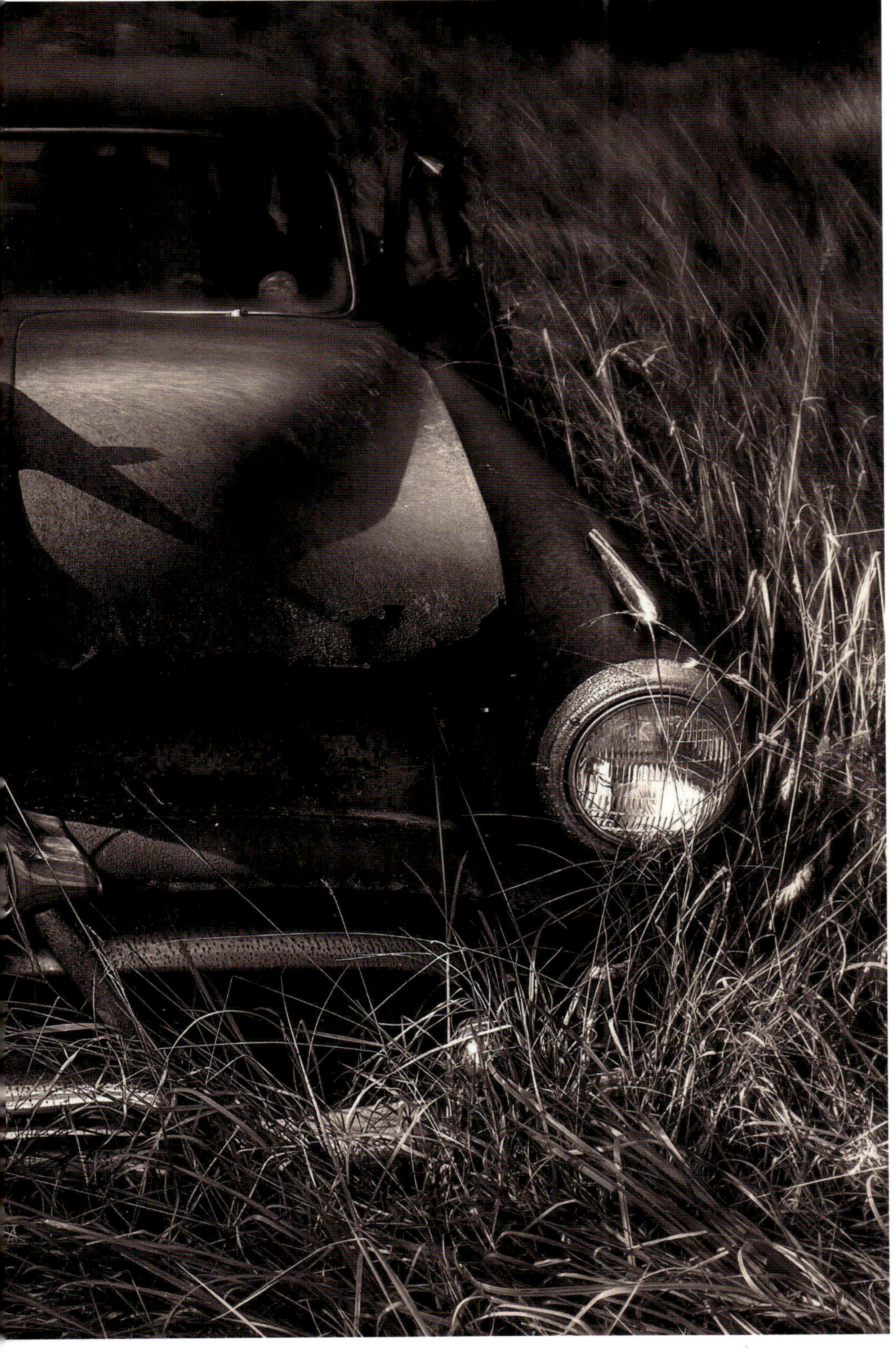

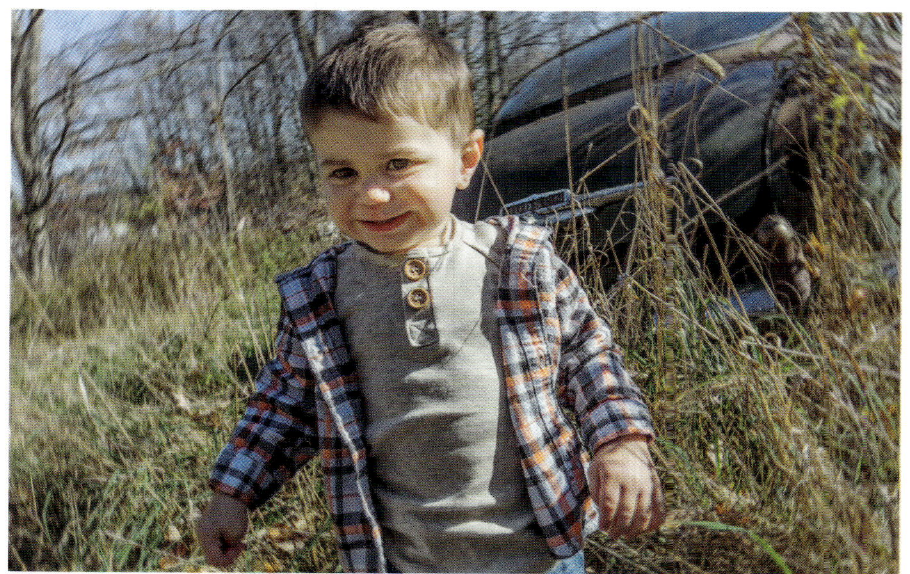

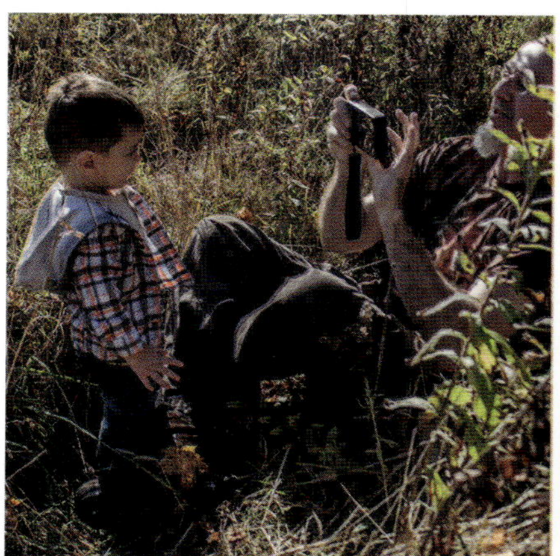

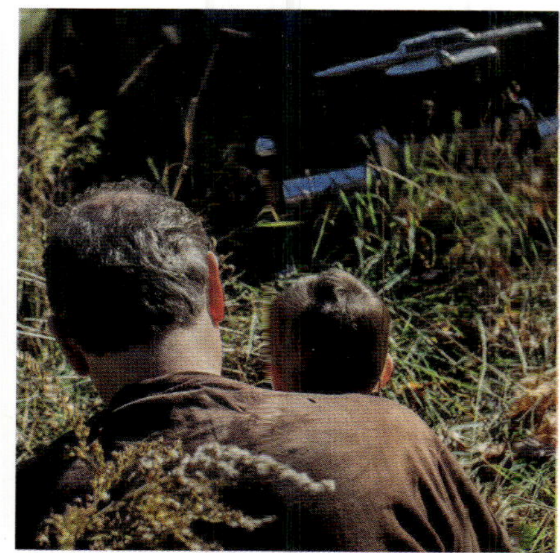

A beautiful scenario played in my mind over and over again, and I was just waiting for the perfect day to bring Hudson out to be photographed with … the Hudson! Holding hands as we walk through the woods, Hudson suddenly spots the car in the distance. He breaks loose from my grip and runs excitedly up to it, squealing with delight, and anxious to commune with his namesake. He stops abruptly, and becomes quietly contemplative in a way far beyond his two years. As he slowly and gently reaches out to touch the insignia bearing his name, a golden ray of sunlight breaks through the trees and illuminates his little hand. All of a sudden, the unmistakable sound of The Mormon Tabernacle Choir swells over the ridge like a scene from a Spielberg movie, and the car's engine starts up and begins to purrrrrrrrr … NOT!!! The truth is, when my wife and I got to Lane's, we had to wake Hudson up from a deep nap. He then proceeded to cry for nearly the entire time we were there! He was inconsolable no matter how many snacks we gave him, and he just couldn't give two diaper-loads about the stupid car. How I managed to get him to not cling to me for more than a few seconds, and even smile for a couple of photos, I'll never know.

A word from Hudson's mom and dad (Bronte and Gregory): "Our son just loves to explore the world with his grandpa! Seeing their adventures together brings us so much joy … memories we'll have forever. It makes us all stop and soak in the wonderful moments of life."

Finally, since Kathleen (my wife, and Hudson's grandmother) took the last two shots in this book, she also gets the last word—and a lovely one at that. "Whenever these two are together, the sun shines bright, and their hearts are light!"